Tastes Like Chicken

Center Point
Large Print

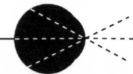

**This Large Print Book carries the
Seal of Approval of N.A.V.H.**

Tastes Like Chicken

A History of America's Favorite Bird

EMELYN RUDE

CENTER POINT LARGE PRINT
THORNDIKE, MAINE

This Center Point Large Print edition
is published in the year 2017 by arrangement with
Pegasus Books.

For complete notes and index,
see the original Pegasus edition.

The text of this Large Print edition is unabridged.
In other aspects, this book may vary
from the original edition.
Printed in the United States of America
on permanent paper.
Set in 16-point Times New Roman type.

ISBN: 978-1-68324-300-7

Library of Congress Cataloging-in-Publication Data

Names: Rude, Emelyn, author.
Title: Tastes like chicken : a history of America's favorite bird / Emelyn
Rude.
Description: Center Point Large Print edition. | Thorndike, Maine :
Center Point Large Print, [2016] | Includes bibliographical references
and index.
Identifiers: LCCN 2016056201 | ISBN 9781683243007
    (hardcover : alk. paper : large print)
Subjects: LCSH: Cooking (Chicken)—United States—History. | Large
type books. | LCGFT: Cookbooks.
Classification: LCC TX750.5.C45 R83 2016 | DDC 641.6/65—dc23
LC record available at https://lccn.loc.gov/2016056201

To my family, the strangest and
most wonderful flock of them all

CONTENTS

Tastes Like Chicken

A Fowl Introduction

O nce, in my student days, a very serious scholar with a very serious mustache at a very serious university looked up at me sternly from a pile of worn treatises on the nature of human progress and mused, "a chicken is an incredible piece of technology."

Even as just a bird, a chicken is an incredible thing. With a population of more than 50 billion, the chicken is the most abundant feathered species on the planet. It thrives on all six major continents, from Iceland to Patagonia, in deserts and forests, on mountain peaks, and in the midst of cities. Thanks to the Chinese, some chickens have even been to space. As the bird can be quarrelsome at times, archeologists believe that the chicken was first domesticated for cockfighting and that the fowl is also a proud descendant of the sharp-toothed and short-armed *Tyrannosaurus rex*. When chickens sleep they sometimes dream, and in their home flocks, the birds can recognize each other's faces. Most incredible of all, a chicken also makes a great chicken dinner.

The methods humans have devised to prepare and enjoy this fowl are almost as abundant as the bird itself. Hungarians like to braise it into *paprikash*, the Senegalese stew it with peanuts and serve it over rice, Mexicans coat it with fiery *mole verde* and like to have a good laugh when foreigners can't handle the heat. All across the globe chicken is skewered and roasted and steamed and jerked, pounded paper thin and coated with breadcrumbs or chopped into little bits and fried up with potatoes. There's no other ingredient quite like it—a food so universal that when you say something "tastes like chicken," almost everyone on the planet will have some idea of what you are talking about.

As a result, most people across the globe would be excited to chow down on the aforementioned fowl-filled menu, but I am unfortunately not one of those people. I am undoubtedly committing the cardinal sin of food writing by telling you this up front, but I am a chicken historian who does not actually like eating chicken. In fact, I've never liked eating chicken (or eating much other meat for that matter). From the time I was very young, there was always something about the texture of flesh, and the idea of the animals behind it that I just couldn't stomach. As a result, some of my earliest memories involve sobbing mournfully at the dinner table while my mother patiently held forth a chicken skewer or a fish stick or a beef taco she expected seven-year-old me to eat. (Spoiler: I never ate them.)

While I no longer cry (that often) while dining and am gradually becoming a more flexible eater following almost two decades of vegetarianism, I still rarely eat chicken. Even after working for some very talented chefs in New York City, and expanding my tastes to include olives of all kinds, thinly sliced hams, and briny oysters on the half shell, in my personal hierarchy of delicious things, the bird is still toward the very bottom.

In this preference, I am clearly very alone. Walk into almost any kitchen or restaurant in the United States and you will encounter a seemingly endless stream of grilled chicken breast and fried chicken and chicken enchiladas and chicken Caesar salad and chicken teriyaki and spicy chicken wings. When one quantifies this incredible fowl cornucopia, my particular eating habits seem even more unusual. Although the world knows my fellow Americans as passionate beef eaters, the citizens of the United States are actually the world's biggest and most prolific eaters of chicken.

Even with people like me skewing the data, in 2015, the average citizen of the United States still consumed over ninety pounds of chicken, which translates to roughly twenty-three birds per person. (For comparison, that same average American ate just over fifty pounds of beef and just under fifty pounds of pork.) Taken as a whole, Americans are eating roughly 5.9 million pounds of chicken every hour of every day. This adds up to over 160 million servings of the bird gobbled up in just twenty-four hours and over 8.6 billion chickens consumed in this country alone over the course of a year. This massive feathered horde is greater than the number of all cows, pigs, sheep, goats, ducks, rabbits, and turkeys eaten annually in the United States combined and comprises almost a full third of the 27 billion chickens eaten in any given year across the globe.

While the sheer scale of America's chicken consumption is incredible to think about, it is even more astonishing considering the fact that these eating habits are entirely new. Well up to the early twentieth century, the average American ate just ten pounds of chicken each year, which meant a family was lucky to have chicken on their plates even once a week for the fabled "Sunday Supper." In fact, for most of Western history, chicken was not even considered a "meat" (more on this later), and instead it was beef that wound up at the center of American dinner plates for most of the nation's history.

Observing this dramatic shift in the country's eating habits, as a culinary historian, the question I have to ask is: Why? Seriously. Why do Americans today eat so much damn chicken? If you're anything like my brother, my friends, or my coworkers, chicken is what's for dinner four or five nights per week and what's for lunch most days in between. If you're the man who helped me sign up for my gym membership or the businesswoman I spoke with briefly on the subway, you eat chicken to the point of boredom, go search for something else to eat, and then end up eating more chicken. Never before in modern history has a food risen so quickly in national eating favor and never before has any country consumed such prodigious amounts of poultry to the point of almost excess.

Raised by two agricultural economists, I've always known there's much more to a dish than what meets the plate. And so I began my search, through cookbook archives and agricultural manuals and the results of poultry science experiments, to unravel the mystery of how red-blooded Americans came to be eating such large quantities of white-meat chicken. The results of this hunt are what you now hold in your hands.

Painted in broad strokes, this is a story of agricultural science and human health, of the economics of feeding a nation and the politics that encircle the making and eating of a food. But on a more intimate level, this is really just the story of dinner. As it has been roasted, baked, boiled, and fried in kitchens across the whole of American history, the chicken's role on the nation's plates has been ever changing. Each generation had their own way of raising, cooking, and enjoying the bird and, in turn, their own understanding of what exactly "tastes like chicken." And so, my sweet readers, without any further ado, let us sharpen our proverbial knives, prepare our historical palates, and dive right into this tale of making and eating a meat in America.

CHAPTER ONE
The Early Bird

A CHICKEN PIE

Pick and clean six chickens, (without scalding) take out their inwards and wash the birds while whole, then joint the birds, salt and pepper the pieces and inwards. Roll one inch thick paste No. 8 and cover a deep dish, and double at the rim or edge of the dish, put thereto a layer of chickens and a layer of thin slices of butter, till the chickens and one and a half pound butter are expended, which cover with a thick paste; bake one and a half hour.

Or if your oven be poor, parboil the chickens with half a pound of butter, and put the pieces with the remaining one pound of butter, and half the gravy into the paste, and while boiling, thicken the residue of the gravy, and when the pie is drawn, open the crust, and add the gravy.

(Paste No. 8: Rub in one and half pound of suet to six pounds of flour, and a spoon full of salt, wet with cream roll in, in six or eight times, two and half pounds of butter.)

—Amelia Simmons,
American Cookery, 1798

The first known American recipe calling for chicken comes from a self-proclaimed orphan named Amelia Simmons. It's directions for making a chicken pie, and compared to other pie recipes that came before it, it's quite boring. It doesn't weigh hundreds of pounds like some Old English versions, nor was it filled with "chicken peepers," young chicks stuffed with gooseberries, as was in vogue during the Elizabethan days, nor were there live frogs and birds inside ready to escape at first cut like pies for "use at Festival Times" in Europe. It's just chicken, butter, water, flour, and beef fat, with a pinch of salt and pepper to taste.

Nevertheless, the concoction was revolutionary. "A Chicken Pie" is the first time anyone in the Thirteen Colonies decided it would be a good idea to write down and share a chicken recipe for posterity. (Ms. Simmons's *American Cookery* [1798] is considered to be the first American cookbook.) While its techniques are decidedly English and its stubborn simplicity distinctly colonial American, its main ingredient originated in a different world altogether. How the chicken made its way across the globe and into Miss Simmons's pies is where this culinary saga begins.

The chicken's story, much like most American stories, is an immigrant's tale, and it begins in

1493, with Christopher Columbus's second voyage to the Americas. In the holds of Columbus's ships, among the seasick mutineers, guns, and clouds of smallpox was a small flock of chickens. The birds' role on the long journey was a simple one: to produce a constant source of fresh eggs and the occasional bit of flesh, both welcome respites from the monotony of salted meat and ship biscuits that was typical fare on long ocean journeys. As far as historians can tell, these birds were the first of their kind to set foot in the New World.

Well before they served on European exploratory vessels, chickens had always been providers. Since the bird's domestication some 8,000 to 10,000 years ago in the jungles of Southeast Asia, humans have made good use of its feathers as ornaments and bedding, its eggs and meat as food, its fighting ability as a great source of entertainment, and in some cultures, a vein of spiritual release. The bird's small size made it conveniently portable as well, and as a result, as one nineteenth-century poultry enthusiast put it, "next to the dog, the Fowl has been the most constant attendant upon Man in his migrations and his occupation of strange lands." From the primordial chicken soup where *Gallus gallus*, the Red Jungle Fowl, mixed with other jungle fowls to become the *Gallus gallus domesticus* the world knows and loves to eat today, the bird was carried by humans in all directions: north on caravans into China, south and east on Malay trading ships into the Pacific, west on merchant vessels crossing the Indian Ocean to Persia and the Middle East.

From the Middle East, the chicken made its way to Ancient Egypt where the image of the brave fighting cock adorned the tombs of pharaohs, and the eggs of the brooding hen, incubated in massive clay egg ovens, fed the slaves laboring upon the Great Pyramids of Giza in the third millennium B.C. From there the fowl wandered to ancient Greece, a culture familiar and fond enough of the bird to ponder, by the fourth century, which came first, the chicken or the egg. And the Greeks in turn spread the chicken throughout the Mediterranean, up into the European continent, and onto the British Isles, where Ceasar first encountered the fowl, still cockfighting away, during his Gallic Wars of the 5th century.

Along the way, the chicken made a very important stop with the perpetually clever and always hungry Romans. This great civilization had a reputation for enjoying lavish feasts, and in addition to enjoying their dolphin meatballs and stuffed dormouse and sow's wombs in brine and lark's tongue pie, the Empire had a thing for chicken. By the fifth century Roman chefs had brought into the world the first omelets, and the concept of stuffing a bird before roasting, while their agriculturalists had bred the bird into the heartiest and tastiest varieties of chicken the world had yet seen.

CONCHICLATUS PULLUS
(STUFFED CHICKEN)

Bone chicken. From the chicken remove the breast bone and the [upper joint bones of the] legs; hold it together by means of wooden skewers, and meanwhile prepare [the following dressing in this manner]: Alternate [inside of the chicken] peas with the pods [washed and cooked], brains, lucanian sausage,* etc. Now crush pepper, lovage, origany,** and ginger, moistened with broth, raisin wine, and wine to taste, make it boil, when done, use it moderately for seasoning and alternately with the other dressing; wrap [the chicken] in caul, place it in a baking dish and put it in the oven to be cooked slowly, and serve.

—*Apicius*,
c. fourth or fifth century A.D.

---

* Lucainian sausage is a type of smoked blood sausage popular among the Romans.
** Origany is a wild type of marjoram.

Early Italian seafarers brought chickens on their journeys of conquest as well, but the Romans believed the bird's eating habits also foretold the outcomes of battles not yet fought. In 249 B.C., the Roman General Claudius Pulcher famously attempted such augury before fighting the armies of Carthage in the bloody Battle of Drepana. When his chickens didn't eat, he threw them overboard screaming, "Since they don't want to eat, let them drink." The general lost the battle and was later fined by the Empire for his fowl behavior.

Many centuries removed from the Romans, even during times of great frustration, Columbus was not known to throw his chickens into the ocean. And although these Spanish ships did not carry enough birds to make chicken dinner an everyday occurrence, Columbus and his men quickly realized they didn't need to worry much about missing out on the bird's characteristic flavor in the New World. When the famed explorer had his first taste of iguana in the Bahamas he mused, "the meat is white and tastes like chicken."

The fact that these reptiles half a world away from the birthplace of the chicken tasted similar to the bird makes perfect sense when looked at from a biological perspective. Munching their way through evolutionary history, researchers have determined that the taste of most of the animals that humans eat is an inherited trait, the product of millennia of changes to those animals' ancestors, and not something that occurred independently in each species. The common ancestor of all tetrapods, or four-limbed animals, which includes fish, amphibians, reptiles, birds, and mammals, must have therefore had a similar flavor to our fowl friend while the "beef-like" and "pork-like" flavor of most four-footed mammals occurred much more recently in evolutionary history. What one can infer from all this science is that the chicken's most famous relative, the sharp-toothed and short-armed *Tyrannosaurus rex*, would probably have also tasted like chicken.

It also makes perfect sense that such chicken-flavored creatures thrived in the New World. To Columbus, tropical Hispaniola was "a miracle" and even the much colder North America in the fifteenth century was, to many settlers, a place akin to Paradise. With the continent's moderate climate, "dainty fine rising hillocks, delicate fair large plains, sweet crystal fountains, and clear running streams," the chicken too thrived. The fowl arrived in small numbers with the first colonists to Jamestown in 1607, and by 1609 the colony had a "very great plenty" of chickens, as many as 500 birds. By 1623, the Plymouth colony to the north already included "many hens," which helped provide broth to feed an ailing Wampanoag tribesman and cemented a partnership that prevented the Puritans from starving to death.

Always an industrious creature, the bird just

kept right on multiplying as the New World grew more and more settled, alongside all the other geese, turkeys, and ducks both native to the Americas and transplanted by European colonists. Within mere decades visitors to the Colonies could not help but be amazed by the "prodigious plenty and variety" of poultry available in the Americas, all of which were roasted and baked and enjoyed in prodigious quantities as well.

As settlements and flocks began to grow, there emerged much advice on the proper way to raise a chicken, an art that had declined dramatically since the height of the dedicated Roman agriculturalist. But most colonial Americans didn't seem to care much for advice. Farmers were warned that one who "carelessly permits his fowls to roost in the adjacent trees will receive very little good from them," but their birds roosted in adjacent trees anyway. Although specialized breeds existed for cockfighting, the vast majority of colonial birds were instead left to their own reproductive devices, causing the chicken to "occup[y] in the poultry yards precisely the position of the cur dog in the kennel."

These mangy colonial chickens quickly earned themselves the illustrious title of "the dunghill fowl," after their inclination to rifle through other livestock's waste looking for their supper. From an agricultural perspective, this practice is in fact essential to building healthy soil, as their pecking breaks up the manure into smaller bits that are better used as fertilizer. Aside from the delicately named "blobfish" of Australia, however, such a title is still among the least flattering an animal has ever earned.

The only consistent care colonial chicken owners seemed to provide their mongrel creatures was to throw out some corn or oats now and again to ensure the birds didn't wander too far off. Such a practice is surprising, however, as most colonial landowners cared so little about their birds that most neglected to even record their chickens as property in their farm inventories. Even the Founding Farmer himself, Thomas Jefferson, found counting his chickens too time consuming and unimportant. Although his stint in the White House brought with it a presidential chicken coop, his records of his holdings at his farm Monticello list only his few prize birds and completely ignore the remainder of his abundant flocks of dunghill fowls.

The one exception to the general neglect a chicken experienced in early America was right before it was eaten. In the weeks prior to a chicken dinner, a colonial landowner would have his chicken minder, typically a female slave if he was rich and in the South or his wife if he was not, hunt down a choice bird and place it in a special fattening coop. These small wooden structures guaranteed that both the chicken could not escape its impending demise and helped to ensure the bird only ate things that would give it the best possible flavor. Fowl last suppers in these coops often included beer, oats, gruel mixed with sand (an element essential to chicken digestion), bread soaked in milk, and corn, a grain that many thought produced meat that "was the sweetest of all others."

And yet, despite the great care it received in the fattening coop, the chicken's place in the early American diet was relatively minor. Sure, some visitors complained that if they ate any more chicken on their travels through the Chesapeake they "shall be grown over with Feathers," but aside from the occasional pie or sliver of salted bird stored away for the long winter, chicken was typically eaten in the colonial household only on rare occasions.

The reasons for this culinary neglect were almost as abundant as the chicken itself. Part of it was straightforward farm economics, in that a dead chicken can't lay any more edible and renewable eggs. As a result, the only birds that were consistently eaten by colonists were spent hens who couldn't reliably lay eggs anymore and excess males beyond the one or two essential to maintaining a healthy flock.

If they were of a certain breed and temperament, however, these males did have a purpose as fighters in the ring. Just like the humans of ten millennia ago who first domesticated the bird, the colonists loved to watch cocks fight. This was particularly true in the American South, where regular cockfighting tournaments filled the bars and hotels in cities like Williamsburg and Charleston, drawing "many genteel people" to commingle "with the vulgar and debased."

The colonial fondness for this particular hobby was inherited directly from the British motherland, whose own royal family had been prominent "cockers" since the 1500s. And with the sport's kingly blessing, betting properly on a prizewinning rooster could earn a man more than enough to buy himself many weeks worth of chicken dinners. Cockfighting even resolved some of the earliest American conflicts. At least one town, Stamford, Connecticut, allegedly owes its name to the outcome of a battle between a bird named Stamford and another named Ayrshire. (Guess who won that fight.)

The largest factor limiting the total number of these chicken dinners in the American diet, however, was that there was simply so much else for colonists to eat. Among the dainty hillocks and crystal fountains of the New World was a conspicuous abundance of wild birds and beasts. Early settlers described clams the size of their forearms and shoals of cod so thick one could scoop them up with a bucket. The skies, wrote one transplant, were filled with flocks of birds "that to my thinking had neither beginning nor ending" and the oceans, wrote another, had an "aboundance of Sea-Fish . . . almost beyond beleeving."

What all this abundance most readily meant to a freshly arrived colonist was dinner. Learning quickly from the examples of the Native Americans, the first settlers shot venison, hunted geese, snared possum, trapped pigeons, harvested oysters, fished for cod, and did almost anything else they could to enjoy the tasty multitude of creatures they encountered on their new continent.

While at first it may have been more convenient for our forefathers to step out on their colonial back porches and shoot something for dinner, living solely off the bounty of the land was just not the European way. That was the unseemly practice of the indigenous, those "savages" who "[ran] over the grass," leaving "the land untilled" and "the cattle not settled." Since the majority of early settlers were English, their idea of a civilized society instead involved large numbers of the cows and pigs and sheep that ruled the pastures back in the British Isles.

These larger domestic animals were brought over soon after the first waves of settlement in the Americas. Much like the chicken, they thrived in the New World. By the time the English arrived in the seventeenth century, swarms of longhorn cattle already overran the Caribbean and the islands were covered, as one Spanish explorer wrote, with "more pigs than I ever saw before in my life." The same multiplication happened on the continent as well, with the bovine population of the Massachusetts Bay Colony booming to fifteen hundred head in just three years and the three sows brought over to Jamestown in 1607 multiplying to over sixty pigs in just eighteen months.

In addition to providing farmers with draft animals, and chickens with manure to gleefully rifle through, what this incredible plenty of larger domesticated animals most readily afforded early Americans was an opportunity to regularly gorge themselves on their favorite traditional meats. While the lower classes back home in Europe were fortunate to see meat once or twice a week, in the colonies "[e]ven in the humblest or poorest houses, no meals are served without a meat course." Per capita meat consumption for the white male topped nearly 200 pounds during this period and even those much lower on the social totem pole demanded meat every day.

The domesticated meats that the colonists ate and preferred were largely dependent on geography and class. New Englanders, who clung desperately to their Englishness, preferred to own and eat a lot of beef. Cattle has long had a tremendous value in Western society—it is thought to be one of the possible origins of the economic term *capital*—and New Englanders treasured it so much that in some parts of the region taxes were "paid in beef."

For its part, the British government was in full support of spreading and maintaining a love of cows in the colonies, so much so that in 1656 the House of Burgesses initiated a program that gave a cow to indigenous Americans who brought their representatives eight wolf heads. Besides aiding in the important task of protecting British colonial bovines from wolves, it was believed that giving native peoples a cow "will be a step to civilizing them and to making them Christians."

Although beef was preferred, colonial New Englanders did reluctantly dine on a considerable quantity of pork, particularly during the winter. This was a result of the pig's incredible adaptability, which allowed it to out-multiply both the chicken and the cow until its numbers in the colonies, as one seventeenth-century Virginian remarked, did "swarm like Vermaine upon the Earth."

The further south one traveled, however, the looser the grip of English culture became. Although Southerners tended to still defer to the traditional English table, their suppers were infused with the Spanish, the French, and the African food traditions that had taken up roots in the region as well. In this culinary melting pot, instead of chicken, it was almost always "pork upon pork and pork upon that," from the daily rations of salt pork and corn given to slaves to the fine tables of Williamsburg, where "scarcely a Virginian lady" breakfasted without "a plate of cold ham." This abundance of hogs was for practical reasons as well as culinary ones; the warmer climate of the American South meant salting and preserving meat was of a matter of greater urgency, and pig flesh is one of the easiest (and tastiest) to cure.

It is because of all of this savory aged pork and thinly sliced beef that the chicken pie was a rare dinnertime dish for an early colonist. And yet still, the chicken had an important role to play at times in the American diet. Even the Founding Fathers got sick on occasion, and it seems for much of history, many have believed that nothing has been better for an ailing body and soul than a hearty bowl of chicken soup.

Apparently early American chicken pies could be sweet as well as savory.

A SWEET CHICKEN PIE

Break the bones of four chickens, then cut them into small pieces, season them highly with mace, cinnamon, and salt; have four yolks of eggs boiled hard and quartered, and five artichoke bottoms, eight ounces of raisins of the sun stoned, eight ounces of preserved citron, lemon and erigo roots, of each alike; eight ounces of marrow; four slices of rinded lemon, eight ounces of currants, fifty balls of forced-meat, made as for umble pie; put in all, one with the other, but first butter the bottom of the pie, and put in a pound of fresh butter on the top lid, and bake it; then put in a pint of white wine mixed with a little sack, and if you will the juice of two oranges, sweeting to your taste. Make it boil, and thicken it with the yolks of two eggs; put it to the pie when both are very hot, and serve it up.

—Susannah Carter,
The Frugal Housewife, 1803

CHAPTER TWO

A Healing Broth

SOUP OF ANY KIND OF OLD FOWL
The only way in which they are eatable

Put the fowls in a coop and feed them moderately for a fortnight; kill one and cleanse it, cut off the legs and wings, and separate the breast from the ribs, which, together with the whole back, must be thrown away, being gross and strong for use. Take the skin and fat from the parts cut off which are also gross. Wash the pieces nicely, and put them on the fire with about a pound of bacon, a large onion chopped small, some pepper and salt, a few blades of mace, a handful of parsley, cut up very fine, and two quarts of water, if it be a common fowl . . . Boil it gently for three hours, tie up a small bunch of thyme, and let it boil in it half an hour, then take it out. Thicken your soup with a large spoonful of butter rubbed into two of flour, the yolks of two eggs, and half a pint of milk. Be careful not to let it curdle in the soup.

—Mrs. Mary Randolph, *The Virginia Housewife or, Methodical Cook*, 1824

By the time President William Henry Harrison undertook his record-breaking hour and forty-five minute long inaugural address on that fateful cold and rainy day in March of 1841, the United States had firmly moved on from the days of Amelia Simmons's revolutionary chicken pies. The country was already on its ninth president, was about to begin its third major war, and had recently acquired its twenty-sixth state.

Harrison, of course, holds the illustrious accomplishment of being the president with the shortest time in office, dying just thirty-two days into his term of what his doctor termed "pneumonia" but what was more likely typhoid fever caught from the nearby Washington, D.C. swamps. Like the Pilgrims who nursed an ailing Wampanoag tribesman back to health, Harrison's physician most likely spoon-fed the dying President generous portions of chicken broth. Such was an integral part of the standard prescription for any sort of nineteenth-century cough, almost always coupled with the most popular remedy of "rest."

President Harrison was not the only one to have need of chicken soup while in the White House. After a disgruntled job applicant shot him at a train station in 1881, President James A. Garfield's doctor provided the ailing American leader chicken soup on his sick bed. Garfield died some weeks later. Following President McKinley's own shooting by an anarchist in upstate New York, among the politician's last breakfasts was chicken broth and toast. He too died some days later. Even when her husband James was healthy, Dolley Madison insisted on serving chicken and okra soup at regular social occasions during his presidency, eventually making even Martha Washington a fan of the concoction. It appears the United States, in sickness and in health, owes a great deal to a chicken's bones in broth.

Chicken soup's use as a panacea in this way has been around since at least the twelfth century, when the famed Jewish physician Maimonides suggested those suffering from everything from asthma to leprosy should sip what is now nick-named "Jewish Penicillin." Even before then, the Ancients had long used the chicken as a veritable clucking pharmacy. Roman scholar Pliny the Elder believed chicken soup could cure dysentery while Roman physician Marcellus Empiricus believed hens' brains could stop nose bleeds and that the bird's excrement was a cure for boils. But as a mild soup, the bird was at its best, prescribed even across ancient Persia and the medieval Arab world as a cure-all.

The English too embraced the healing power of this medicinal broth, although they used it more often to help a weak stomach than to cure a common cold. The difference among the English, however, was that although they may have recognized the chicken as a valid food source, chicken was not an everyday food. It was widely believed well up until the seventeenth and eighteenth centuries that chickens are better for sick men than healthy ones, and that, as one popular health manual declared, "unlesse a man after eating of it, use extraordinary exercise, it will do him more hurt then good."

CHYKENNS IN CAWDEL

Take chikenns and boile hem in gode broth and ramme hem up. þenne take zolks of ayrenn and þe broth and alye it togedre. do þerto powdour of ginger and sugur ynowh safroun and salt. and set it ouere the fyre withoute boyllyng. and serue the Chykenns hole oþer ybroke and lay þe sowe onoward

CHICKEN SOUP

Take chickens and boil them in good broth and press them close together. Then take egg yolks and the broth and mix it together. Add powder of ginger and enough sugar, saffron, and salt; and set it over the fire without boiling; and serve the chickens whole or divided and pour wine on top.

  —The Chief Master Cooks of King Richard II, *The Forme of Cury*, c. 1390

• • •

What instead was meant to be eaten on daily terms by the British was beef. Lots of beef. "The climate makes them terrible and bold," proudly penned the English poet Daniel Defoe in 1703, "and English beefe their courage does uphold." Even before Defoe, the Isles' great passion for meaty bovines had been well documented by history. Since the age of Caesar, it has been widely held that cattle was the true source of the country's wealth and the inhabitants of the British Isles were long renowned throughout Europe as the "beef-eating, beer-drinking Britons."

The love of beef was readily transferred over to the New World as the English colonists, scared, cold, and alone in strange new lands, tried to replicate, as best they could, their beloved dinner tables from back home. This was why the early English settlers of New England revered beef above all and explains, to some extent, why chicken for them was a food of last resort.

But unraveling how the meat of cows came to be the preferred meat of the English-speaking world, like solving any riddle of a culture's food preferences, is no easy task. At its most basic origins at least, it can be deduced that this love of beef is to a large extent ecological. Eating a lot of meat, as opposed to eating a lot of plants, tends to occur in places with low population densities on large areas of land that are either not used or unsuitable for other crops. The windswept plains of ancient Great Britain and much of northern Europe easily met these requirements. With a geography well suited for meat making, the British readily developed a fondness for meat eating.

An eating preference bluntly described by the predominantly plant-eating Romans as "barbaric," the meat-heavy diet of the North was further proof of the inferiority of these peoples and therefore that Caesar should continue his quest to conquer them. To the Italians, the northern "flesh devourers" were "much more stupid than the southern" and those that "feed much on plants" were "more acute, subtil [*sic.*], and of deeper penetration." And while the Romans may have been smart, the carnivorous Britons were undoubtedly strong. Perhaps this is why the Roman Empire eventually gave up their conquest of England and just built a wall; after all, as one Englishman claimed around the time of the American Revolution, "you find more courage among men who eat their fill of flesh than among those who make shift with lighter foods."

While the medieval British diet may have contrasted heavily with that of ancient Rome, the inclination to excessively feast was certainly shared. The English nobility religiously followed God's words to Noah that "everything that lives and moves will be food for you" and overloaded their groaning tables with whole carcasses of beasts and game birds. One dead pheasant quickly led to another, and soon the competition for throwing a bigger and better feast became the original dinner party war, a culture of one-upmanship that caused King Edward II to issue a decree in 1283 to restrain "the outrageous and excessive multitude of meats and dishes which the great men of the kingdom used in their castles, and by persons of inferior rank imitating their example beyond what their stations required." What their stations required were specific kinds of meat, the choice cuts going to the rich while the "umbles," typically the entrails of a deer, went to the poor. If you were relegated to eat this "humble pie" at a medieval banquet, you could deduce what your host thought of you and your place in the social order.

On a daily basis, early English food preferences were regulated less by royal decrees and more by a concept of healthy eating known as Galenism. Galen, the father of Galenism, wasn't an English-man, nor was he even a citizen of the medieval world. Aelius Galenus, or Galen of Pergamon, was a prominent Greek physician and philosopher in the second century A.D. A skilled surgeon and contemporary to the likes of Hippocrates, Galen was also a prolific writer on the subjects of health and sickness of the human body. (So prolific in fact, some historians attribute his lasting influence to the fact that he wrote so much, not necessarily because he wrote so well.) Spreading rapidly from Ancient Greece, through the Arabs and the Italians, Galenic ideas eventually came to dominate Western medicine for almost 1,300 years after Galen's demise.

Galenism as a concept of health was built around an idea called "humoral theory," which claimed that the human body was made up of four basic essences known as the four humors, or temperaments. These temperaments were choler, blood, phlegm, and black bile, each consisting of a different combination of the essential character-istics found in nature: hot, cold, moist, and dry. (Blood was considered hot and moist, phlegm moist and cold, choler hot and dry, while black bile was cold and dry.)

To maintain health and vigor, an individual strove to balance their humors, which they largely did through cooking and eating. Foods, like human bodies, were believed to have these same essential qualities; sugar, for instance, was considered to be hot while salt was hot and dry. If your temperament was choleric, your body had extra choler and you would gravitate toward eating foods as hot and dry as you were, mainly fried or spicy things, to keep healthy. As a phlegmatic person, by contrast, you were believed to crave the cold moisture of sweets and dairy products that matched your specific temperament. The way a food was cooked also affected its health value; boiled mutton was considered to be bad for phlegmatic persons while roasted baby goat was better for the young and hot than for the old and cold.

It is from this way of understanding the body that the medieval English derived their now famous aversion to raw fruits and vegetables, and their great love of pies. Under Galenism, these edible plants were typically considered cold and moist, two traits that would certainly harm the warm body when eaten too much. Anyone who chose to eat fruit, wrote one seventeenth-century health guru, did so "more for wantonnesse then for any nutritive or necessary good which they bring unto us." In order to avoid harming a great many eaters, the majority of old British recipes call instead for cooked fruits and vegetables in the many delectable varieties of baked tarts that came to characterize English cuisine. These spilled over into the New World and quickly became as American as Amelia Simmons's chicken pies.

The body's ability to absorb the cold and moist or hot and dry characteristics of its food was particularly potent when one ate animals. The English believed the blood of the animals, also part of Galen's universal system, "doth not only contain the Spirits, but the very Humour, Dispositions and Inclinations of the Creature." Eating a cow provided an eater with a cow's humors, while

41

eating a chicken provided a chicken's humors. Individuals seeking certain traits for themselves were thus recommended to eat certain meats, "as he that feeds on beefe is strong; he that feeds on venison, is nimble." And the more similar you were to the creature you were eating, the more easily absorbed its characteristics were, meaning land-living cows and pigs were better for a healthy dinner than flying birds or sea-dwelling fish.

It was from Galenism then that the chicken received its early reputation among the English of being a food better for a sick man than a healthy one. Aside from the occasional English stomach ache, chicken's popularity was also not helped by the fact that these early Europeans literally thought that you are what you eat, and since the time of Shakespeare the English have equated cowards with chickens. The act of soldiers fleeing a battlefield in the Bard's tragedy *Cymbeline* is described to the audience as, "forthwith they fly chickens."

The chicken too, more specifically the rooster, was also the national symbol of France, England's biggest rival. During the Roman Era, by some linguistic twist of fate, the Latin word for Rooster, "*gallus*," was the same name the Empire gave to "a man of Gaul." Although historically used as a taunt by France's enemies, the symbol of the Gallic cock made a marked resurgence as a Christian symbol during the French Revolution in the eighteenth century. Whether or not it was adopted out of an ancient sense of irony, the Gallic rooster is still held as the French national symbol today, an icon celebrated more often than not with a feast of roast chicken or a generous helping of *coq au vin*.

From this popular English understanding of the bird, as a symbol of cowardice (and of the Gallic French), chicken was not something a proud Englishman wished to become, and therefore not something that he wished to eat. "No soldier can fight unless he is properly fed on beef and beer," claimed instead one famed military leader in 1704. Plump capons, castrated roosters whose lack of sexual organs cause raging hormones and gargantuan growth, were actually the only form of chicken believed to provide any form of good sustenance. According to one manual, "hennes in winter" got close to the capon, but still "they do not make so stronge nouryshement." This aversion to chicken was bolstered by the fact that the well-bred Roman fowl was a long-forgotten memory of agricultural history, which meant early English chickens, the ancestors of the early American mongrel birds, were scrawny and decidedly not delectable.

What this all entailed was that chicken was simply not "a meat." In its earliest recorded definition, "meat" was in fact not used to specify animal flesh. According to the *Oxford English*

Dictionary, the term "meat" originally meant primarily "food, as nourishment for people and fodder for animals," and secondarily "a fundamental, core, or customary requirement." This is the origin of the word "nutmeat" and why, when you read the 1611 King James Bible, God tells Adam and Eve that he has "given [them] every green herb for meat." The cultural preference toward what is now considered meat eating necessarily caused "required foods" to become "the flesh of animals used as food" starting in the fourteenth century.

But chicken was not a required food; it was only for sick men and those of weak constitutions. As an early English health manual explains, "there are two sorts of flesh, the one four-footed, and the other that of Fowle," with only the former being considered "butcher's meat." The distinct category of fowl to which chicken belonged stood just above the less nourishing "white meats" of the poor, namely chicken eggs, cheese, milk, butter, and other dairy products. The early chicken found itself in a strange predicament—it was considered an animal food outside of meat, a somewhat nourishing flesh that was in no way desirable to eat.

What was required eating for the British however was all this beef, conveniently supported by Galenism. "Yong beefe . . . is natural meat for men of strong constitutions" and it "bringeth more strong nourishment than other meats," as "may plainely be perceived, by the difference of strength in those that commonly feed of beefe, and them that are fed with other fine meats." If such reaffirming praise wasn't enough, the Yeoman Warders, better known as "Beefeaters," have stood guard at the Royal Palace and the Tower of London since their founding by King Henry VII in 1485, being fed as much as two pounds of meat per day and serving as symbolic watchmen of the realm. The English were a strong people and so they consumed beef; the English consumed beef and so they were strong.

As beef "is a good meate for an Englyssheman," beef was also a good meat for an English colonist newly minted as a citizen of the United States. Where the English had their national symbol of John Bull, the people of the United States had Uncle Sam, a national symbol also born out of a great fondness of meat. During the War of 1812, as one version of the legend goes, a meat packer by the name of Samuel Wilson sent barrels of pork and beef marked "U.S." to the troops stationed along the Canadian border. In gratitude toward these shipments, troops began joking that these barrels were gifts from "Uncle Sam." The symbol became so widespread so rapidly that by 1813, less than a year after Samuel Wilson began his meat deliveries, an army recruiting poster proclaimed, "If Uncle Sam Needs, I'll be Glad to

Assist Him." One nation, under God, indivisible, with salt pork and roast beef for all

This pork that Uncle Sam was peddling was a bit of a healthy eating conundrum for both American and English eaters, as has always been the case with the pig. While the rich and the warriors wallowed in beef (and mutton as well, which was plentiful only in England thanks to productive woolen industries that never managed to take off in the American colonies), the lower classes of England consumed much less of these meats, and much less meat in general, hence their great excitement at the meaty bounty of the New World. The butcher's meat dined upon by the middling classes in England was typically pork. As a four-footed beast that lived its life on land, the hog fared quite well in Galenism's nutritive assessments. In fact, "above all kinds of flesh in nourishing the body," declares a sixteenth-century health manual, "Galen most commends pork."

Like in the Americas, in Great Britain the pig's incredible ability to quickly gain weight with little to no human care also made its economic appeal undeniable. This was particularly true for members of the lower classes, whose diets regularly consisted of large amounts of bacon and salt pork. But the fact that the poor could afford ham was reason enough for the rich to avoid it. As one eighteenth-century English agriculturalist admits "[the pig] is one of the most profitable that an inhabitant of the country can rear," but he goes on to declare that "of all the quadrupeds that we know . . . the Hog appears to be the foulest," in that "all its ways are gross" and "all its inclinations are filthy." It should therefore not be eaten if at all possible. Such derision at the pig's natural proclivities, some historians claim, may also be part of the origin of the Halal and Kosher bans of pork in Islam and Judaism.

More than just being considered disgusting, the pig was also the smartest animal raised for its meat, making it one of the largest nuisances of the Middle Ages. During this era of legal history, animals could be persecuted for their wrong-doings alongside their human counterparts. Too smart for their own good, and with a voracious appetite for anything, swine accounted for half of all recorded animal executions in medieval Europe. In 1379, for example, a group of pigs was convicted of murder for trampling the son of a sow-herd, and in 1567 a sow was publicly executed for devouring a four-month old girl. As animals conveyed their traits through their flesh, pork might have been nourishing but it also "hurteth them that be subject to the Gout and Sciatica, and annoyeth old men, and idle persons."

Not one to stray far from its roots, the pig continued on with its legal troubles after it crossed the

Atlantic. Left to roam throughout the American woods just like the chicken, that is "without any Care of the Owners," pigs rooted up farms, destroyed crops, and generally sowed discord among the early colonists. In an attempt to control these wayward beasts, a Massachusetts court declared in 1633 that "it shall be lawfull for any man to kill any swine that comes into his corne." By 1635 the colony had established animal pounds to house the growing multitude of feral hogs, but by 1636 the pig problem had become so bad that it became legal "for any man to take them, either alive or dead, as hee may."

With the continuation of the pig's disruptiveness came the continuation of the negative characterization of those who enjoyed it. Although rich seventeenth-century Virginia planter William Byrd often dined upon fried pork, he remarked that the poor residents he encountered on a journey through the backcountry of Carolina dined "so much upon swine's flesh" he felt it made them "extremely hoggish in their temper, and many of them seem to grunt rather than speak in their ordinary conversation." The same rhetoric was regularly used to describe poor American blacks, whose poverty led them to eat pork more often. As one American doctor wrote, the pig was "peculiarly appropriate for negroes on account of their habits of life."

These superior and inferior categorizations of

animal foods in the British Empire were not only matters of class but also of gender as well for both man and beast. According to yet another old English health manual, "certainly that of the male, doth far excel the flesh of the female" for eating, "as for example: the Oxe flesh is better then [*sic.*] the Cowes flesh." Women and their proper nourishment are rarely mentioned in early English dietary regimens. When they are, the emphasis is on a woman's overwhelmingly weak constitution and the resulting need to avoid foods that might harm it. If a woman is pregnant, a fifteenth-century medical treatise warns her to avoid the strength and salaciousness of "Bull's flesh or ram's or buck's or boar's or cock's or gander's," as they were a direct threat to both her health and that of her unborn child.

Chicken and "white meats" therefore became the foods of women and the poor (and even sometimes simply the "bookish"), while the blood and strength of the red meats were meant for rich and powerful men. These ideals that you are what you eat, or rather you should eat what you are, have infused themselves into our cultural psyche and linger on into the present, even after five hundred years of culinary and social change. Today, after all, attractive young "chicks" are supposed to enjoy their dainty chicken Caesar salads while hunky "beefcake" men should chow down on giant bloodied steaks.

• • •

As it turns out at the end of this long explanation of medieval dietary regimens, Galenism wasn't actually that good as a model of medicine. In fact, it missed a great many physiological truths about the human form, the most damning of which was the absence of any explanation of the circulation of blood in the body. When the English physician William Harvey discovered this important facet of human physiology in 1628 he dealt Galenism a fatal blow from which it could not recover.

But the fall of Galenism as a medical science was not the same as the fall of Galenism in its practical application. Purging and leeching and puking and balancing the humors had made people feel better for centuries and there was no reason to believe they would stop just because one man suddenly knew about circulation.

The same was true for food and the ideas surrounding a balanced diet. But unlike colonial farmers dealing with their chickens, the eating public desperately wanted advice. When medicine had long consisted of purging and leeching and puking, eating correctly was one of the few means one could really feel in control of one's health.

In England, the first of many to fill the void left by the death of the ancient regimen was George Cheyne, an obese Scottish physician who revolutionized the diet book genre in the early eighteenth century with his "milk and seed diet."

Key to his guidelines was a message of abstention from meat. Such temperance in eating, Cheyne claimed, had helped him to shed excess weight and regain his health. Despite (or perhaps because of) their heavy contrast to English meaty ideals, Cheyne's diet books were among the most popular in British history.

The United States, a century later and just as President Harrison was slurping his last cup of soup, experienced its own efforts at dietary reform led by a doctor named William Alcott and a minister known as Sylvester Graham. While these men would go on to lead the first eating advocacy movements in American history, their efforts didn't begin with food. Colleagues in conviction, the pair blusteringly and belligerently railed upon all the sinful ways of the American populace throughout the 1830s and 1840s. Alcott declared vehemently against procrastination, under whose reign "every thing in human character goes to wreck" and against courtship that was too free and conversation "which is too exciting." Supported by his cult of followers known as "Grahamites," Graham urged the populace to abstain from alcohol and to avoid masturbation at all costs. The stimulation of the brain during such acts of self-affection was even greater than during natural arousal, he claimed, leading men and women to inevitably go insane.

Influenced by each other, both Graham and

Alcott together came to the conclusion that the true source of America's decay was its diet. Side by side with his propensity for lecturing women about their chastity and feeding people his so-called whole wheat "Graham Crackers," like Cheyne, Sylvester Graham eventually set his reforming sights on the meat course. At this time, while continental Europeans were blown away by the meat-eating of the British in the seventeenth and eighteenth centuries, with "more flesh spent in two or three months in London" than in an entire year in Venice, the nineteenth-century English were flabbergasted at the meat put away by US citizens. Describing an American town to a European audience during the mid–nineteenth century, English writer Anthony Trollope claimed, "A population in America would consume double the amount of beef which it would in England."

Such was unacceptable to the reformers. "Flesh-eating," Graham declared, "impairs the intellectual and moral faculties, and increases the influence of the carnal nature of man over his mental and moral nature." You are what you eat after all, and the United States was viciously dragging itself into bestial damnation with every morsel of meat it shoved into its mouth. Particularly bad was still pork, which Alcott held to be "one of the worst things that ever entered a human stomach" and was the one true cause of leprosy. Although still not a meat, our favorite bird did not escape the attacks of the reformers either; according to Graham, cholera was, without doubt, caused by "chicken pie and excessive lewdness." The only option for salvation from all of these food-borne ills was therefore abstaining from flesh. A vegetable system, Alcott wrote, was clearly the only way to "advance the happiness of all."

Unfortunately for these reformers, raging against the meat with no guiding health principle besides "morality" was a decidedly uphill battle. Thanks to the opening of the Great Plains and the rise of large industrial meat-packing complexes in the Midwest by the mid–nineteenth century, pork and beef were growing cheaper and more abundant by the day. And while Galenism might have been dead by the time of Alcott and Graham's reforms, a more universal dietary truth may well be the fact that nothing angers a meat-eater more than a self-righteous vegetarian.

Although the American public desperately wanted dietary advice, still in limbo from the loss of their ancestors' eating practices, abstaining from eating animals was clearly not the advice they wanted to hear. Outside of his parishoners, Graham often had difficulty in speaking throughout New England due to the angry mobs of butchers and bakers that showed up at his events. Even the reformers acknowledged the difficulties they faced in their campaign to improve American eating habits. Alcott himself admitted that his admired colleague Sylvester Graham was "more successful in obtaining disciples than in keeping them." After all, Alcott believed, "mankind were too strongly wedded to their lusts," primarily a love of meat, "to yield them up entirely and forever."

William Alcott published his own vegetable-based cookbook in 1846 and, unsurprisingly, it contains no chicken recipes. Conceding that "since people will continue for some time to use animal food," he does provide instructions on cooking an egg, which is one of the animal foods Alcott deems "least objectionable."

"EGGS"

Eggs are almost entirely pure nutriment, and when not cooked too much, are easy of digestion. When over-done, however, they are exceedingly difficult of digestion, especially their white or aluminous part. The last coagulates at about 160° of Fahrenheit's thermometer; and when once coagulated, is no longer soluble by the gastric juice. It is also said by some that when hard boiled, they tend to constipation of the bowels; whereas when very slightly boiled, they are known to be laxative.

This last is the state in which we ought to eat eggs, if we eat them at all. Some suppose they are best raw; but this going to the other extreme. They should be boiled just long enough to coagulate slightly the greater part of the white, while the yolk still retains its fluidity.

—William Alcott,
The Young House-Keeper, 1846

CHAPTER THREE

The General Chicken Merchants

SOUTHERN FRIED CHICKEN
Put in frying pan equal parts of lard and butter; roll the pieces of chicken in cracker dust and dip in egg then dust them again; drop in boiling fat and dry brown. Mince parsley and put in the gravy with a cup or cream.

FRIED CHICKEN AND TOMATOES
Fry chicken in boiling lard; when done, put in sliced tomatoes and fry; take up; season with salt, pepper and a little sugar.

—*Union Recorder*, Milledgeville,
Georgia, August 9, 1887

Things were heating up in Washington, D.C. in the summer of 1861. The first shots of the Civil War had been fired at Fort Sumter in April, and by May Yankee troops began amassing around the northern capital. "On to Richmond!" the headlines shouted and the Union leadership complied. By mid-July some 35,000 enlisted men found themselves packed tightly into railroad cars to be shipped south to fight.

The going was slow and the summer was hot. Tempers flared and squabbles readily broke out among the undisciplined and nervous young men as the locomotives wound out of the city. The Battle of Bull Run, the first skirmish of the Civil War, had already been announced and was just days ahead of them. Sweaty, tired, and scared, when these hungry Yankee troops arrived at the Gordonsville, Virginia railway station the aromas that greeted them must have seemed nothing short of heavenly. As their trains hissed to a stop, just outside their windows were a handful of African American women who held up trays loaded with coffee, freshly made pies, and crispy fried chicken.

Long before the Civil War, Gordonsville had always been a small town at the crossroads of American history. It started as just a single tavern at the intersection of the two main highways of colonial Virginia. George Washington, Thomas Jefferson, and James Monroe were among the ranks of the travelers who stopped in for hard cider and glad tidings of the new nation they were building. A post office, a blacksmith, and a mercantile shop soon joined the tavern, followed later by the railroads, shipments of produce, and prosperity.

The fried chicken and pie came not long after.

Black citizens vending foods in this way was a common occurrence in the South even before the Civil War and Emancipation. With the permission of their masters, slaves would take to the roadsides in town and country alike to sell their delicious wares to hungry travelers and earn themselves a small income. The practice was so common that one visitor could not help but remark as early as 1779 that, "I know already that chickens or other fresh meat can't be had but in exchange" with the "Negroes who are the general chicken merchants."

All roads in the Old Dominion led to Gordonsville, making it the center of the universe for culinary-minded African Americans. This was particularly true after the state's two main rail lines finally met in the town in the 1850s. The locomotives would pull in and the women would hold their trays of piping-hot fried chicken up to the windows, letting passengers pick and choose what part of the bird they wanted—five cents for a back, ten cents for a wing, fifteen cents for a leg or a breast. (The legs were always the best sellers.)

The food wasn't just cheap and convenient—it was delicious too. "The eating houses on the railways in the South are, almost without exception, abominable," wrote one Yankee making his way from Washington to Mobile, Alabama via train in 1868. "It took me several days to learn the secret," he continues, "but I found at last that the surest way of satisfying the appetite, and also the cheapest, is to patronize the colored women who throng around the cars at the principal stations with nicely cooked chicken, eggs, and sometimes hot coffee."

Serving up tasty fried chicken—crispy on the outside, juicy on the inside—to the thousands upon thousands of troops and increasing numbers of civilians who would eventually pass through Gordonsville during the Civil War was no easy feat. Although it has long been one of America's favorite ways to eat chicken, making fried chicken from scratch every day is an incredibly laborious process. First the chicken must be properly killed, either with an ax to the neck or a knife to the brain, and then properly plucked while still warm, with the extra feathers carefully singed off, and then properly dressed and then correctly butchered.

For those who haven't had the opportunity to butcher a chicken themselves, it's a very delicate and gruesome task. As a nineteenth-century ladies' magazine details, first, "cut off the feet where they join the fleshy part of the leg," then "put a slit just through the skin and take out the crop and windpipe, breaking the latter off at the end and cutting the gullet off as far down as possible," then "make the usual opening from the breastbone to the vent and around it, cutting through the fat but not into the intestines," among other steps that include emptying the insides, removing the gizzard, and clearing the carcass of as much fat as possible. Only from there, the cooking can begin: brining the meat, rolling it in breading, and then dropping it into glistening hot oil. Because of this intensive preparation involved for relatively little food, many African American serving women in the period after Emancipation often refused to cook chicken for their employers. (Many white homemakers without serving women did the same.)

There are many twists on the classic Southern fried chicken recipe, be it buttermilk-brined, cayenne-breaded, or double fried in pork fat. All such interpretations however can be traced back to the two original schools of preparing the dish: Virginia Fried Chicken and Maryland Fried Chicken.

Mrs. Mary Randolph, the original white and middle-class star of Southern food, had a particularly famous fried chicken recipe. Considered the earliest written example of Southern Fried Chicken, this Richmond native ascribed to the Virginian technique of frying the bird in a deep pot of what was typically bubbling hot lard. Her recipe was apparently so good that when an enslaved blacksmith named Gabriel Prosser organized an ill-fated slave revolt in Richmond in 1800, he intended to make the very talented Mary Randolph his queen in his proposed republic, presumably so she could make him this fried chicken every day.

At the same time, just across the Potomac River in Maryland, cooks preferred instead to use a shallow cast-iron skillet, in which the bird was pan-fried and then covered with a lid, meaning the meat was steamed as well as crisped. Famed American gastronome James Beard once claimed, "there is no other American chicken recipe quite so internationally famous as Chicken à la Maryland" (another name for Maryland Fried Chicken), but both variations of the dish, modified in whatever way a home cook thought best, obviously still tasted delicious when served with hot biscuits and doused with a generous portion of cream gravy.

FRIED CHICKENS

Cut them up as for the fricassee, dredge them well with flour, sprinkle them with salt, put them into a good quantity of boiling lard, and fry them a light brown; fry small pieces of mush and a quantity of parsley nicely picked, to be served in the dish with the chickens; take half a pint of rich milk, add to it a small bit of butter, with pepper, salt, and chopped parsley; stew it a little, and pour it over the chickens and then garnish with the fried parsley.

—Mrs. Mary Randolph, *The Virginia Housewife, or Methodical Cook*, 1824

Maryland Fried Chicken

1 young chicken (3 lb.)
4 tablespoons water
salt and pepper
1 cup fine bread crumbs
1 cup flour
¼ cup butter
2 eggs, slightly beaten
¼ cup pork fat

Cut chicken in pieces for serving, wash and dry. Season with salt and pepper, roll in flour, dip in slightly beaten eggs diluted with water, and roll in crumbs. Saute in butter and pork fat in heavy frying pan until browned on all sides; cover and place in moderate oven (350° F) ½ to ¾ hour, or until tender. If chicken weighs more than 3 pounds, add ½ cup hot water to pan in oven. Serve with cream gravy made from drippings in pan, substituting light cream for milk.

To Make Cream Gravy

2 tablespoons meat drippings
2 tablespoons flour
1 cup light cream
½ teaspoon salt
⅛ teaspoon pepper

Heat meat drippings lightly and stir in flour; gradually stir in light cream, and stir until mixture boils and thickens, then cook about 3 minutes longer, stirring occasionally; add seasonings. Place over hot water to keep hot and cover tightly to prevent crust from forming. Approximate yield: 1 cup sauce.

—The New York Herald Tribune Home Institute, *America's Cook Book*, 1943

Traced back far enough, fried chicken is part of the culinary traditions of Great Britain, more specifically Scotland, where the bird was preferred battered and deep-fried in pig fat. This came in heavy contrast to the dominant cooking techniques of the rest of the British Isles, where meats were overwhelmingly enjoyed after being roasted for hours over a massive fire. Such was considered the highest technique of British cuisine; in fact, it was once widely held that "in comparison with other nations, the English are most commended for roasted meates."

This skill might have been natural to the people of England—"You may be made a cook but you must be born a roaster," declared famed French gastronome Jean Brillat-Savarin—but they also used a multitude of innovations to enhance this culinary technique. Some Englishmen and women preferred the wonders of mechanical engineering to aid in their cooking, building weighted turning-jacks to continually rotate spits over their kitchen fires. Others believed it was the labor of small, innocent creatures that best flavored their supper, forcing a young child or a turnspit hound to continually turn their meats. This breed of dog, also known as the "Vernepator Cur," is now extinct, which is a pity, because it apparently had tremendous culinary talent. As a 1536 treatise on dogs remarks, "A certain dog in kitchen service [is] excellent. For when any meat is to be roasted they go into a wheel, which, they turning about with the weight of their bodies so diligently look to their business that no drudge or scullion can do the feat more cunningly."

Even without kitchen dogs, the some 145,000 Scots that made their way to the American South in the eighteenth century still managed to cook up platefuls of golden, delicious fried chicken for their English brethren. The almost half a million enslaved Africans forcibly taken to the United States also brought with them their own similar version of the dish, coated in fiery chilies or smothered in zesty curries and fried crispy in searing palm oil. In the Colonial South, where the enslaved were most often forced to be in charge of the plantation kitchen, African traditions met Scottish palates and an American classic was born.

The birds that found themselves fried in this way for the street merchants' trays or the plantation supper tables were most often the slaves' own. In the brutal system of slavery, slave rations were almost never adequate to get a human being through a week of hard labor. When the salt pork and corn were gone, hungry slaves were left to procure food in whatever ways they could, be it through hunting or cultivating small gardens or often raiding their master's stores.

In an effort to protect the livestock of white people from hungry enslaved people, in 1741 the Carolinas revised their slave code to make it illegal for slaves to own hogs, cattle, or horses. This statute became the gold standard of slave codes, and was readily adopted by the rest of the South. Conveniently missing in the text of the law was the chicken; dunghill fowls were of so little value to colonial landowners that they didn't record them in their inventories after all. (Such an allowance seems to be universal commandment of slave codes; in ancient Palestine Rabbis forbade low-level workers to sell wool or milk but chicken and eggs were just fine.)

As a result, yardbirds, as many in the South came to call chickens, moved into a place of increasing importance for the enslaved African. Savvy entrepreneurs traded their chicken's eggs, feathers, and meat with their masters or became the chicken merchants that thronged the markets in nearby towns. In some instances, slaves even earned enough money from selling these wares to buy their own freedom (as curious as such a transaction may seem). In their small way, this ingenuity marked the beginning of the bird's transformation from a backyard scavenger into today's multi-billion-dollar industry, one that, as we will repeatedly see, was continually built on the backs of the poor and the desperate.

Although during slavery those in bondage were understandably hesitant to eat their feathered opportunities, thus losing the eggs and income their chickens were routinely providing, there's still something apparently heavenly about how chickens taste. And in many ways, the bird has always had a connection to the divine in the African tradition. Just like the Romans, peoples in ancient West Africa went crazy for cockfighting, and adopted the chicken for use in religious ceremonies. The Mande of Senegal believed the bird had the gift of prophecy while the Yoruba of Nigeria came to believe that the first chickens accompanied the god Obatala and together their scratching brought life upon the Earth. In the racially mixed American South, the lowly chicken was elevated to the status of the "Gospel Bird," consciously chosen to be the crispy centerpiece of the religious social events that dominated the Sunday afternoons of Southern blacks and whites alike.

But not all Southern chickens wound up fried, even in Gordonsville. In 1862 the Army of Northern Virginia commandeered Gordonsville's famous Exchange Hotel for use as a medical facility, and over 70,000 wounded soldiers from both sides would eventually be treated there by the war's end. All these sick and wounded men, of course, required a lot of chicken soup. Indeed, shipments of chicken to the some 20,000 wounded following the Battle of Gettysburg amounted to one thousand pounds a day in the weeks following the fight, where hospital cooks and doctors boiled them into broth or steamed them into innocuous slabs of flesh for the sick, wounded, and dying. The amount sent to Gordonsville over the course of the war was presumably even greater.

Knowing the demands of the infirmaries at the height of the conflict, and staying true to their Galenic roots, the US War Department declared that the chickens obtained by the army were not permitted "for the ordinary carnal uses," but rather only for infirm soldiers and their "hospital purposes." Both the Union and Confederate governments instead aimed to keep their beefy and manly soldiers fed with as much meat as they could afford, which was actually in such small amounts, and was so difficult to keep fresh that it occasioned some of the biggest complaints from the enlisted men. Even after it started to "rust" with mold, pork largely sustained those fighting for the South while inedible salted beef and bread fed the northern soldier.

Getting enough food for soldiers during the conflict was not an easy task, however, particularly on the Confederate side. It's money, men, and food that win wars, and in the South good things to eat grew increasingly scarce as the conflict raged on. With their economy largely dependent on huge harvests of tobacco and the tufted outputs of King Cotton, even before the Civil War the region had relied heavily on food imports from the increasingly productive agricultural lands of the American Midwest. Northern blockades cut these shipments off and Confederate government policies, which called for farmers to give all their "excess" food to the army, virtually destroyed any incentive for farmers to produce more marketable food surpluses. The thrift of current and former slaves at the helm of the camp stove kept troops fed better than they would have otherwise, but hunger was still rampant. The Union, with their Midwestern meatpacking cornucopia, were a bit better off, but still, "an army is a big thing," explained one Yankee officer in 1863, "and it takes a great many eatables and not a few drinkables to carry it along."

When the government didn't provide, and generosity of the locals was hard to come by, like hungry slaves, soldiers often resorted to theft to feed themselves. With agricultural fields ravaged by battles and forests cleared of game, almost no Southern town could keep a chicken or a cow for very long when either army was near. Of course, well-off journalists writing from the safety of New York were appalled that "chicken roosts are invaded without remorse by men who, previous to enlistment, would not have taken a pin's worth from a neighbor without permission," but soldiers had bigger things to worry about than uppity editorialists. Although theft was punished in both armies by flogging or public humiliation, Yankees and Confederates still went out on regular "chicken stealing" expeditions as their commanding officers turned a blind eye.

While all these chicken thefts may have caused the government a good deal of trouble after the end of the Civil War—angry Southerners who could not have cared less about the life and death of their family's dunghill fowls just months before now petitioned endlessly for compensation for their lost birds that were "left defenseless by the laws of war"—even in times of peace, there never was quite as American a pastime as chicken stealing. Hardly a week went by that the nineteenth-century media did not report on a massive chicken heist or ring of chicken thieves operating in the vicinity of a municipality's hen flocks. Doctors, ministers, German factory workers, older women, chicken farmers, coyotes, large frogs, Italian chefs, and even author Mark Twain were all among the ranks of those who reportedly raided American chicken coops.

The problem was that no matter who actually stole the birds, the only group these charges stuck to was African Americans. Such a seeming proclivity of the black race was part of what became known as the "The Great Chicken Question" of the late nineteenth century. Great debates were held, editorials written, even professorships in "Chicken Ethics" were endowed to understand why, as one essay put it, "in the breast of every colored man," there was "a mysterious, powerful, and ineradicable yearning for chickens." Given the context of slavery, opportunity, and the celebratory "Gospel Bird," it is understandable that enslaved and free Africans flocked to chickens as a source of sustenance and economic empowerment. But so too did rich and poor whites alike, groups that would continue to raise and eat the chicken for decades to come. In the nineteenth century however, it was widely held, even in the most educated circles of white America, that "were the negro to be wholly cut off from chickens he would probably pine and die."

So rampant was the belief that all blacks were fowl addicts and uncontrollable chicken thieves that convictions were almost guaranteed in such cases. Like their English forebears, Americans were unafraid of letting their livestock take the stand and bear testimony in criminal proceedings. In 1876 a black woman in Virginia was accused of stealing a chicken. As part of the prosecution, the mother of the chickens in question was brought to court to see if she could identify those birds as her offspring. The biddy somehow managed to convince those present, beyond a reasonable doubt, that she recognized that those were indeed her progeny that were stolen. As a result of the hen's testimony, the human defendant received thirty-nine lashes.

Despite the racism inherent in these court proceedings, of all groups in the United States, African Americans certainly had more reason to steal chickens than most. Plantation slavery with its endless hours of hard labor was a life filled with misery and hunger. This system, by its very construction, meant that the enslaved had few other options but to steal livestock and poultry in order to survive. As one slave explained before the outbreak of the Civil War, ". . . dey take all our labor, and steal our chil'ren, and we only take dare chicken." The policies of much of the country in the post-slavery era, which kept African Americans largely without the ability to find decent, well-paying work and even own property, didn't offer much improvement.

Even as prominent African Americans were pressured to advocate for the end of chicken thefts by blacks, attempts at this so-called "chicken reform" grew ever more violent as each American with their own coop increasingly acquired a shotgun to defend it. A good portion of chicken thieves that were caught raiding a hen house alive in American history quickly ended up dead at the hands of a trigger-happy police officer or fowl vigilante.

With the rising death toll came the mounting public outrage. "It seems to be considered the right thing to do to shoot a man caught stealing," wrote one editorialist in 1874 after a chicken thief was killed in California, "We have more anxiety in providing punishments for men who steal the almighty dollar than for those who take a human life." In New York, people pushed back too. "It is an awful thing to think that a few fowls can outweigh a human life. It is frightful to see an armed officer of the law recklessly shooting a paltry offender who hesitates, or even refuses, to be arrested." The response to this pacifism was equally harsh. "What diamonds are to one man chicken is to another. . . . A dead thief is well disposed of, say I." What's more, "I can only say that I hope more chicken thieves will be shot and killed. I also hope all sorts of thieves, burglars, thugs, yeggmen, panhandlers, embezzlers, and other scum and vermin will be killed off."

With chickens steadily garnering higher prices among America's growing urban populations by the late nineteenth century, public policy seemed to follow the "chickens as diamonds" philosophy. If an alleged chicken thief happened to survive, the punishments were harsh, up to life in prison for some repeat offenders, a sentence most often given to African Americans. As the years rolled on, government-sponsored sterilization programs were even launched in states like Oklahoma to prevent these same degraded "chicken thieves" from reproducing. Under these racially charged laws a three-time chicken thief would be castrated but a three-time embezzler would not.

Today the cultural connection between African Americans and fried chicken is still a difficult one, a cliché fraught with centuries of brutal violence and inequality perpetuated at the dinner table and beyond. But the women of Gordonsville did not let such stereotypes get in the way of their delicious endeavors. As the Civil War subsided and commercial train service returned to the small Virginia town, Gordonsville's waiter-carriers managed to keep visitors fed and happy for decades to come. The period after Emancipation was a time of great confusion on the role of newly freed African Americans and these Virginian women were admired not just for their cooking but also for their entrepreneurship. Although little is known about their day-to-day lives, what is remembered is how these vendors made work for themselves, supported their families, and, as one historian put it, "built houses out of chicken legs."

Well into the early 1900s, travelers heading north to Washington or south to Richmond would often change their routes just for a chance to pass through the town, a place that affectionately became known as "The Fried Chicken Capital of the World." After enjoying a classic meal of Virginia Fried Chicken along its railway tracks in the 1920s, one journalist couldn't help but remark, "there was never such a place as Gordonsville. There were never better cooks. It is a fact that nowhere else on earth is chicken fried as it is here. It is an art."

Although the bird is stewed in addition to being fried, this chicken recipe comes from the earliest known cookbook written by an African American.

CHICKEN GUMBO

Salt and pepper chicken before frying it. Take a chicken, separating it from all the joints and breaking the bones, fry the chicken in one and a half tablespoonful of lard or butter. First well mix the chicken in dry flour, let the fat be hot, put chicken to fry until brown; don't burn chicken. After fried put it on in soup kettle with half a gallon of hot water, one and a half quarts of green ochre cut into thin pieces, throwing the end away, and let the whole boil to three pints; season with pepper and salt. Chop half of an ordinary sized onion fine, and fry it with chicken; chili pepper chopped fine if added is nice when liked.

—Abby Fisher, *What Mrs. Fisher Knows About Old Southern Cooking*, 1881

CHAPTER FOUR

Of Chicken and Champagne

CHICKEN SALAD, AMERICAN STYLE
Cook a four-pound chicken in some
stock; the time allowed for this varies
considerably, according to the age of the
chicken, but the usual length of time is
about two hours. When the chicken is done
put it into a vessel, pour its own broth
over, and let it cool therein; remove it, and
begin by lifting off all the skin and white
parts from the breasts; cut the meat into
dice from five to six-eighths of an inch,
and lay them in a bowl, seasoning with
salt, pepper, oil and vinegar. Chicken salad
may be prepared either with lettuce or
celery the latter being generally preferred.
Choose fine white celery, wash it well,
drain and cut it across in one-eighths of an
inch thick pieces or else in Julienne; dry
them in a cloth to absorb all the water
remaining in them. Put at the bottom of a
salad bowl intended for the table some
salt, pepper, oil and vinegar; mustard can
be added if desired; mix the seasoning in

with the celery. For lettuce prepare an ordinary lettuce salad. Lay the pieces of chicken on top, and cover the whole with a layer of mayonnaise sauce; decorate the surface with quartered hard-boiled eggs, anchovy filets, olives, capers and beets; place some lettuce leaves around, and a fine lettuce heart in the center.

—Charles Ranhofer,
The Epicurean, 1894

Although the South was left in ruins following the Civil War, prosperity returned quickly to the industrialized North. And as the nineteenth century waned, trains, steel, and oil rapidly replaced plows, fields, and crops as the engines of the American economy. Soon the output of this great industrial machine had surpassed even that of Great Britain, making the United States of America the richest republic in the world. One nation, under God, those at the very top of the capitalist heap rejoiced, and by 1880, the richest one percent of Americans had amassed nearly fifty-one percent of the nation's wealth.

If one happened to be rich enough to sit upon the rugged shores of Rhode Island's Newport Harbor on any summer day in this Gilded Age, by all reports the sights were magnificent. As the sun gently beat down on the tranquil bay, troops of ladies marched briskly through the streets as dashing financiers and commercial princes took to the helms of massive yachts to "skim the crystal brine, lapped in day-dreams and buoyant with mirth." Such spectacle, remarked one commentator, truly proved that "Yachting is the poetry of sea-faring," a poetry fueled largely by the heaping plate of chicken salad that graced every vessel's well-crafted galley.

After these rich white knights docked their pleasure boats for the evening, they robed themselves in black tie and attended one of the numerous balls held at the many fine hotels in the small Rhode Island town. And as a German brass band produced boisterous music and a "fine display of beauty, ranging from the intellectual New-England blonde to the impassioned Louisiana brunette" paraded past, these bankers again dined on chicken salad.

And when these financial barons returned to the Big Apple, as sunburnt as sea captains and ready to retake their positions at America's burgeoning financial helm, there was plenty more poetic nourishment to greet them. Among the young rabbits with mushrooms, green turtle steaks, exotic Brazil nuts, and the other hundred items that graced the lunch, late-lunch, early-dinner, dinner, and late-dinner menus of New York City's finest hotels were, of course, sumptuous plates of this white, fowl mush.

Every dish has its moment, and for chicken

salad it appears that this moment was in the opulence of the late nineteenth century. It is impossible to exaggerate the multitude of Victorian-era affairs in which an illustrious guest might have encountered plates of this spread. Heading downtown to Delmonico's for dinner? The famous restaurant's renowned French chef Charles Ranhofer made a particularly elegant version of the dish, tastefully garnished with romaine hearts and anchovies. Spending the weekend at a joyous convention in Richmond? The bill of fare was sure to contain plates of chicken salad among its offerings of saddle of venison, stewed pigeons, and English ducks with olives. Attending a grand and glorious ball down in South Carolina? An affair of any esteem would not be complete without the customary cohort of rowdy and often unwelcome "chicken salad annihilators."

To accompany their chicken salad, the upper-class drink of choice was very often champagne. A luxurious beverage in its own right, since the days of Marie Antoinette herself, nothing has connoted affluence quite like the combination of birds and bubbly. Its union of flavors is so divine it has even been immortalized in poetry; the moment of two noble young lovers finally reuniting is described by an English writer as "And we meet with champagne and a chicken at last." Even more important, such a drink can accompany the many other dishes at a lavish bird-centric banquet, as any variety goes well with the increasingly popular chicken croquette or slices of cold cut chicken or even, on occasion, boiled fowl.

> TO MAKE CHICKEN CROQUETTES:
> To one chicken and one pound of veal (cold) chopped very fine, almost to a paste, add one-half a chopped onion, one tablespoonful parsley (chopped), one saltspoonful mace, and one egg; take the same quantity of stale bread crumbs until the bread absorbs all the gravy; add that to the meat. The mixture must be quite smooth and thin; if not thin enough add a little cream or milk; it whitens the croquettes; roll the croquettes egg-shaped or cone-shaped in an egg beaten with a tablespoonful of milk, then in bread crumbs dried in the oven; fry in boiling grease in a deep pan; when done put on brown paper to absorb the grease.
> —*The New York Times*, August 28, 1881

While it may have been exceedingly fashionable to eat chicken salad in the Victorian era, enjoyment of this food was nowhere near universal in urban America. In the latter half of the nineteenth century, only if one's heels were better heeled than average did one have the privilege of encountering this dish around every ornate corner.

Although today chicken is incredibly cheap, all throughout the 1800s in American cities, it was exorbitantly expensive. As a point of comparison, in 1865, chicken in New York City markets cost 25 cents per pound, roughly $3.75 in 2016's currency, the same as a pound of pork sausage or just less than a pound of sirloin steak. During this time, when one bought a pound of sausage or a pound of sirloin steak from a butcher, one received roughly a pound of edible meat. In contrast, chicken well up until the 1950s was sold only in its whole form, very often with its head and feet still attached. With little to no processing done before the consumer took the bird home, one pound of chicken in the market roughly translated into just one quarter of a pound of meat and three quarters of a pound of chicken bones and blood and guts. A true pound of chicken meat at this time was therefore essentially four times the price of a pound of sirloin steak.

The high prices were largely because it was very difficult to find big quantities of good chickens in cities. Yes, the United States has been overflowing with these feathered creatures since colonization, and throughout the 1800s poultry was always available in the market, but the supply of birds came and went with the seasons. Because chickens naturally lay more eggs in the spring, there were typically more young birds available at that time, with larger and more mature "roasting" birds available in late fall and early winter, conveniently in time for Thanksgiving and Christmas. Prices rose and fell accordingly.

What's more, the practical American farmer still largely raised *Gallus gallus domesticus* as just a side business and with the age-old intention of simply using a chicken to make an easily renewable egg. The birds that managed to make their way into the kitchen, as in the colonial era, continued to be limited largely to those spent hens or the unproductive male "spring chickens."

And getting any of these birds to market was quite the ordeal as well. By the 1880s, there were thousands of small farmers with chickens primed for the eaters in east coast cities like New York and Philadelphia, but there were not yet highways or motorized vehicles to help them send their birds to the city folk, just horses and carriages, and the limited numbers of railroads in existence charged farmers high prices for the small numbers of chickens they were shipping. Profits on the birds were often incredibly low and so farm families with a side flock or two had very little interest in producing more birds or sending away what birds they did have.

As a direct result, the price of chicken in the city skyrocketed to exorbitant heights. A few pragmatic people responded to these tremendous prices by building urban chicken houses and raising their own birds, but Victorian upper classes had the resources to be very un-pragmatic. It is not surprising then that common convention of the nineteenth century held chicken to be an item "sought by the rich because [it is] so costly as to be an uncommon dish."

Most modern eaters spending a fortune on chicken probably wouldn't turn it into what is considered more of a deli-case delicacy today, but the Gilded Age's preference for chicken salad was a very strategic one. With advances in the railroad by the end of the century, large meat companies and independent dealers moved farther and farther afield in their pursuit of birds, and started scouring farms in the Midwest looking for suitable chickens for America's hungry cities. Once gathered in groups of four or five thousand, the birds were packed into a freight car and sent through Chicago and onward to the east coast.

While the birds most often arrived in urban areas alive, clucking and squawking and causing general disturbances in a city's railroad yards, the "disassembly line"—devised to industrially slaughter, pack, and ship the nation's beef and pork in the Midwest—was gradually being applied to the chicken too. Chickens sent on these long journeys alive always lost a considerable amount of weight due to stress, which did not bode well for prices. Poultry retailers often paid young men to ride the trains and continuously feed the birds fattening foods, but, like getting Americans to be vegetarians, it was a perpetually uphill battle to keep those chickens profitably plump.

To ensure a certain weight of bird, chickens were increasingly killed and packed in ice before being loaded on the train destined for the east coast. These chickens became known as "cold-storage birds," and their existence led to the second "Great Chicken Question" for nineteenth-century pontificators to pontificate, a debate that raged this time among fancy chefs and hotel owners. The issue: whether a bird should be sold in the market drawn or undrawn, that is, with its innards outside or in.

Chickens with their guts still intact weigh more, meaning they could be sold at higher prices to benefit farmers and dealers, and keeping the birds whole prevented contaminants from getting inside the meat. On the flip side, if the chicken is left in its whole form, some advised, "certain gases will generate in the entrails" and subsequently "render the flesh unhealthy and its taste bad." A bird with a foul or musty taste was always a cook's biggest fear when buying a chicken for roasting. With the bird popped into the oven whole, one could not tell if the bird was truly bad until it was served on the table. Hidden decomposition generated "the nasty odor which follows the carving knife's track." This risk was especially grave with cold-storage Midwestern birds traveling up to two thousand miles in an undrawn condition.

The second "Great Chicken Question" was thus the reason that chicken salad was the standby for the high-class hostess and high-minded hotelier alike. No matter how bruised or battered or smelly a chicken arrived at market, when minced to bits, mixed with enough pungent mustard and vinegar, coated with a huge quantity of creamed egg yolks, and then tastefully garnished with anchovies and a romaine heart, not one gilded guest would be the wiser.

Chicken salad, as it happens, was also an excellent choice for the upper-crust ladies attending these affairs. Meat in the Victorian era had already caused a tremendous uproar with Graham and his cracker crusade, and it still continued as an anxiety-inducing food item for the proper society woman. Chicken, having long been the lighter selection for the fairer sex, would certainly assuage these nervous lady diners. The fact that the dish was white as well, a Victorian symbol of purity, was certainly an added bonus.

But even at the hand of the most skilled kitchen servants and chefs, eating fowl in whatever form in a city was a very brave thing to do. This was still the 1800s after all and there were a lot of ways an expensive, status-laden, morally appro-priate chicken could kill you. Such unfortunate "victims of the salad" were regular fodder for the national papers, especially when a mayor and his family died from food poisoning or an opera singer succumbed to a chicken bone caught in her strong, well-trained throat.

As chicken flesh was known to be "heir to numerous ills," there was no single cause of all of this fowl-borne illness. This was decades before the widespread understanding of germs, so most of the sickness was attributed to what was generally referred to as "ptomaine poisoning," pseudoscientifically described as wayward alkaloids found in foodstuffs. (Modern medicine has rejected this theory.) How those alkaloids got into that chicken depended upon whom you asked. Some people became sick after eating a feathered victim of chicken cholera, while others received indigestion from consuming a bird that had received "bad food and improper ventilation." Sometimes "poultry [was] not properly fed during the Summer season, but allowed to roam at will," resulting in tainted meat, or other times a bird was simply too old or too young or poorly marketed or just plain bad. The cure for a bad chicken's harm to the stomach was, of course, chicken soup, along with some much-needed rest.

The easiest way to avoid all this unpleasantness and death was for a would-be chicken salad eater to avoid those cold-storage birds and to buy their chickens alive. This was often both the cheaper and safer route, but not always the most convenient. The next best thing then was to witness the death of one's dinner; as popular women's magazines warned, "if the house-keeper is too dainty to see her chicken prepared in market . . . she must run the greater risk of eating diseased or decomposed poultry."

Either way, a skilled chicken purchaser had to know how to choose the right chicken, but what was "right," again, varied considerably depending on whom you asked. A bird's color mattered to some, but not to others. Certain consumers believed that a chicken was much tastier if it had experienced the timeless pleasures of a fattening coop while others advocated for a lifetime on a strict meat and buttermilk diet. To identify a young bird, some eaters sought "skin as smooth as that of a debutante," while others were on the hunt for pin feathers, new feathers growing under the skin, which were "as sure a sign of youth as a baby's first teeth."

And then there was also the matter of a chicken's breeding, with some diners preferring a tender and flavorful bird shipped all the way from chicken-loving France, and others seeking a famous Philadelphia broiler. Raised in a small area and on a rich diet, these Philly birds were, as one commentator wrote "plump, tender-meated, juicy and sweet flavored," and, as a result, "often beyond our pocketbook."

Choosing a good chicken breed for supper became even more difficult after Queen Victoria got her hands on a few the birds in the mid–nineteenth century. Like all good monarchs, the Empress of India had a passion for collecting extraordinary chickens, the effects of which would reverberate at dinner tables the world over.

Although flourishing rather well after she assumed the British throne in 1837, the young Queen still relished her time spent out of the public eye with her beloved Prince Albert. Among her preferred escapes was her royal menagerie, a bestial collection that was constantly growing as brave English voyagers returned from far-flung corners of the globe with lions and tigers and other exotic beasts for their queen. In 1842 Victoria received a peculiar gift from one of her intrepid explorers: two male and five female Cochin China fowl from the Far East.

The Queen and her consort had never seen the likes of these "Shanghai" birds before, with their slender legs, elongated necks, and vibrant auburn feathers, all ending with the dramatic flourish of a green-black tail. Such elegant creatures made quite the contrast to scruffy native British chickens, and Victoria was smitten. She built these prize birds a grand aviary and would spend hours lounging in front of their enclosure. She soon called for more exotic chickens to be brought for her viewing pleasure, and sent these birds' eggs to her appreciative royal relatives throughout Europe, starting a royal fad of chicken-keeping across the Continent.

The society papers quickly got wind of the Queen's new hobby and the commoners grew excited. The Queen was a trendsetter after all, ushering in the era of the "white wedding" when she wore the color to marry her beloved Albert, and by 1845 the English too started collecting exotic chickens. Americans got wind of what the British were doing and the "Hen Fever" rapidly spread across the pond.

What started with just a handful of aficionados already interested in collecting and breeding the bird quickly grew to a mania exhibited with much ado at the 1849 Boston Poultry Show. The great chicken exhibition was, without doubt, the event of the year. Over ten thousand men, women, and children attended the show, whispering and gaping and delighting as "the cocks crowed lustily, the hens cackled musically, the ducks quacked sweetly, the geese hissed beautifully, [and] the chickens peeped delightfully." The event lasted three full days and was, as one con- temporaneous commentator declared, "indeed a magnificent exhibition."

From Boston Public Garden, the exotic chicken fascination quickly grew into a plague that infected everyone from senators to governors, the old and the young, those who sought chickens with long shank bones and those who looked for the springiness of their wings, as well as doctors, lawyers, preachers, farmers, the rich, the poor, and the "white, black and gray." By the early 1850s, as one account tells it, the whole of the United States was "more or less seriously affected by this curious epidemic." The inaugural chicken show hatched a second show in Boston the following year, and then a national show in New York. Within the next half-decade, local and regional exhibitions were popping up throughout the country, all featuring an ever-growing number of new, exotic, and expensive chicken breeds.

With the populace already drooling over the flocks of regal Cochins before them, in 1852 one prominent New England breeder shipped nine of his finest Brahma chickens directly to Queen Victoria herself. Developed in the United States from a hodgepodge of Asian chicken varieties, the Brahma was a large, strong, and vigorous bird with a glorious cacophony of white, black, or gold feathers covering even its legs and feet. It turned chicken fanatics' heads, including Victoria's, who was apparently overjoyed at the gift. With the Queen's approval, the Brahma quickly became the "King of All Poultry," and almost overnight the going rate of $13 for a pair of fowls at the 1849 show in Boston, that many believed to be already ludicrous, swelled to $1 for a single egg and up to $125 on a duo of fancy birds, the equivalent of $30 and $3,750, respectively, in 2016.

As a result, the chicken market grew extravagantly in a matter of months, and people who had never met a chicken before in their lives were lured to the craze by legends of birds the size of ostriches and as fearsome as tigers. (More often than not, unfortunately, these breeding novices found that those exotic eggs they had just spent their life savings on produced baby ducks or even turtles instead of chickens.)

But as quickly as the Victorian fascination with fowls spread, almost inexplicably the fancy chicken bubble burst. Where once these chickens were so valuable fanciers hired bodyguards to protect their coops, prices now plummeted rapidly to the point that they barely covered the freight costs of shipping the fowls over from Asia. "You can't get rid of these birds!" wrote one disgruntled chicken owner in 1855 as the pandemic receded. "It is useless to try to sell them; you can't give them away; nobody will take them. You can't starve them, for they are fierce and dangerous when aggravated, and will kick down the strongest store-closet door; and you can't kill them, for they are tough as rhinoceroses, and tenacious of life as cats." One fancier at least found a delicious way to properly dispose of what was once a feathered fortune: a glorious

"Shanghai" dinner, where his birds were broiled, stewed, curried, and coddled, and then served up to a cohort of other former chicken aficionados.

This is perhaps how this particular aficionado "curried" his Shanghais.

WHOLE CHICKENS CURRIED

Put the chickens whole into a saucepan, with a little pepper, salt, and a few pieces of pork; cover them with cold water. When about half done, add a cup of rice and a little more water if required. Let it boil until the chicken is quite tender, then put the chicken on a dish, and mix with the gravy a large spoonful of curry, stir it in well, and turn it over the chicken

—Elizabeth H. Putnam,
Mrs. Putnam's Receipt Book and Young Housekeeper's Assistant, 1849

Many a fowl speculator lost a fortune after the implosion of the "Hen Fever" but the world as a whole learned an important lesson in the incredible genetic gymnastics that *Gallus gallus domesticus* is capable of. As a companion on man's great journeys, this ability to adapt has always been an integral part of the global success story of the chicken. Thanks now to dedicated breeders in the United States and England, through choice crossing and re-crossing, the chicken became gargantuan and robust as Jersey Giants, stocky and rugged as Buckeyes, docile and devoted as Wyandottes, and mottled and multi-purpose as Plymouth Rocks. If a chicken aficionado needed a chicken that was big or small, fat or thin, docile or aggressive, dull or vibrant, in a few generations, with some choice mates, the chicken could make it happen.

The wondrous variations the Hen Shows were producing by the mid–nineteenth century quickly led many a research-minded individual to concede, "Poultry has been too much undervalued as a means of study." Scientists had just begun to investigate the inheritance of certain traits in plants and animals and those who saw the glorious diversity and rapid reproduction of chickens could not help but conclude that the birds provided "the best possible subjects for observing the transmission or interruption of hereditary forms and instincts."

The father of evolutionary theory agreed. Seeing the fantastic variations of hens and roosters during the "Fever," Charles Darwin readily trained his scholarly eye on our feathered friend. By studying the results of chicken breeding experiments, and quantifying the minutiae of the resulting chickens' varying forms, within a decade Darwin had cemented his radical theories on species change. What may have started with Darwin's famous finches ended with chickens and the world would never be the same.

For those more concerned with dinner, the Hen Fever produced as equally wonderful results. Although the United States Department of Agriculture had yet to be established, meaning no grand surveys of the nation's fowl population had yet been undertaken, just by the sheer popularity of the Fever in the mid–nineteenth century it can be concluded that the number of American chickens had grown dramatically. With more chickens came the first real egg boom, which meant that what was considered a great "thinking food" was now increasingly a democratic food as well. Cheap eggs were, remarked one editorialist in 1854, "the practical and excellent issue of the poultry fever." And for this reason, and this reason alone, the country should "Let it rage."

Chickens bred for eating also started to abound, led by the Brahma, a bird that could reach a weight of up to eighteen pounds and would be the most popular eating bird in the country well until the 1930s. Chicken-centric feasts were quickly filled as well with the flavors of large Jersey Giants and the English imports of plump Orpingtons and hardy Dorkings. The variation exploded the world over too, with the bird becoming mottled and streamlined as Russian Orloffs, delicate and fluffy as Japanese Silkies, pompous and crowed as Golden Polish, and jet-black and menacing as Indonesian Ayam Cemani. There are over one hundred recognized breeds of chickens today, at least two dozen of which can be traced back to the ecstatic poultry celebrations of the Hen Fever. The majority of these varieties are now coveted as "Heritage Chickens," and enjoy a place of prestige among modern breeders and "farm to table" food enthusiasts.

Although breeding standards would be soon developed and enforced by chicken associations, throughout much of the mid–nineteenth century, individual chicken owners largely multiplied their flocks according to their particular poultry preferences. Some liked their Brahmas golden, while others preferred them white. Certain chicken breeders enjoyed raising chickens with robust breasts while others preferred to own tremendous egg-layers. Yet others bred their chickens to have long legs while still others focused on developing exceedingly elegant beaks. As a result, even when choosing from among the same newfound breed of bird in a Victorian urban market, the attributes that made a superior chicken varied considerably.

There were only a few ways to identify a truly bad bird when attempting to make chicken salad, however. Any sign of putrefaction was definitely not a good thing, and so popular periodicals also sought to publish definitive guidelines for understanding a chicken's basic biology. *Good*

Housekeeping, for example, was an excellent source of advice. While on the outside, the bird's "youth and tenderness are to be judged by a small comb, smooth shanks, soft, thin skin, and an easily bent breast bone," and on the inside, among a multitude of other traits, "the entrails . . . should be almost empty, round, firm in texture, and showing little red veins here and there." Chickens that are fresh have "full, bright eyes, pliable feet, and soft, moist skin," while old fowls can be identified by their "long thin necks and feet and the flesh on back has a purplish shade."

Housewives weren't the only people to read ladies' magazines, however. The dangers of these pre-dead chickens, as one food writer put it, "lie in misrepresentation," a skill that chicken dealers readily mastered. During the 1880s and 1890s, purchasers expressly sought chickens with skins that looked rich and golden, thinking that this characteristic indicated a bird's superior flavor. Chicken merchants quickly caught on to this trend and began painting their birds with yellow substances, ranging from flower petals to sulfur, or reducing their birds' diets to only milk in order to achieve this desired color. While its methods are now subject to the regulations of the Food and Drug Administration, contemporary poultry purveyor Perdue Farms does something quite similar with its birds by including marigolds in the company feed. This produces the golden skin, the "chicken Man-Tan," that many still attribute to a more delicious chicken.

Besides stench, which dealers took care of by generously sprinkling charcoal dust and other potent deodorizers over their products, another very common way to determine a chicken's freshness in the markets of both nineteenth-century New York and particularly Paris was by looking at the feet. These would be glossy when a bird was fresh, but got progressively grayer as time wore on. Obviously the older a chicken was, the lower a price it was able to command. In response, one entrepreneurial Frenchman invented a paste that, "when rubbed on the legs, brought back the original . . . gloss, and completely erased the tell tale date of death." The man swiftly became rich and retired, leaving behind him the exceedingly lucrative and dubious profession of the "painter of poultry legs."

Another matter of vital importance to both consumers and their poultry dealers was the weight of the bird. The heavier a chicken, the more valuable it is, which obviously lent itself to further deception on the part of chicken merchants. Those same young men paid to ride the trains to keep the birds fat could also be paid to starve the fowl for days and, just before arrival at market, feed the ravenous chickens a combination of chicken food mixed with gravel. Grotesquely hungry, the birds would sometimes eat enough to double their own body weight in a matter of minutes, effectively doubling the dealer's profits.

Anyone going about their purchases of course knew "to refuse to buy a chicken with its crop full of sand and corn." This was easy enough when the chicken was drawn, but increasingly difficult after the US government officially sanctioned undrawn poultry as the fittest for consumption in the early twentieth century. Hearing the news, the poultry dealers of New York rejoiced and continued to stuff between 150,000 and 300,000 pounds of sand and rock down chickens' throats each week. Even enjoying a plate of carefully minced chicken salad after this particular decision must have been a very brave choice.

Another popular dish at this time, and through most of American history, was the classic Chicken Fricassee, which also graced many a fowl-filled banquet in the mid–nineteenth century.

MR. DEMOREST'S
CHICKEN FRICASSEE

Prepare a couple of nice plump chickens; joint them, dividing the wings, side, breast, and backbones, and let them lie in clear water half an hour; remove them then to a stew-pan, with half a pound of good, sweet salt pork cut up in pieces; barely cover with water, and *simmer* on the top of the stove or range for three hours; when sufficiently tender, take out the chicken, mix a tablespoonful of flour smoothly with cold milk, and add a little fine dried or chopped parsley, sage, and thyme, or summer savory, and stir gradually into the liquor; keep stirring till it boils; season with pepper and salt to taste; and then put back the chicken and let it boil for a few moments in the gravy; garnish with green tops of celery.

—Jane Cunningham Croly, *Jennie June's American Cookery Book*, 1870

CHAPTER FIVE

The Poor Man's Chicken

VEAL BIRDS

Wipe slices of veal from leg, cut as thinly as possible, then remove bone, skin, and fat. Pound until one-fourth inch thick and cut in pieces two and one-half inches long by one and one-half inches wide, each piece making a bird. Chop trimmings of meat, adding for every three birds a piece of fat salt pork cut one inch square and one-fourth inch thick; pork also to be chopped. Add to trimmings and pork one-half their measure of fine cracker crumbs, and season highly with salt, pepper, cayenne, poultry seasoning, lemon juice, and onion juice. Moisten with beaten egg and hot water or stock. Spread each piece with thin layer of mixture and avoid having mixture come close to edge. Roll, and fasten with skewers. Sprinkle with salt and pepper, dredge with flour, and fry in hot butter until a golden brown. Put in stewpan, add cream to half cover meat, cook slowly twenty minutes or until tender. Serve on small pieces of toast, straining cream in pan over birds and toast, and garnish with parsley. A thin White Sauce in place of cream may be served around birds.

—Fannie Merritt Farmer, *The Boston Cooking-School Cook Book*, 1896

While the rich in the Gilded Age steadily amassed fifty-one percent of the nation's wealth, and enjoyed chicken salad and champagne on every pleasure yacht they sailed, the bottom forty-four percent of Americans shared just one percent of that same prosperity. What's more, waves upon waves of immigrants kept streaming in; by 1890 New York City was home to more "Irish than Dublin, more Italians than Naples, and more Germans than Hamburg." These hungry souls stirred up competition for industrial jobs and steadily pushed down working wages. As the nation as a whole became richer, the gap between the rich and the poor only widened.

Rising income inequality translated to growing social unrest. Labor became organized and calls for "godless socialism" and the radical redistribution of wealth were increasingly heard on factory floors. The great captains of industry, most considering themselves good Christians, were not pleased with these attacks against their money and their Bible. There needed to be a way to smite down this impending crisis of industrialization, while at the same time uplifting the downtrodden and maintaining the financial blessings that had been bestowed upon the likes of the Carnegies and the Rockefellers.

This great wealth had, in part, come from innovation, from making old processes new and new processes more efficient. From the view atop great mountains of cash, it appeared that those living in poverty weren't lacking in resources, they were simply not using what they had as efficiently as possible. "The salvation of the poor," reformers concluded, "must come from better every-day living." If the application of scientific management had brought improved efficiency to the factory worker, such streamlined processes would surely allow the poor to climb out of abject poverty.

Nowhere could this sermon be more effectively applied than in the kitchen. "Half the struggle for life is the struggle for food," remarked one nineteenth-century Boston businessman, and indeed, by 1887, one half of a working-class family's income was spent on feeding itself. If this amount could be reduced in any way, the poorest Americans could afford better clothes and better homes and, with a warm body and full belly, socialism would lay its head down to rest and never rise again.

No one believed in this particular culinary gospel more than agricultural chemist Wilbur Olin

Atwater. A native of upstate New York and the son of a Methodist who learned the ways of the world at a Methodist university, his work too was inspired by the Christian faith. A dogged scholar and humorless researcher, when writing about his work with foodstuffs, Atwater often quoted the phrase, "if we care for men's souls most effectively, we must care for their bodies also."

In his youth, the first place Atwater sought the divine was in the chemical composition of American corn, which he studied using cutting-edge techniques developed in the German laboratories he greatly admired. For the better part of the last half-century, Germany had been on the forefront of food and agricultural science. In 1816, when a massive volcanic eruption in Iceland darkened the skies and caused worldwide crop failures during what became known as the "Year Without a Summer," Germany was among the hardest hit by sudden famine. Knowing what true hunger meant, that generation of scientists and farmers focused their work on finding better ways to produce and consume food.

Before these researchers set to work, no one really knew what happened to foods once they hit the stomach. With Galen long gone, it was assumed that if one ate the right amount of things that one liked one could be healthy. Everything ended up the same in the body so it would be fine to simply live on "bread alone," if one liked that sort of thing. The Germans didn't agree. Led by a particularly talented and bold chemist named Justus von Liebig, these scientists applied rigorous analyses to foods, the human body, and cooking. In their laboratories they broke down edibles, discovering them to be made of fats, proteins, and carbohydrates, and put graduate students in giant metal boxes they called "calorimeters," calculating the amount of heat the human body generated when doing everything from sleeping to running to eating.

Justus von Liebig has since rightly earned himself the title of the "Father of Organic Chemistry," but he was also a bombastic man, with flossy hair and a great eye for neckwear, and often used his platform as a high-profile scientist to talk about his favorite subject, "the juice of flesh." These are the liquids that come out of meat when it is cooked. To Liebig, there was valuable nutriment to be found in these juices, and ordinary cooking wasted them. Teaching the poor how to prevent this loss would necessarily better their health, so Justus widely advocated home cooks to sear meats to retain all nourishment. Although this culinary concept has zero basis in scientific fact, many cooks today still believe that searing meats really does help to "seal in the juices."

Not content with just advocacy, Liebig soon founded the Liebig Meat Extract Company, and started bottling and selling this "juice of flesh" to pharmacies. Pulped and extracted from the cattle of South America, Liebig claimed that "meat teas" made from his concentrated meat juices were as therapeutic as chicken soup. If properly applied, he explained, the extract could cure even ovarian inflammation and typhus fever.

At first doctors were thrilled. The "whole medical profession owe[s] a deep debt of gratitude to Liebig for having put into their hands a means of giving their patients the nutritive parts of animal food in a remarkably concentrated form," exclaimed members of London's Royal Medical Society in 1865 and these extracts quickly became staples of the Victorian pantry. Unfortunately for Liebig, nutritional science progressed beyond his work and discovered that the "juice of flesh" actually contained little nutriment at all. Being almost as savvy at public relations as he was at chemistry, Liebig quickly changed his marketing message: meat juice is just plain delicious. His meat extract company, now known as Liebig Benelux, still exists today.

Atwater, a more modest man, continued his work in the States, his focus shifted from American corn to American fish and in the second half of the 1880s he rigorously applied German methods to understand the composition of more than fifty species of them. Atwater's detailed work eventually took him to Germany itself, where he became inundated with the gospel of calories and constituents. (He avoided the juice of flesh.) In Atwater's eyes, the world had finally discovered a unified field theory of food, and its applications to everyday life were immediate and profound. The differences between cheap foods and expensive foods dissolved under chemical analysis. A protein was a protein was a protein and a fat was a fat, which meant that if the poor could be taught to eat more efficiently and effectively, it would be the path to their salvation.

Atwater returned to the United States invigorated. He immediately ran to the pulpit declaring, "the cheapness or dearness of different foods must be judged by comparing, not the prices per pound, but the costs of actual nutrients." He went about setting up his own food science laboratory at his alma mater Wesleyan University, equipped with its own state-of-the-art calorimeter filled with graduate students, and over the course of his career doggedly recorded the constituents of over one thousand edible items. His findings he presented to the public in food values tables and in wildly popular articles that made him one of the most famous scientists in the country during the late nineteenth century. Atwater's ideas reverberated strongly within the reform-minded community too. "Knowing what to eat," echoed a popular magazine, "should be almost as exact a science for every intelligent adult in this age as for an engineer to know what to feed his engine to secure it the most effective service."

The most effectual portion of the meal to apply Atwater's ideas was the meat course. Even when the urban poor were having trouble feeding themselves, they still ate a lot of animals. According to an 1874 survey of Massachusetts's workers, almost half of working-class families ate fresh meat at two meals a day, which was quite a feat given their low wages and how erratic the supply of fresh meat was to cities at this time. And their meat of preference was still largely beef; even after all these years, as one nineteenth-century newspaper proudly proclaimed, the citizens of the United States were still "essentially a hungry *beef-eating* people."

The problem wasn't the beef though. According to Liebig, proteins were the only constituents that became human muscle and thus were the only true nutrients in food. Pound for pound, foods with more protein were therefore more wholesome. Atwater agreed, and in him the nation's hungry citizens had finally found the beef-eating messiah they had been looking for. As Atwater wrote in 1894, "A pound of lean beef, a quart of whole milk and a pound and a quarter of potatoes contain the same amounts of actual nutritive ingredients," but ultimately the nutrients found in the pound of beef, "are, for ordinary use, more valuable."

The problem was rather that Americans were

eating expensive beef. The porterhouse steak, the rib roast, and the sirloin all were readily snapped up by consumers, leaving butchers to grumble that the "very best portions of the carcass were not 'popular', and could hardly be disposed of at any price." "Even a laborer on the street or a negro will come in and ask for porterhouse steak," growled another meat vendor. "[N]obody wants anything else." The solution for Atwater and his ilk was simple: "If the American people . . . would ask their butcher for the 'breast,' 'chuck,' and 'shoulder,' which are quite as nutritious, and much more economical than the favorite cuts, it would improve the general heath, and be a source of saving."

This substitution campaign, sacrificing one's favorite rump roast for the sins of one's budget, would be markedly easier if Americans knew how to properly prepare the less popular cuts of meat. Unfortunately, they didn't. Thanks to its fine streams and dainty hillocks, the country had always managed to produce massive quantities of low-cost meat that the rest of the world could only dream about. American cooks typically fried or boiled up these massive hunks of flesh and threw them on a plate with little garnish or skill. As one visiting French chef wrote in 1865, "in the United States the national cooking is the worst known." Charles Dickens, after a brief tour of the country, came to the same conclusion, as did the proprietor of a famous cooking school in New

York. In 1879 she threw up her hands and decried, "In no other land is there such a profusion of food, and certainly in none is so much wasted from sheer ignorance, and spoiled by bad cooking."

But, in the new science of foods, it didn't really matter what dinner tasted like. America's eaters had to be taught not to enjoy their food but rather to produce meals with the maximum nutriment for their bodies. Food was fuel and public cooking schools with their science of home economics sprung up to teach people how to properly use it. As the 1896 *Boston Cooking-School Cook Book* declares, through this science of cooking "mankind will eat to live," as opposed to living to eat, and "will be able to do better mental and physical work, and disease will be less frequent." At last, Paradise could be found on earth, and it would be achieved through counting calories!

The growth in chicken consumption owes a great deal to these scientific crusaders out to save the impoverished American eater. For the first time in Western history, ideas about healthy eating put the lowly chicken on the same playing field as beef and pork. Atwater studied chicken meat, quantified its fats and proteins, and placed it up in the same column of his food values tables as beef, pork, fish, and shellfish, all of which were concluded to also contain generous portions of protein.

The playing field still wasn't even, however. Old social preferences on what meat to eat still held, even though the lens with which to view them was no longer humoring the humors but rather calculating the constituents. Beef was now, as one cookbook declared in 1882, a "Bible and chemically sanctioned food, purposely designed for man" that is "very satisfying to the stomach and possesses great strengthening powers." Pork still did "not generally meet the approval of intelligent people and is almost entirely discarded by hygienists" and remained enemy number one of health reformers. The most famous pork-hater during Atwater's time was John Harvey Kellogg, a man who not only invented corn flakes as yet another attempt to prevent Americans from touching themselves but also consistently campaigned against eating pig, an animal he liked to describe as an "animated mass of physical defilement." And the chicken was still idling on the sidelines. It provided ample protein like the rest, but even Atwater's tables demonstrated that the bird didn't provide nearly enough calories, pound for pound, to compete with the red meats.

What's more, in the age of budget-oriented substitutions, chickens weren't a very budget-friendly choice. When one didn't raise chickens, the bird was still quite an expensive food item to purchase, pound for pound. As a result, chicken was very often the focus of chefs cooking mock foods, dishes that were made to look and hopefully taste like another.

There are a multitude of reasons for making food substitutions like this—to impress a guest, to subvert a religious law, to save money, to bring back nostalgia for foods made distant by time and geography, or just to have fun. The English were big fans of mock foods, particularly around the meatless days of Lent. Despite not being considered meat, chicken had never been permitted on fasting days since the seventh century. (In the ninth century the rules were relaxed a bit to allow fish, but never birds.) The English counterpoint to Mrs. Mary Randolph was one Mrs. Maria Eliza Rundell and her very famous *A New System of Domestic Cookery* (1824), which taught the English how to turn the swim bladder of a cod, a common food in the Victorian era, into something that looked like a young chicken. This recipe would have been a good one for the Lenten season. A century earlier one of Mrs. Rundell's culinary predecessors had instructed the English how to transform tripe, or pig's stomach, into mock cock's combs, a dish that was both unusual and less welcomed on the tables of the devout.

COD SOUNDS TO LOOK LIKE SMALL CHICKENS
A good maigre-day dish. Wash three large sounds nicely, and boil in milk and water, but not too tender; when cold, put a

forcemeat of chopped oysters, crumbs of bread, a bit of butter, nutmeg, pepper, salt, and the yolks of two eggs; spread it thin over the sounds, and roll up each in the form of a chicken, skewering it; then lard them as you would chickens, dust a little flour over, and roast them in a tin oven slowly. When done enough, pour over them a fine oyster-sauce. Serve for side or corner dish.

—Maria Eliza Rundell, *A New System of Domestic Cookery*, 1807

TO MAKE ARTIFICIAL COXCOMBS

Take Tripe, without any Fat, and with a sharp Knife pare away the fleshy part, leaving only the brawny or horny part about the thickness of a Cock's Comb. Then, with a Jagging-Iron, cut Pieces out of it, in the shape of Cocks Combs, and the remaining Parts between, may be cut to pieces, and used in Pyes, and serve every whit as well as Cocks Combs: but those cut in form, please the Eye best and, the Eye must be pleased, before we can taste any thing with Pleasure. And therefore, in Fricassees we should put those which are cut according to Art.

—Richard Bradley, *The Country Housewife and Lady's Director*, 1732

• • •

By the time Atwater had been baptized in the fires of his culinary crusades, many low-income cooks in the United States were already making a very popular dish called "the veal bird." This is simply veal pounded flat, wound around a stick, and seasoned to taste like chicken. From a culinary perspective, when pounded flat, veal and chicken breast are pretty similar in terms of flavor—that is, they both have very little of it. Breaded, seasoned, and deep-fried in the same way, it's very hard to tell if a young cow or a piece of chicken actually ended up on your plate.

That's what made this substitution so wonderful that even the *Boston Cooking-School Cook Book* included it among its recipes. (This cookbook would eventually become one of the best-selling tomes in American history.) In an almost complete reversal of contemporary food status, while chicken was expensive at the time of the American Industrial Revolution, veal was then one of the cheapest meats in the market. An automated milking machine had been recently invented, causing the commercial dairy industry to take off. With more dairies came more veal calves, whose regular births keep dairy cows producing their milk. Like male chickens, male calves are more of a farm nuisance than anything else and so, after four to five months on their mother's udder, they are typically shipped off to the dinner table.

In the age of the industrial revolution and the veal bird, a lot of times when people of all stripes thought they were buying chicken they were actually getting veal or pork or even rabbit anyway. Of course, it was hard to pass off a baby cow as a chicken when the bird was being sold in its whole form in market, but the rise of eating-houses and the beginnings of processed foods made the illicit substitution easier and cheaper. The first chicken sausages and premade potpies and even chicken salads, particularly those that made their way into poorer parts of the city, were almost never actual chicken. Canned chicken, which was growing popular in the 1880s, was notorious for actually being "Bob veal," calves less than four weeks of age that were considered too young to be sold as proper veal by butchers.

These Bob veal calves were causing such a hubbub among eaters at this time mainly because the country was beginning to see an animal's welfare as yet another factor to consider when choosing meat for their supper tables. Great Britain had passed the Cruelty to Animals Act of 1876, and although the US government wouldn't follow suit until 1966, anticruelty societies were gaining considerable traction throughout the United States in the late nineteenth century.

In the poultry market, the primary issue these groups confronted was the common practice of many poulterers of plucking chickens while the birds were still alive, the reasoning being that such an act preserved the integrity of the meat. If you wait too long to pluck a chicken after it has been slaughtered, the flesh becomes rigid and the feathers become increasingly difficult to remove. The alternative to live picking usually involves scalding, which often cooks the birds slightly. Nineteenth-century eaters, in general, preferred dry-picked chickens, which were considered better in quality and were also more expensive.

What thus resulted was a culinary-ethical dilemma that most Americans have confronted at some point in their lives when eating animals, the Victorian version being choosing between a superior bird treated poorly and an inferior bird that had experienced a more humane dispatching. But, as history proves, taste and what would today be considered animal cruelty have often gone hand in hand. The English bulldog, for example, was bred for the traditional English blood sport of bull baiting, a practice in which the dog repeatedly attacked a restrained cow for hours before its death. While later banned under the government's animal cruelty statute, for many centuries this custom was actually a requirement of any beef that went to market, as it was thought the bovine's final hours of terror considerably improved its postmortem flesh. Such a practice comes in sharp contrast to modern views on meat quality; humane slaughter legislation is often passed, in part, because it is now held that a more humane dispatching enhances the quality of meats being produced in the United States.

Standards of the treatment of animals were different in the kitchen as well. Putting any and all lobster-boiling guilt to shame, royal cooks in 1300 in France were in possession of a recipe called "How to Roast a Chicken and Make it Live Again." To make this peculiar dish, the cook was first instructed to pluck a chicken while it was alive, coat it with spices and seasonings, and then gently rock the bird into a delicate slumber. The chicken would then be served on the table flanked by a few of its already cooked brethren. When one nobleperson started carving into the already roasted fowls—"Squawk!"—this still-kicking bird would pop back to life. At this point, the chef actually kills the creature, stuffs its throat with mercury and a tasty sauce, and roasts it over an open fire. When carving for the second time, the mercury in the throat produces a mild clucking sound from the now dead bird, hence making the chicken live again.

This recipe was in many ways excessive; who has the kind of time anymore to lull a chicken to sleep for the purposes of macabre dinner theatrics? What most concerned consumers were forced to do was instead to take poultry dealers by their word that the bird was killed before its feathers were forcibly removed. While as dubious as food poisoning caused by ptomaines, such claims may very well have been the pinnacle of the achievements of the poultry rights movement. Thanks to the same semantics that allowed slaves to own chickens, the bird is not mentioned in the 1958 Humane Slaughter Act, nor for that matter any subsequent legislation regarding humane slaughter methods, meaning that even today there is little to no oversight over the pain and suffering a chicken experiences as it wends its way through the slaughterhouse to your dinner plate.

Another way to avoid cruelty toward chickens in the industrial era and beyond was simply to return to imitation foods yet again. By the early twentieth century, butchers seized on the trend of a fake bird and started skewering cubes of veal and pork and selling it to their customers as "mock chicken." All the eater had to do was bring the meats on a stick home, coat them in bread and egg crumbs, and then brown and simmer, finally eating the meat like a drumstick. Since chicken was so expensive in cities by the 1930s, the name of these skewers morphed into "city chicken" just in time for the Great Depression. Packages of pork, skewered and labeled in such a way, can still be found and enjoyed from supermarkets in some parts of the Midwest.

Contemporary entrepreneurs have embraced the idea of mock chicken as well, cooking up fake meats from nonanimal sources that they hope, someday soon, will really "taste like chicken." A protein is a protein is a protein after all and, if this fake chicken is seared properly, perhaps even Justus von Liebig would be pleased by the flavor and nutrition of this chicken-free flesh.

CITY CHICKEN

Take one pound veal steak, one pound pork tenderloin. Cut in pieces about one and one-half inches square. Put alternately a piece of veal, then a piece of pork on wooden skewers that are used for rolled roast, until six pieces are used. Roll each "chicken" in cracker crumbs and beaten egg. Brown well on sides, season well. Put in roaster, add two cups of water, cover and bake two hours. When done add a cup of rich milk to make the gravy.

—Mrs. Mary Morton, "Household Hints,"
The Washington Reporter,
November 27, 1926

CHAPTER SIX
America's Egg Basket

NO. 39. SPANISH OMELET.

Emilia Lundberg,
2400 South Flower Street, Los Angeles

One cup boiling milk, butter the size of an [*sic.*] eggs, yolks and whites separate, pepper and salt. Pour the boiling milk over the butter and crumbs. When cool add the yolks of the eggs beaten light; add salt and pepper to taste. Beat whites until stiff and dry, cutting and folding them into first mixture. Have omelet pan hot, and butter sides and bottom. Turn in mixture, spread evenly, place on range where it will cook slowly. When well "puffed" and delicately browned underneath, place pans on center grate of oven to finish cooking the top. Spread with tomato sauce before folding. Serve at once on a hot platter. Garnish with parsley and tomato sauce around omelet.

Tomato sauce: Cook two tablespoons of butter with one tablespoon of finely chopped onion, until yellow. Add two cups of tomatoes, a small piece of red pepper. (One tablespoon sliced mushroom or minced ham may also be added.) Cook until moisture has nearly evaporated. Season with salt and Cayenne pepper. This will make two large omelets, each sufficient for five persons.

—*Los Angeles Times Cookbook*, 1905

Sea breezes and sunshine were the only things sailing medical student Lyman Byce was seeking when he left the cold of Canada for California in 1878. His final destination was a small area just north of San Francisco known as Petaluma, a region so nice that when Europeans arrived they assumed the local Miwok peoples were calling it "Oh, the Fair Valley" when the Miwok were actually just referring to it as "side hill." A century earlier, the Spanish too were very fond of *péta lúuma* with its abundant timber and good soil, establishing Rancho Petaluma and turning it into a major agricultural center of their short-lived west coast empire.

By the time Byce arrived, Rancho Petaluma had been shortened to just Petaluma, but its role as an agricultural center was ever growing. Tales of enormous gold nuggets had drawn over one hundred thousand souls to California between 1848 and 1855. While very few miners ended up filthy rich, many of those who fed them certainly did. Legends of the region's natural riches were surpassed by stories of cattlemen roaming the streets in $1,000 suits, of prostitutes making $50,000 a year from their backyard gardens, and of humble dry goods stores turning men into millionaires.

Demand for edibles in San Francisco skyrocketed along with food prices. Even with local farmers plowing ahead at full speed, their outputs weren't nearly enough to feed all the new hungry mouths. Food had to be sent over on ships from the east coast (the transcontinental railroad hadn't been completed yet) and imported from foreign producers in China, Chile, and the Kingdom of Hawai'i. With the region flooded with hungry single men, who were apparently unable to light a camp stove to save their lives, the same square meal in Seattle that could be had for $0.25 now cost a man $1.50 or more in San Francisco. Like the King of Hawai'i, the farmers of Petaluma who hadn't abandoned their posts to pan rivers for gold were making a fortune sending fruit and milk to feed hungry miners.

In the era of the forty-niner, a single chicken egg was almost as valuable as gold; men wrote home to their families complaining that while they could get a pound of beef for around twenty-five cents, a single egg cost him upward of $1, or roughly $30 in today's currency. The people of Petaluma capitalized on this. Among their orchards and dairies, each farm family had their own small flock of chickens and all the eggs they didn't eat they sent down river into the big city. In just three months, the small town could sell some 250,000 eggs, but even that wasn't enough to satisfy the ever-growing demand.

Simply producing more eggs was not that easy however. Egg prices were high around San Francisco well up until the 1880s because there was no real poultry industry in California, or anywhere else in the country for that matter. The way most eggs made it to market on the east coast was the same way the chickens did—through a massive crowdsourcing of all the farms east of the Mississippi. Chicken dealers would go from flock to flock, eventually gathering up enough eggs to make a dozen, and enough dozens to make a case, and then shipped them eastward on the vast networks of canals and growing number of railroads. It wasn't a perfect system by any means. Eaters in Washington, D.C. often complained that it was easier for them to find months-old eggs coming from states along the Mississippi, which were brought in by speedy rail and barge, than fresher, local eggs from nearby farmers, which were transported via slower horse and cart, but the coordination on the east coast was still much better than the sparse infrastructure of California.

Entrepreneurial souls out west did attempt to start their own chicken farms, but each eventually failed. The first difficulty an aspiring nineteenth-century chicken producer faced was in procuring enough chickens. A good hen will lay an egg every other day, or a bit more, on average, but if a farmer wants to increase his or her flock size, it takes a few weeks for the lady chicken to lay enough eggs (that are not collected for sale) in order to make her start brooding. From that point, she will sit on them for three to four weeks and then spends the next six to ten weeks raising these baby chicks to maturity, during which time she doesn't feel the need to lay any more eggs.

Farmers have long known that the best way to get a chicken to keep laying is to immediately take her eggs away from her. Some of these eggs are eaten while the rest are set aside to hatch in whatever artificial incubators a given civilization has at hand. Some 3,000 years ago the ancient Egyptians had their massive egg ovens, which were simple clay brick structures filled with eggs and heated by a central fire. If properly trained, a single individual using such an incubator could hatch 40,000 to 80,000 eggs at once by carefully monitoring the fire's temperature and turning the eggs twice daily, mimicking the care of a mother hen. Similar heated buildings have also been found in China dating from roughly 500 B.C., although, given their culinary proclivities, the ancient Chinese were probably hatching more ducks than chickens.

Medieval Europeans had their own incubators as well, albeit on a much smaller and rudimentary scale, typically wooden boxes heated by fires or rotting manure. When European nobles heard about the egg ovens of the Egyptians in the early eighteenth century, they immediately sent for these experts to build replicas on their grand villas throughout the continent. Although many Egyptians obliged, the Europeans could not manage to find the same success in hatching chickens. The major drawback of primitive incubators, both large and small, was that it was incredibly difficult to replicate the hen's consistent heat of roughly 100° Fahrenheit for the entire twenty-one or so days it takes to hatch the baby chicks. Too cold and the eggs do not develop; too hot, and with too much humidity, one had created a very expensive and convoluted way to hard boil hundreds of eggs at once.

Unable to replicate the Egyptian's skill, Europeans turned instead to their mechanical ingenuity, using fermentation or steam radiators or grain alcohol to try to achieve regulated temperatures. Each of these eventually failed too. People in the United States found their own distinctly American versions of incubating, and for a brief period in the mid–nineteenth century a Chicken Soup Hot Spring, which was used to hatch baby chicks by submerging the eggs in the warm water, was one of the major tourist attractions in the state of Nevada. Apparently, with a dash of salt and pepper, whatever minerals leached into that spring made the water taste exactly like chicken soup.

The chickens themselves weren't helping the cause in California either. Even if an aspiring chicken farmer managed to get them in a decent enough quantity for any sort of economy of scale, the would-be hen keeper quickly found, as one poultry expert declared in 1855, "fowls, in any large number, will not thrive." Poultry diseases are (and continue to be) particularly rampant and especially deadly when birds are in any sort of big group.

Another difficulty was that feeding lots of chickens was an expensive enterprise. A couple of chickens in the backyard can be left to peck around for kitchen scraps and insects. Chickens in a large mob need to be fed and that food needs to contain essential nutrients and animal protein. ("If fed on grain alone they become remarkably fat, sicken and die," wrote one fowl philosopher in 1860.) "The great difficulty generally attendant upon rearing and keeping large numbers [of chickens] is that of providing them with suitable food," explained one west coast agricultural magazine. This was especially true when the price of a pound of flour was jumping from $8 to $85 in a single year. At least one Californian, drawn to the pleasures of the hen, spoke of spending most of his waking hours scrounging through garbage cans to find enough food for his birds. For these various reasons, farmers have been advised since the age of the Romans to never keep flocks exceeding 200 chickens.

To meet the hungry demand, eggs were coming in instead from across the China Sea and from Boston on the only sea route available, a four-month journey that took the eggs all the way around Cape Horn of South America and then up to the west coast. Even well beyond the point of freshness, the substantially lower price of Boston eggs made them preferable to those produced locally. Although agriculturalists may have lamented the state's exorbitant egg prices, there was still no economic incentive to start a local chicken industry.

This was very unfortunate for the eaters of the west coast. The first rule of egg eating has always been that newly laid eggs are best. As an egg ages, its yolk and albumen (the white) become increasingly watery and, subsequently, increasingly bad tasting. While contemporary eggs may appear fresh, unless you have your own flock of chickens, they are almost never newly laid.

When straight from the chicken, the texture and flavor of an egg, even raw and sucked straight from the shell, are incomparable. The French chefs of the seventeenth century knew this and more, often adjusting their recipes not just to the age of the egg but also the season during which it was laid. (Summer eggs, being laid during insect season, were "very bad to eat" as compared with spring or winter eggs.) There's a legend in professional kitchens that the one hundred pleats in a chef's toque, also known as his or her fancy chef's hat, represent the one hundred ways to cook an egg in French cuisine. Although no one today, not even the most famous of French chefs, is sure this rumor is true, there's no denying the firm French conviction that "all cookery rests on the egg." Eggs are the binder in the classic *crème brûlée*, the wash on a golden *pâte à choux*, the leavening assistant in a *soufflé*, but old school French chefs would also poach egg yolks in sugar syrup, scramble them whole with orange and nutmeg, and fluff them into perfect omelets, the dish one renowned chef known only as Stacpoole declared to be "the thing that is as French as a Frenchman, and which expresses the spirit of our people as no other food could express it."

Americans have always had a love-hate relationship with French food. Although early colonists rejected the apparent opulence of French cookery, the very first and most famous restaurants in the United States, including Delmonico's, all served up French cuisine to the American upper classes. At-home cooks attempted to cook

French food as well, resulting in large demand for good French cookbooks, like La Cuisine Française, *which had multiple printings in the late nineteenth century. Given his tendency to eat iguanas, it can be concluded that Christopher Columbus never prepared the following egg dish created in his name.*

OEUFS À LA CHRISTOPHE COLOMB

Portions: For five persons

6 Poached eggs
¼ lb. Jelly of meat
6 Toasts
Butter
¼ lb. Paté de foie gras

Time: ½ hour

Preparation: 1st. Make a small toast about 2½ inches in diameter and 1 inch thick, fry them in butter, lay over a coat of "paté de Foie Gras" about ¼ inch thick, taking care to leave a hole in the middle. 2d. Dispose them on a warm dish and place upright on each toast in the hole menaged in the "paté de foie Gras" an egg poached and carefully shelled. 3d. Let melt in a sauce pan ¼ lb. of "Jelly of

Meat" and ¼ fresh butter, mix well the whole, don't allow to boil and pour over the eggs.

—François Tanty,
La Cuisine Française, 1893

Although not everyone was quite as jazzed about egg artistry as the French, the enjoyment of the chicken's egg has definitely not been limited to just the fans of the Gallic cock in the Western world. In ancient Rome it was customary to start the meal with some sort of egg dish, be it soft-boiled, hard-boiled, made into the first omelets, or fried, leading to the popular Latin trope *ab ovo usque ad mala*, translated to "from eggs to apples," meaning from beginning to end. In Renaissance kitchens from Italy to England, an egg would be poached in milk or wine, stirred into a frittata with a little pork blood and spices, creamed with saffron, or hard-boiled with salt and pepper, sliced, and strewn over fish.

A particularly popular Renaissance preparation method was the roasted egg, which was set down raw to cook besides a blazing fire or buried in hot ash. Depending on the amount of time it spent lounging by the heat, the egg's insides would gain a caramel color and an immense depth of flavor. To cook an egg in this way required much skill; without proper attention, an egg next to the heat for too long could explode or would be cooked only on one of its halves. The English cooking public must have known this quite well, making William Shakespeare's insult, "Truly, thou art damn'd, like an ill-roasted egg, all on one side," particularly cutting. Another variation of this was to impale raw eggs on a searing spit (the heat cauterizes the albumen around the punctured shell) and set that above the flames. Perhaps a turnspit hound helped the English cooks rotate this unusual staff diligently above the fire, but at least one cookbook author at the time thought that eggs on a spit was "a stupid concoction."

Egg cookery has expanded as far as the chicken itself. Almost every world cuisine has whipped up delicious homages to the chicken egg, from the *shakshuka* of North Africa, a tasty breakfast dish of eggs baked with fiery tomato sauce, to the shredded eggs sprinkled over Indonesian *nasi goreng*, that archipelago's famed fried rice. The beginnings of these culinary traditions may have come with the bird as it traversed the globe those many thousands of years ago, or they may have come before, with the eggs of wild birds. Even in a culinary sense, we will probably never know which came first, the chicken or the egg.

From an evolutionary perspective though, we actually do know the answer: the egg came first, laid by a creature that was not quite yet a chicken. And the fact that other birds also lay eggs was immensely helpful to hungry Californians in the

1850s. The Pacific coast had long been a super-highway for migratory sea birds, many of which would stop to nest on the Farallon Islands, a collection of jutting and rocky sentinels standing just thirty miles outside the San Francisco harbor. One of these species was the common murre, a bird that looks something like a flying penguin and has the convenient characteristic of not defending its nest when chased off. In 1849, a man remembered by history as Dr. Robinson took his boat out to the Farallones and filled it up with the murre's distinctive large blue eggs. When he brought them back to San Francisco, diners just ate them up, enthralled by the speckles splashed on the eggs' pointed shells and the fiery red yolks that were contained within. Although their flavor was decidedly fishy, the eggs were still "rich, delicate, and altogether desirable—dropped, fried, boiled or cooking in any of the hundred ways known to a Frenchman."

From his first journey, despite having broken half of his original trove of murre eggs, Dr. Robinson made enough money to buy a pharmacy and to start a Farallon egging company. Seeing his success, one of Dr. Robinson's neighbors soon copied him and almost overnight the murre egg rush was on. Donning their cotton sack "egging shirts," intrepid men from rival egging companies would risk life and limb scrambling over sharp rocks, climbing sheer cliff faces, and fending off aggressive seagulls to gather up their shelled quarry. Egging season would begin each year in May with the eggers stomping on all existing murre eggs, thereby ensuring the ones they gathered were freshly laid. (If sat upon for a single day, they claimed, the eggs would be unfit for market.) By the time the season was over in August, the companies gathered as many as 500,000 eggs, an astonishing number coming from a bird that typically lays only one egg in a single season. The prices the eggs would reach in the San Francisco market were up to $1 a dozen, also not a measly sum when eggers could gather hundreds of eggs in a single day.

But with more money came more problems for eggers, and the business soon became too lucrative for friendly competition on the islands' cramped and jagged shores. In the summer of 1863, a small city news headline in San Francisco declared, "War in Earnest at the Farallones." Independent Italian eggers had attempted to land on the islands to start that year's egging in early June, only to be blocked by the established Farallon Egg Company. The disgruntled Italians shouted that they would land on these islands "in spite of hell" and returned to do just that the next morning, this time a little bit drunk and also with guns. A legitimate battle ensued and ultimately two men were killed in the conflict, one on each side. The leader of the invaders, one Captain D. F.

Batchelder, was ultimately convicted of murder and sent for a year in state prison.

Despite continued tensions between rival egging interests, the ravaging of the Farallon murres continued for decades, even after an 1881 government mandate officially prohibited egging companies from visiting the islands. With lighthouse keepers and independent fishermen keeping the tradition alive, summers in San Francisco continued to be "gull egg" season well into the early twentieth century. The now less-common murre are only just beginning to recover on the Farallones and they have the disorganized chicken farmers of California to thank.

Eventually, when the murre eggs dwindled and food prices stabilized, the incentives returned for starting a California chicken industry. Following the completion of the transcontinental railroad in 1869, eggs were now more quickly shipped across the country in massive, stuffy railway cars that had an environment very similar to a hen's nest. Eggs carried by these hot locomotives had about a one in twelve chance of actually carrying a growing baby chicken, and bartenders at the best hotels on the west coast were growing tired of breaking eggs under the table to make their drinks for their customers. Boston eggs suited when nothing else was available but hotelkeepers were now willing to pay a premium for fresher, locally produced eggs.

And that's when Lyman Byce came along, a man who may have been studying medicine but who was really born to be the king of the hen men. By the time he had arrived in Petaluma at the age of twenty-six, he had already built a great many things, from a potato digger to an acoustic telephone to a surgeon's lancet. Byce had grown up with a flock of chickens on his family farm in Ontario, and at the age of sixteen had made his first attempt at producing a reliable mechanical incubator. His dreams of rest and relaxation in Petaluma were quickly cut short when he came upon a prototype of an incubator made by a local dentist named Dr. Isaac Dias. The machine brought hens back on Byce's mind and within the year the young man had built what would become the world's first commercially viable artificial incubator.

The Dias-Byce contraption was quite the thing to behold. An octagonal box raised off the floor on four ornate legs and carved from sturdy California redwood, it had the appearance of an eccentric coffee table more than anything else. Byce had solved the problem of consistent heat by affixing a combination of a coal lamp and a mechanical regulator to the bottom of his egg box and had installed glass doors on each side of the contraption for easy access to the up to 650 eggs inside. The only work an owner of Byce's incubator was required to do was play the role of dutiful hen and turn the eggs twice daily.

The fashionable and practical incubator caused an immediate sensation. Bringing it on a grand tour of agricultural fairs throughout the country, crowds of men, women, and children would gather around Byce and his machine to watch tiny beaks and feathered bodies poke through their shells, "wet and bedraggled and evidently convinced so early that life at best was but a burden." Knowing that hens weren't always enough, to garner even greater attention Byce started hatching more exotic fare, like ostriches, silkworms, and alligators, at exhibitions. His stunts worked, and his contraption's reputation grew. The throng surrounding Byce and his boxes was so immense at the 1879 Sonoma-Marin Agricultural Society Fair that several women fainted in the rush to get close enough to see the demonstration of the machines.

While Byce found a way to make the incubator effective, a Danish farmer by the name of Christopher Nisson found a way to make it profitable. A longtime resident of Petaluma, Nisson had dabbled in potatoes and cows before beholding the possibilities of this new mechanical heating machine. In 1879 he bought several of the hatching boxes and filled them up with all the eggs he could find. The incubators were so effective, hatching almost ninety percent of Nisson's eggs, that a handful quickly turned into a fleet and soon the great Dane was hatching hundreds of chicks each week.

Within the year, Byce established an incubator factory and Nisson's ranch was home to the world's first commercial hatching company. Unable to possibly raise all the chickens he was hatching, Nisson started selling them to his neighbors, who in turn hired Nisson to establish operations to raise their birds on their own property. Within the decade, Petaluma had six more commercial hatcheries, a handful of feed mills to feed the rapidly growing numbers of chickens, and scores of carpenters that catered exclusively to the building of chicken houses. At the time of Byce's invention in 1879, the chickens of California were producing some 69 million eggs each year; by 1889, that number had jumped to 164 million. It was at last time to make money off "hens' eggs alone."

The way Nisson and his comrades maneuvered around the Romans' 200-count cap on chickens was with what they termed their "colony scheme" of raising poultry. If birds wouldn't survive in one massive flock, why not break the massive flock up into separate smaller colonies of birds, each with their own moveable "colony houses" equipped with feeders and waterers and nesting areas? The birds weren't enclosed in any way but rather left to swarm freely inside and outside around their own colony, which was moved regularly to ensure the chicken manure and scratching was evenly spread throughout the farm. At the end of each season the hens that had survived the past few months of disease and thefts by America's still passionate chicken thieves would be merged back into one colony of chickens and the process would continue on its merry way.

By the early 1890s as well, a prolific variety of the White Leghorn breed of chicken had been shipped cross-country. This bird produced an unheard-of 200 eggs a year and is today still considered one of the best laying breeds. Petaluma's poultry farmers pounced on these chickens and soon great flocks of Leghorns colonized every corner of the fair valley, clucking their way through the countryside like massive squawking snow drifts.

Seeing how the small town teemed with such feathered promise, thousands of outsiders began flocking to Petaluma—Germans, Irish, Swedes, Danes, Russian Jews—all eager to escape the confines of the city and to try their hand at the chicken business. To these migrants and many others, having a chicken farm in the beautiful hillocks of Petaluma was akin to achieving the American dream. "Here I went at my own speed," remarked one grower, "on my own place, outdoors in an area of great beauty." Watching their neighbors go at their own speed by increasing the size of their farms and hiring more laborers and buying shiny new pieces of equipment was evidence enough, and by 1904 nine out of every ten inhabitants of Petaluma was involved in the chicken industry.

But it wasn't just in California. Despite the Gold Rush being long over, American demand for eggs was seemingly implacable; even after the United States produced 10 trillion eggs domestically in 1901, it still imported some 180 million more from countries like Canada, Spain, China, and Italy. Unlike other agricultural products, egg producers would get paid every day or week, and not just at the end of harvest, making it easier for them to budget and to make ends meet, and so egg-hungry dreamers in the North, the South, the East, and the West all went wholeheartedly into the raising of chickens.

This was aided in large part by the rapid spread of variations of Byce's incubator and the fact that baby chicks could now be shipped directly from the hatchery to a farmer's doorstep. A quirk in chicken genetics entails that a freshly hatched chick does not require food for the first forty-eight hours of life (they ingest what remains of their egg's yolk before hatching), which means they can travel forty-eight hours sans nourishment without any ill effects. No one is sure who did it first but as early as 1883 chicken hatcheries would pack these little balls of fluff into corrugated boxes and ship them anywhere within a two-day railroad distance. The results were immediate, and between 1880 and 1890 the population of birds throughout the country leaped from 102 million to 258 million.

Needless to say, the turn of the twentieth century was a good time to be a pastry chef in America. The cookery of the United States had always enjoyed a fine selection of cakes, puddings, and creams, but suddenly cookbooks were embracing a Frenchman's love of the egg, and overflowed with directions for transforming this increasingly cheap and plentiful commodity into cookies, mousses, soufflés, and meringues. These nouvelle collections could be flipped through in newly established soda shops, which served up decadent ice cream sundaes, another great invention of the late nineteenth century. Early processed foods, such as Nabisco wafers, also owed a debt to the cheap egg, as did nineteenth-century photographers, who relied upon albumen paper, coated in an emulsion of egg whites and salt, to make their prints. Companies that produced this paper often went through as many as 60,000 eggs in a single day.

CHOCOLATE SOUFFLÉ

Half a pint of milk, two ounces of Walter Baker & Co.'s Chocolate, three tablespoonfuls of sugar, one rounding tablespoonful of butter, two tablespoons of flour, four eggs.

Pour the milk in the double-boiler, and place on the fire. Beat the butter to a soft cream, and beat the flour into it. Gradually pour the hot milk on this, stirring all the time. Return to the fire and cook for six minutes. Put the shaved chocolate, sugar, and two tablespoonfuls of water in a small pan over a hot fire, and stir until smooth and glossy. Stir this into the mixture in the double boiler. Take from the fire to cool. When cool add the whites of the eggs, beaten to a stiff froth. Pour the batter into a well-buttered earthen dish that will hold about a quart, and cook in a moderate oven for twenty-two minutes. Serve immediately with vanilla cream sauce.

—Maria Parloa, *Chocolate and Cocoa Recipes*, 1909

As America succumbed to a national egg-stravaganza, nowhere put more of its eggs into one basket than Petaluma. Hiring themselves a public relations expert, they branded themselves the "Egg Basket of the World" and began an extensive marketing effort across the United States touting the wonders of the Petaluma hen. For as little an investment as $4,000, one could purchase 1,000 chickens and all the chicken-raising fixings, and be well on the path toward bucolic independence. "Even a moderately industrious farmer could expect to make a profit of $1.00 per hen per year," they declared. Thousands answered the Call of the Hen and between 1900 and 1920, the town's population doubled.

Now outgrowing even the hungry San Francisco market, Petaluma eggs could be found all throughout the United States, Europe, and South America. Fashionable housewives in New York paid premiums for "Petaluma Extracts" and the President of the United States and the King of England both breakfasted on Petaluma eggs. By 1915, the town was shipping out an estimated 120 million eggs at prices that reached upward of thirty cents a dozen, or just over $7.00 in 2016's currency.

But this was not enough, and Petaluma and its farmers shamelessly threw themselves further into promoting the egg game. In August 1918, with an egg parade led by an egg queen and a glorious egg ball, they ushered in the first-ever National Egg Day, a celebration that their public relations guru had just invented. In 1919, harking back to the good old days of Rancho Petaluma, the town held yet another grand "Egg Fiesta," with a chicken rodeo, an egg scramble, an egg and chicken barbeque, and a second egg parade presided upon by a new and presumably even more beautiful egg queen. Outside of these festivals they invited in film crews to witness the solemn procession of eggs leaving the Petaluma rail station, inducted advertising men into the Order of the Cluck Clucks, and created pro-motional films of women doing calisthenics in a giant frying pan that was later used to cook a massive omelet.

By all public accounts, this relentless promotion was working. By the mid-1920s, one in every fifty eggs in the United States was raised in Petaluma, and with its whole populace singlehandedly focused on the chicken, slowly but surely the town became the richest of any its size in the country. But a closer look at Petaluma's shiny and glorious nest egg revealed its fine cracks. Despite the Petaluma Chamber of Commerce's repeated assurances that chicken farming could transform a "man of small means" into a "country gentleman," raising chickens remained a tough business. The birds were fickle, still prone to sickness and death, and profits were in no way guaranteed. A farmer may be independent but independence meant weathering every hardship, handling every emer-gency, and constantly preparing for each terrible contingency that might occur. A random plague could kill off all of their chickens, a sudden price collapse render their eggs completely worthless, or a freak storm wash all of a farmer's birds and hopes into the river and out to sea.

Every single success story in Petaluma was

built on the backs of one hundred failures. After spending decades watching his neighbors go bankrupt, one experienced poultry man declared, "I would not advise anyone unversed in poultry culture to give up a situation, however poor, in order to do in for poultry-keeping as a means of livelihood." Just like the forty-niners, there wasn't always money to be had in gold or the golden egg, but rather in providing the wood and feed and marketing that supported it. As one writer put it, "raising chickens or producing eggs was in fact seldom more than a particularly arduous form of gambling." A good chicken farmer was told, above all else, to keep up with the times. And the times, they were a-changing, rapidly and without remorse.

CHAPTER SEVEN
Calories and Constituents

CHICKEN GELATIN
2575 Calories

1 3- to 4-lb. Chicken
3 hard-cooked eggs
1 lb. cold cooked tongue
Celery-salt
1 tablespoonful granulated gelatin
2 tablespoonfuls cold water
1 pint clear brown stock

Roast the chicken. When cold slice and lay in a mold with alternate layers of sliced tongue and occasional slices of hard-cooked eggs; season with celery-salt. Soak gelatin in cold water five minutes and dissolve in boiling stock. Pour it over the meat. Let stand several hours in a refrigerator before unmolding. This recipe will serve at least eight persons. *Miss Estelle Claeys, 5107 Page Bldg., St. Louis, Mo.*
—*Good Housekeeping*, August, 1917

Even with eggs now readily available up and down the west coast and beyond, by the beginning of the twentieth century eating in the United States had become a much more difficult affair. Inflation was outstripping wages year after year, and between 1897 and 1916 the cost of living in the United States had increased by nearly a third. A series of industrial depressions and shortfalls in crop yields in the early 1900s elevated food prices to all-time highs, and the poor were feeling the crunch.

In an attempt to combat the impending food crisis, many municipal authorities began to distribute Atwater's Food Values Tables more aggressively in working-class neighborhoods, but to no avail. Malnutrition and hunger were so rampant as World War I began to escalate that in 1917 the postmaster of Chicago reported that children were writing to Santa asking for food more than any other item that Christmas. Earlier in the year, the United States had officially entered the global conflict, pushing commodity prices up even further. Food riots soon broke out in New York, Chicago, Philadelphia, and Boston. Just a few months later, the unrest of a famine-stricken populace brought down the Tsar and helped the Bolsheviks seize power in Russia.

Worldwide, it was becoming increasingly clear as the conflict raged on in Europe that "the great economic problem of the near future is the feeding of man." Although the Western world was well familiar with the massive famines that had swept across China and India in the late nineteenth century, the ravages of World War I had, at long last, brought hunger upon "the white race" of Europe. Money, men, and food were still what were needed to win wars in the early twentieth century, and as this war progressed, the European Allies were slowly but surely starving.

In August 1917, Congress passed the Lever Act, also known as the Food and Fuel Control Act, granting the government unprecedented control over the nation's food supply and establishing the US Food Administration. This new agency's charge was to organize and maintain food supplies at home to make sure there would be enough to feed American soldiers and their allies abroad. At the helm of this fledgling bureaucracy was a skilled administrator by the name of Herbert Hoover. Long before his party promised all Americans a "chicken for every pot" in the presidential election of 1928, Hoover had spent decades as a successful international mining engineer and financier. Feeling compelled to give back for all his good fortune, in 1914 he had begun what would become three difficult years of overseeing privately funded food relief efforts in war-torn France and Belgium. Since the Food Administration was also tasked with maintaining supplies at home while feeding the starving European continent, Hoover's move to the head of this organization was an obvious one.

As "white flour, red meat, and blue blood" still comprised "the tricolor flag of conquest," white flour and red meat were the foodstuffs most sought after for the blue-blooded fighting men on the front. After all, "diet is destiny," declared one contemporaneous commentator, and, most importantly in a time of war, "beef makes savage." The problem of course was that white flour and red meat were also the cornerstone of the average white American's diet. Similar to the belief that blacks would quickly die without chicken, some at the time claimed that whites could not live very long without ample supplies of wheat bread.

But hungry Europeans and American fighting forces were in dire need of all such commodities. By the end of the war, the American soldiers stationed in France were consuming over nine million pounds of food daily and all the while the people of Europe were facing severe food shortages. "The moral is clear," wrote one government official in 1917, "we must reduce our own consumption. Our highest obligation in this war is to make sure that we do not fail our allies in their hour of need, just as our deepest duty to ourselves is to plan today, intelligently and patriotically, to provide against the possible shortage of next spring."

In this dire light, Atwater's great doctrine of substitution shone brightly. If the eaters on the home front could replace their beef with protein-rich chicken, fish, or beans, and their wheat with corn, barley, or oats and still remain healthy, there would be enough of these combined staples to send to war-ravaged Europe.

Although the Lever Act did give the government the power to requisition any and all foodstuffs from citizens deemed necessary for the war effort, the benevolent Hoover firmly believed that "the spirit of self-denial and self-sacrifice" would lead all Americans to gladly change their eating habits and thus provide a surplus of supplies at home to send abroad. Eaters were implored to go meatless on Mondays, wheatless on Wednesdays, and sweetless on Saturdays, which they more or less did, with varying degrees of enthusiasm.

Although even in 1915, as one food journal reported, "most people do not consider chicken as meat," hungry Americans were increasingly told to substitute poultry for their regular hearty portions of beef and pork. The chicken found itself in Group Two of the Food Administration's edible categories: "meat and meat substitutes, or protein-rich foods," along with fish, milk, cheese, eggs, and beans.

This suggestion to substitute with chicken, however, in an era with some of the highest food prices the country had ever experienced, many found laughable. Like it had been for the past century, chicken prices remained incredibly high during the war. Although the US government appropriated $150,000 in an attempt to increase poultry stocks, production remained relatively constant and prices were pushed even higher by the substitution campaigns. "Lots of us would like to be 'rationed' very frequently with chicken and rice," scoffed one editorialist in Georgia.

A World War I era recipe calling for chicken and rice, this one from a pair of cookbook authors who took the government recommendations to heart.

TOMATO GUMBO SOUP
Bones and gristle from chicken or turkey
2 quarts cold water
1 cup okra
1 tablespoon chopped pimento
1½ teaspoons salt
½ cup rice
2 tablespoons fat
1½ cups tomatoes
¼ cup chopped parsley

Soak bones and gristle in the cold water 1 hour. Then boil slowly 1 hour, in same water. Strain out the bones and gristle and add other ingredients to the liquid. Boil this mixture slowly ¾ hour and serve.

—C. Houston Goudiss and Alberta M. Goudiss, *Foods that Will Win The War and How to Cook Them*, 1918

But Americans are a thrifty bunch and it seems very few can resist the call of the hen. Backyards flocks, which municipal health departments had been slowly pushing out of cities to prevent the spread of avian illnesses among humans, began to hatch again in large numbers, aided by the efforts of the Food Administration. "In time of war" declared a government propaganda poster, raising one's own chickens was "a patriotic duty." (This wasn't because Americans should turn wholly to chicken, mind you, but rather that "the back yard chicken will help the meat supply while the pig is growing.")

This miniature "return to the land" movement was also spurred on by the fact that in 1918 the government decided it was okay to ship chickens by mail. This practice continued long after the war, and by the 1920s millions of mail-order chicks were whizzing throughout the country in trains, trucks, and later planes to be delivered to one's front door by a friendly neighborhood postal worker. In the 1920s and 1930s, as much as half of the chicks produced at commercial hatcheries in the United States were sent out to small farmers and backyard enthusiasts in this way.

It wasn't enough that Americans were supposed to eat more chicken and eggs during the war however. The government wanted them to also know why the fact that chicken was "19 per cent protein, 16 per cent fat, and 1 per cent mineral matter," and that each pound of it supplied "1050 units of energy" was supposed to be good for them. "Food Will Win the War," the government declared. And to preserve the integrity of land of the free, they believed, "the health and happiness of the future depend largely on the education of the people respecting scientific nutrition."

How this science had been interpreted had varied wildly since the days of the juice of flesh aficionado Justus von Liebig. Right up there with baseball and chicken theft, fad dieting has always been one of America's favorite pastimes. Before the First World War the country had become successively passionate about vegetarianism, all-meat diets, diets avoiding "fermentations, carbohydrates, and hydrocarbons," low-protein diets, and single food diets. In the self-controlling Victorian era, fasting had its time in the sun, as did the long-standing belief that "too much fruit and vegetables should not be eaten." A diet known as Fletcherism reached a popular zenith too at the beginning of the twentieth century, a principle of eating espoused by Horace Fletcher, the "Great

Masticator," who vehemently believed that "nature will castigate those who don't masticate." At each meal, eaters were meant to chew each bite one hundred times, swallow its juices, and unceremoniously spit out all the remaining "fibrous matter."

By the time of the First World War though, the government had decided that the calorie would be the cornerstone of their dietary messages. In a basic scientific sense, a calorie is just a unit of measurement, namely the amount of heat required to raise the temperature of one gram of water by one degree Celsius. It first came to use in France in the eighteenth century under the famed chemist Antoine Lavoisier, who helped determine the importance of hydrogen in combustion, developed the metric system, and became the father of modern chemistry, all before he lost his head rather abruptly to the French Revolution. The principle of the calorie migrated throughout various non-food-related scientific experiments in Europe, eventually becoming the standard by which the Germans were quantifying their metabolic studies and foodstuffs. Wilbur Atwater was the one who then brought it to the United States and began writing about its use in measuring the values of American foods.

The calorie, believed to be so convenient and so universally applicable, became the foundation of the Food Administration's work. The value tables that Atwater had diligently calculated throughout his lifetime were adjusted according to sex, age, weight, occupation, and race, and were distributed throughout the country in popular magazines. The Food Administration even went so far as to quantify the whole of the agricultural output of the United States in terms of its caloric value, which they believed would help them better plan their rationing not by amount of food but by the "actual nutriment" of all foods.

Despite its seeming universality, these scientific ideas about eating were not the easiest for the citizens of the United States to swallow at first. The calorie is the gold standard of everything we put into our mouths today, but when it was first widely applied in the 1910s people were writing to the US government assuming that this calorie was "a new type of explosive discovered by the war department" or "the name of a new breakfast food."

The government found that the best way to influence their citizenry's eating habits, besides having the citizens become meatless Monday vigilantes (which many did and some still do), was to rely on the increasingly important field of home economics. This course of study in home-making had been educating women on how to make their households the most productive possible since the *Boston Cooking-School Cook Book* taught cooks how to make veal birds and had continued with great fervor during the reforms of the Industrial Era. As the pressures of the Great War began to be felt in the United States, "every home economics teacher is asking herself today, 'How can I best aid in my community in the national movement toward food conservation?' "

The answer to that question could be found in the kitchen. Americans were still pretty terrible cooks at this point, and these professional home scientists now had reason to say that "food may not only be spoiled in the cooking," but that "it may be wasted in cooking" as well. At-home cooks were told to pay close attention to the fats and proteins and carbohydrates of their foods to make each meal the most nutritious possible. Boiled down from its scientific verbiage the message was clear: "Avoid Fancy Cooking."

Even without the resource constraints of the war, the Gilded Age banquet was already well on its way to becoming the one-pot meals these cooking advocates were championing. Foodstuffs were increasingly expensive, and social restructuring meant full-time cooks and serving women were getting harder and harder for the upper classes to come by. The proverbial housewife, her budget strained and now tasked with washing the clothes and sweeping the floors and mending the sheets *and* cooking the dinner, in turn found herself increasingly drawn to the message of home economists. By the war's end, labor-intensive and time-consuming chicken salad feasts had given way to one pot chicken gelatin casseroles, generously seasoned with government-endorsed calorie counts.

Despite the caloric glory of a well-prepared chicken gelatin, increasingly pressed home-makers, like their serving women before them, would often avoid chicken dishes and the layers of plucking and gutting and trussing that they still involved. Precut beefsteaks or perfectly formed pork sausages, when they were available, required much less preparation and were therefore much more to a busy home cook's liking. What's more, even though the wartime government recommended using more chicken, as the Food Administration's chief statistician pointed out, there were still a lot of parts to the bird that just don't get eaten, twenty to forty percent of it in fact. This, he believed, "explains in part why the total contribution to the nutrition of the nation by poultry is so comparatively small." Buying a whole chicken was a wasteful thing and during the First World War, where an efficient diet was a patriotic duty, there was no room for waste.

But one question remains: did it work? Did food conservation really help win the war? Did these nutritionally balanced, economized meals like chicken gelatins and tuna casseroles galvanize the home front? The answer is sort of. There's no denying that food helped keep the allies fed and in fighting order, but the increases in supplies to be shipped overseas came largely from increases in production rather than from decreased consumption. The beef-heavy rations, to the troops at least, may have actually even been excessive; the average US soldier who came back from the frontlines was twelve pounds heavier than when he had left.

While the American fighting men may have gained weight, American women during the war were increasingly encouraged not to. Over-indulgence was definitely not in line with home economic principles, and thus 1918 saw the momentous publication of Dr. Lulu Hunt Peters' *Diet and Health with Key to the Calories*, a book that taught women for the first time that scientific eating could help them to "reduce." Enthralled by this new concept and encouraged by an increasingly visual media that emphasized images of slender young women, "the picture of a chicken," as one publication actually phrased it, calorie counting quickly became the new national craze.

By the 1920s, health-conscious restaurants started advertising their food's calorie counts, and newspapers started regularly sponsoring national "diet derbies," reporting weekly updates to an enthralled American public about the weight loss progress of groups of "fat women." Chicken and its low calories were prominently featured on such high-profile weight-watching menus, which were conveniently prepared not by the contestants themselves but by a hospital's kitchen staff.

What's more, after the war, trim and "healthy" waistlines now became much more of a national concern than food conservation. Aside from battle, in the 1910s the number one cause of death in the United States had started to shift from infectious to chronic diseases, such as heart disease and cancer. Early nutrition scientists were starting to detect links between such ailments and life-style, and Americans became concerned. Almost immediately "eating began to change its status from that of a major indoor sport to a portentous ritual upon which our lives, our dispositions and our very figures are considered largely to depend."

Slowly but surely, the obsession over nutrition science and calorie counting and weight watching grew, and by the end of the Roaring Twenties no one in the United States could rightly assume calories were a new breakfast cereal anymore. Surveying the rapidly changing state of American eating habits, one columnist in 1930 could not help but remark, "man, and perhaps more particularly woman, no longer eats what he likes in nonchalant abandon, fancy free. He eats what is good for him, on some scientific or pseudo-scientific hypothesis."

In a land where now "the gourmet who is a

curiosity, the dietician who is a prophet," many voiced concerns that this single-minded focus might not be the best for American cuisine. One dietician even remarked, rightly so, that "we in the United States have not given full respect to flavor," but most eaters seemed to be too concerned about their waistlines to notice. The main course of the American salad had dawned and you can rest assured that on top of that bed of lettuce would soon be a whole bunch of low-calorie, protein-rich chicken. But not just yet.

Another one-pot meal, again featuring chicken and rice.

CASSEROLE OF CHICKEN AND RICE
1 two to four pound chicken
¼ cup flour
¾ cup rice, boiled
¼ cup chicken fat
3 cups chicken stock
1 small onion, grated
1 cup milk
salt and pepper, as needed

Cook chicken until nearly tender in salted water to cover, using a closely-covered kettle and simmering slowly, or cooking in fireless cooker. When done, separate it into sections and thicken stock with chicken fat and flour mixed, adding the milk and more salt and pepper, if necessary. Mix together the boiled rice and thickened stock, add onion and place in casserole in layers with chicken. Set the whole in oven and cook slowly from forty to fifty minutes longer. If desired, the chicken can be baked until tender in a slow oven, if it is first disjointed, then placed in a bean pot, covered with salted water and cooked gently for four hours.

—Mrs. Ida Bailey Allen, *Woman's World Calendar Cookbook*, 1922

CHAPTER EIGHT
The Kosher Chicken Wars

ROAST CHICKEN

Stuff and truss a chicken, season with pepper and salt and dredge with flour. Put in a roasting-pan with two or three tablespoonfuls of chicken-fat if the chicken is not especially fat. When heated add hot water and baste frequently. The oven should be hot and the time necessary for a large chicken will be about an hour and a half. When done, remove the chicken, pour off the grease and make a brown sauce in the pan.

—Florence Kreisler Greenbaum, *The International Jewish Cookbook*, 1919

It was nearing six o'clock when Barnet Baff asked his son Harry to take over their West Washington Market poultry shop for the evening. Barnet had received a message that he was needed for some business down the street. Bundling up against the November cold, he stepped outside into the Manhattan darkness. The market was usually subdued by this time in the autumn evening but Thanksgiving was just two days away and the cobblestone streets hummed with shoppers gathering goods for their holiday feasts. In the dim flicker of the streetlamps, Baff surveyed the hustle and bustle with satisfaction. Even with the war in Europe, 1914 would be yet another good year for his chicken business. Lost in his own thoughts, he didn't notice the two young men waiting for him up ahead, hat brims down and pistols drawn.

Such lack of caution was unusual for Baff. He was, after all, a man who was used to being a target. Pig-headed and business-savvy, the Jewish-German immigrant had been universally hated by most of the city for more than a half decade, starting immediately upon his entrance into the poultry receiving business in 1908. At the time, the receivers were the most powerful individuals in the city's growing live chicken trade. These receivers were the middlemen. They assessed the quality of the birds arriving daily by rail, offered the shipper what they deemed a fair price, and then trundled the birds off to retailers and butchers.

To protect their lucrative interests, in 1906 the receivers of New York had organized themselves into the Live Poultry Commission Merchants' Protective Association and quickly earned themselves a ruthless reputation. The Association fixed wholesale chicken prices, strong-armed retailers into buying only from them, and paid slaughterhouses to refuse to provide their services to dealers the Association had blacklisted. Membership in the Association was "voluntary" for New York City receivers in the way feed is "voluntary" for raising chickens. Dealers that refused to cooperate were threatened, and another poultry store with conveniently lower prices would be opened just around the corner in order to drive the wayward merchant quickly out of business. When offered membership to this Association, Barnet Baff refused.

Outside of New York City, chicken trusts were nothing new, as price fixing had long helped farmers to maintain a minimum income per bird. In the absence of such practices, prices would deviate wildly, soaring during the winter when birds were scarce but plummeting during the spring and summer when all the newly hatched chicks had matured enough to eat. Aside from the Gospel Bird and the occasional chicken gelatin, throughout the 1920s average per capita consumption of chicken was just ten pounds per year in the United States, and such low demand made the unpredictability of prices worse.

But most Americans back then weren't Jewish and most chicken markets weren't in New York City. It has been said that "a hundred million Sabbaths have begun on Friday nights throughout the Jewish universe with a roast chicken" and by the time the Association was formed it was well known in New York City that every Jewish family was purchasing at least one live chicken per week. Thursdays in West Washington Market came to be known as "chicken day" for Jews and Gentiles alike.

Chicken is a popular choice for the sacred Friday night Shabbat dinner largely because, if slaughtered correctly, the bird is undeniably kosher. The word "kosher" itself derives from the Hebrew word *kasher*, meaning fit or proper, apt descriptors for an ancient set of rules determining what foods are fit for the Jewish people to eat. Chickens are not mammals and so completely avoid the cloven foot, chewing cud requirements of larger animals. (Both of these traits are possessed by cows but the cloven-foot pig does not chew its cud, which is the primary reason pork is not considered kosher.) The chicken is also not a carnivore nor is it a scavenger, attributes which prevent eagles, vultures, and guinea fowls from even getting remotely close to a kosher kitchen. And like in the rural South, even the most impoverished of Jewish people could afford to raise a flock of chickens in whatever part of the world they found themselves, making it the universal standard of the celebratory Sabbath.

Since the establishment of the first Jewish community in New Amsterdam in 1654, the city had grown accustomed to the Friday night prayers of the Israelites. Well up until 1825, the number of Jews in the city remained small enough for a single synagogue to accommodate both their worship and kosher slaughter needs. But by the second half of the nineteenth century, fleeing the anti-Semitism of Russia and much of Eastern Europe, streams of Jewish immigrants were flooding the shores of Ellis Island. By 1855, one synagogue had blossomed into twenty, and the Jewish population was more than four thousand. By 1915, this number had exploded to over four hundred synagogues in the Lower East Side neighborhood alone and the population reached over 1.4 million Jews scattered throughout the five boroughs of New York City and New Jersey.

With more Jews came a greater demand for kosher meat. A Jewish housewife of the middle-class sort would go down to the poultry market each week before Sabbath to select her live bird. Observing the kashrut, the kosher laws, she would then bring her chicken to a trained and registered *shochet*, a kosher slaughterer. He, in turn, would properly prepare the bird with a blessing, a quick cut to the throat, the removal of all blood, and an inspection to determine that the meat wasn't torn or sick and was indeed truly kosher.

A much older kosher chicken recipe.

GIBLET PIE

Make your pastry as follows: three quarters of a pound of suet chopped very fine, rub this smoothly into one pound of flour, add a teaspoonful of salt, one of ginger, and mixed with sufficient water to make a paste, strew with flour and pound well with the rolling-pin, then roll out very thin, repeating this three times, line the pudding bowl with this pastry, which should be about one-quarter of an inch in thickness; put in the following giblets: two pounds of meat, cut very small, the necks, wings, gizzards, livers, and heart, that has been split open and the skin taken off the brain, and the feet skinned and the claws chopped off; all to be cut up small. Season with marjoram, thyme, parsley, onions, pepper, salt, mace, ginger, and a few potatoes out in very thin slices, with hard boiled eggs. Then cover the top of the basin with the above paste, and tie tightly in a cloth, put in boiling water and boil for three hours.

—Mrs. Esther Levy, *Jewish Cookery Book on Principles of Economy*, 1871

Those pragmatic individuals of the Jewish faith but of little means skipped the expensive market and just kept chickens of their own, just like they had back in Europe. The Lower East Side wasn't a quaint village in Poland, however. A brief tour of the tenements in the 1880s and 1890s would reveal entire ornithological parks packed away in basements, buzzing in gardens, squawking on rooftops, and squirming in the corners of extra bedrooms. In addition to the occasional supper, the birds produced noises and filth that even the most seasoned New Yorker was unaccustomed to. "Indescribably vile" is how one journalist described it in 1877.

Municipal authorities attempted to cut down on this practice, as dense flocks of birds tend to spread nasty strains of avian flu to humans, but largely to no avail. Everyone in the city knew when a health raid was underway in the Lower East Side because coops of chickens could be seen roaming the city streets uptown until the inspection ceased, at which point the crates would be rounded back up and the birds returned to their bedrooms and backyards.

The fight against Jewish flocks quickly grew to be too much for city officials. Under the urging of increasingly powerful rabbis, municipal authorities built more slaughterhouses and poultry markets catering to those of the Jewish faith. But the immigrants kept streaming in and demand for live chickens regularly outstripped supply. In 1889, with much pomp and circumstance, the expansive West Washington Market was opened in what is now Manhattan's Meat Packing District to accommodate all these hungry kosher mouths. Just south of the city's main railroad yards, the market received ten to fifteen cars of chicken a week in the 1890s, carted in from upstate New York and Connecticut. This number expanded to over 7,000 cars annually by the outbreak of the First World War, and eventually there would be over 35 million chickens gushing in on crowded locomotives from the Midwest and increasingly the Mid-Atlantic each year. New Yorkers were quick to dub the feathered bazaar "Chicken City."

Although neighbors complained of the stench and the noise and the chaos of the live chicken trains, there was no such thing as a cold-storage bird in the kosher poultry trade. Most observant Jews in the nineteenth century refused to eat any chicken that they did not personally bring to the butcher alive and flailing. Getting the bird from the farm to the dinner table consisted of roughly fifteen distinct steps at this point, with the bird passing from growers to dealers to railway men to catchers to receivers to dealers to butchers. In between, there was more than enough room for fraud and abuse in the increasingly lucrative sale of kosher goods.

Moreover, Jews of different ethnic backgrounds preferred to only purchase foods from those of the same background, leading to a massive proliferation and fragmentation of kosher enforcement and meat shops. Butchers who were known and trusted to have the finest products could charge a premium on their goods, which often angered

Jewish eaters, who would in turn boycott those same butchers for their high prices. Boycotts readily turned into angry mobs and the New York police department often had to be called in to control the irate eaters roaming the streets of the Lower East Side, their crates of chickens in hand. And the clucking cherry on top for this tumultuous market was the Association, whose strong-arm tactics were pushing up chicken prices by as much as five to ten cents per pound, a full fifty percent increase from the eighteen to twenty-two cents eaters were accustomed to.

And then Barnet Baff came along, whose dealings were almost as cutthroat as those of the Association itself. Baff made deals with farmers to ship directly to him, cutting out the dealers and handlers. To bring the birds from the trains to his shop, he hired a fleet of trucks, cutting out the chicken drivers, too. Eventually he opened his own kosher slaughterhouse, eliminating his need to work with independent butchers and distributors.

Baff's business acumen was successfully threatening the livelihood of everyone involved in the New York City kosher chicken trade. The Association was not pleased. In 1912, they took it upon themselves to try to force Baff out of the market by suing him for nonfulfillment of a contract. Baff immediately countersued and accused the association of operating under a trust. The judge sided with Baff, sending eighty-seven other poultry dealers to jail.

The next year, unscathed from the legal proceedings, Baff made a deal to work with the fledgling poultry worker's union before any of the other retailers had the chance to. What was left of the Association hit back, tipping off the city that Baff was one of the worst offenders when it came to selling those chickens filled with rocks and sand that made poor chicken salad. The city looked into it and instead indicted some of Baff's accusers on fraud charges. Baff, who was indeed one of the biggest perpetrators of this scam, slipped by yet again unscathed.

The poultry men countered again by blackmailing Baff and threatening violence against him and his family. Baff responded by expanding his sales directly to consumers, cutting out retailers. Soon Baff's stores were ransacked while his horses and chickens were poisoned. The store of one of his chief collaborators was burned to the ground, and a failed bomb was placed under Baff's summer home while another was set off in the doorway of his store. Baff proceeded to open another store uptown.

Barnet Baff was successfully running his competition out of business and the Association was at its end. Every effort they had made to ruin him only made the "Kosher King" even bolder. It appeared the Association needed to do something much more permanent to deal with Mr. Baff, and in early 1914 some one hundred New York poultry dealers convened with the sole purpose of creating a very generous "Kill Barnet Baff" fund. (They eventually collected some $4,200, the equivalent of a whopping $100,000 today.) After filtering through several locales to do the deed—at the Brooklyn market, at his store at 109th Street, at his market at 80th Street—a particularly angry poultry man by the name of Joseph Cohen and his two hired Italian guns concluded that the West Washington Market would be the best place to dispatch Baff. After all, at this point everyone in Chicken City who wasn't involved in his schemes hated the poultry man and "not one would lift his finger to frustrate the plot nor ever 'squeal' about what might be seen in connection with the murder."

With the false phone call placed about some business down the street on that cold November evening, the two gunmen stood in wait in a back alley. As Baff approached, the two youths sprang out and sent a bullet straight through the chicken man's heart before scampering off in a waiting getaway car. Despite the bustling market, as predicted, no one the police interviewed seemed to know a thing about the shooting. Barnet Baff was pronounced dead upon arrival at the nearby hospital.

Baff was only the first casualty of the great

Chicken Wars that would rock New York City for the next twenty years. Brooklyn slaughterhouses would be bombed, rabbis' assistants kidnapped, and poultry men gunned down in the city's markets or while eating dinner in Lower East Side restaurants. Almost immediately upon entering the chicken industry for himself, Baff's son Harry found himself in a violent dispute with some 6,000 independent poultry dealers over his cutthroat practices. Even Joseph Cohen, the ringleader in Barnet Baff's murder, would himself meet a violent end, shot to death as he sat on the front porch of his Brooklyn home.

The escalation of this violence and mayhem in the 1920s was simply because all people in New York, not just those of the Jewish faith, were starting to eat more chicken. World War I boosted fowl sales through its nutritional campaigns while the Roaring Twenties saw increased demand from the rising ranks of the American middle class. New York City restaurants were no longer just the domains of the rich, as they had been since their beginnings in the early nineteenth century. Already facing decreased demand and public scrutiny for their excess during the hardship of the war, most highbrow eateries could not withstand the prohibition of alcohol that went into effect in 1920. *Coq au vin*, after all, is a considerably less appetizing dish without all the *vin* and thus these eateries went into a swift decline.

In these establishments' ornate ruins sprung up restaurants of a different kind: the automats and cafeterias that catered to middle-class, white-collar workers who were slowly realizing that dining out could be fun. If chicken dinner had once been a luxury to treat our families to on occasion, as early as 1921, chickens were now seen as a means for restaurants to expand their higher-end menus during the winter months. Eating out was still an extravagance, so why not eat an extravagant meal of roast chicken while there? Coupled with the steady Jewish demand, chickens were needed in greater quantities and of a more uniform quality than ever before by restaurateurs seeking to attract a broader clientele. Reliable dealers in turn were ever more important.

With more requests for chicken came more money for those racketeers that managed to rule the roost, all orchestrated under the strict control of the newly organized New York Live Poultry Chamber of Commerce. This was created in 1926 as an attempt to better the conditions of those working in the poultry industry, but quickly evolved into a reincarnation of the then-defunct Association. The Chamber set prices and levied a tax of a few cents on all chicken sold by any of its members, which consisted of nearly every butcher and dealer in the city by the end of the decade. Half the proceeds went into the Chamber's coffers and the other half so the firm could "hire gorillas."

Price-fixing of chicken, even at one or two cents a pound, was incredibly lucrative when over twelve million carloads of the bird were reaching New York City annually by 1930, with over half of those destined for kosher slaughter. But such control requires strict collaboration on prices and weights, which is where the Italian mob came in. The Chamber had their hired guns spy on butchers and retailers, threaten them when they didn't comply with orders, and poison the chickens and disable the trucks of those who the Chamber thought weren't playing nice. Dealers were only allowed to purchase birds from their specific merchant and could only sell them to butchers on the Chamber's list. Deviation was not tolerated. Members testified that young men would come by to tell them, "If you don't buy from the right place, you'll get a good beating," and if they went ahead despite the threats retailers had their hands broken.

In this treacherous kingdom built on chicken legs, everyone involved knew the trail of blood always led back to Arthur "Tootsie" Herbert. By the end of the 1920s, with his impeccable style and perfect movie-star hair, Tootsie was an imposing figure in the world of New York City racketeering. Born to a kosher butcher in the Lower East Side, he had spent his youth charming his way up the ranks of the city's organized labor. By his mid-twenties, Herbert had his eyes set on the Chicken Drivers' Union.

The Local 167 of the International Brotherhood of Teamsters, Chauffeurs, Stablemen, and Helpers of America, as the Chicken Drivers' Union was more formally called, was unique to New York City. Nowhere else on the planet had developed enough of a poultry trade to warrant the organizing and unionizing of the chicken drivers, those who were engaged solely in the "hauling and delivery of chicken, ducks, geese, and turkeys." Despite never having driven chickens in his life, with charm and wit and the threat of violence, Tootsie Herbert managed to get himself elected as business agent of the Local 167 at the age of 24. Not long after, he abolished the union's elections all together.

To strengthen his chokehold over New York's chicken industry, he assigned his brother Charlie to be head of the Local 440, the *Shochtim* Union, comprising of those trained in the ways of proper kosher slaughter. With a rap sheet as bad as his reputation, Charlie quickly molded the union into an organization more to his and his brother's liking, one with no meetings, no elections, and zero connection to any rabbis concerned with keeping the city's chickens *kashrut*.

Together, the Herberts trailed poultry trucks, kidnapped defiant *shochtim*, and even bombed the home of one insolent Brooklyn dealer, severely injuring him and three members of his immediate family. The market men of the 1920s had a special song they liked to sing about the Herberts' "reign of terror." Sung to the tune of "Sing a Song of Sixpence," it goes:

Sing a song of *shochtim*, how we love to sing
Four and twenty gangsters, done up in a sling
When the markets opened, Tootsie came around
And all the people ponied up one cent a pound.

The New York City government did not take this ditty lightly. The violence and corruption had grown so rampant in the chicken trade that even officials of the Commission of Health had started extorting money from kosher slaughterhouses that wanted to renew their permits each year. Enough was enough. After a tired and scared Brooklyn dealer filed a lawsuit against the Live Poultry Chamber of Commerce in 1928, which alleged that the organization was operating under a trust (which it was), the US Attorney's Office began to look into the city's violent chicken rackets.

The investigation into kosher chicken's dark underbelly eventually went to court, a seven-week affair that was, by all accounts, a complete circus. With eighty-six members of the New York Live Poultry Chamber of Commerce, the Official Orthodox Poultry Slaughterers of America, and Local 167, among other poultry trade groups, charged with "conspiracy to restrain commerce in violation of the Sherman Anti-Trust Act," this was the largest number of people accused in a single case up to that point in American history. The court had to build a six-tier set of bleachers in the middle of the courtroom just to accommodate them all. Attendance was spotty and the accused themselves almost never filled their uncomfortable seats in what the press had started calling "the chicken coop." Government witnesses proved too afraid to testify—"I received an injury to my jaw," remarked one, "and it affected my memory"—while others used their time on the stand to provide lengthy Hebrew lessons for the non-Jewish in attendance.

The only things lighter than the tone of the trial were the sentences themselves. Even with sixty-six of the eighty-seven defendants convicted, ring leader Tootsie Herbert received just eight weeks in prison, his brother only two. Within months of their release, the Herberts were back at it again, this time with their accomplice Joseph Weiner, a Bronx-born racketeer and business agent of the Local, who helped to expand the Herberts' empire to include feed and coops in addition to assault and battery.

Tired of dealing with ever-escalating chicken prices and the general atmosphere of terror in the city's poultry markets, the exasperated New York commissioner of markets asked a young and enthusiastic special prosecutor by the name of Thomas E. Dewey to look into the Herberts' financial accounts. Such a route had helped the Federal Bureau of Investigation recently bring down notorious gangster Al Capone, more specifically by tracing down thousand-dollar checks for—what else?—"chickens" in Chicago, so the New York government hoped such tactics would help them to capture actual chicken men.

The tracking proved quite easy for the eager Dewey, a man whose drive and ambition would eventually lead him to become governor of New York State and eventually a candidate for president in 1944. Within six months, Dewey had discovered some $40,000 in embezzled union funds in Tootsie's accounts. The older Herbert and two other members of the Local 167 were promptly brought to trial for fraud.

Ever faithful to their cutthroat dictator, the members of the union rallied around Toostie. "If they embezzled it, then we'll raise more money for them to embezzle," one of their leaders piped off in a speech. Their unusual support was in vain however. Herbert and his two comrades all pleaded guilty to their charges, with Tootsie heading to jail for seven years for his crimes. (Being a big fan of assault and battery, Weiner had been previously thrown in jail after attacking a chicken dealer with a sawed-off billiard cue.)

Tootsie Herbert's sentence proved to be the death knell of New York City's great kosher chicken rackets. His brother would continue to be as big of a mobster as ever, but even before Tootsie's sentencing, the brothers' power had been steadily waning with each passing year, hence their need to embezzle money instead of extort it. By the 1930s, live chickens were giving way to much more convenient dressed poultry, even in the city's kosher households. Presumably second-generation Jews were growing tired of funding this chicken war with those extra few cents paid for live chickens, and were also much less strict in their orthodoxy than their parents. Fortunately for these chicken eaters, a revolution in the way chicken was raised was well underway in the Mid-Atlantic, a transformation that would eventually mean chicken on every day before and after the Sabbath as well.

This recipe comes from a recipe contest held by the largest weekly Jewish news-paper, The Jewish Examiner, *in the 1930s in New York City.*

IMITATION CHICKEN LIVER
By Mrs. S. Horowitz
1427 Pitkin Ave., Brooklyn, N.Y.

1 stalk celery
2 carrots, medium size
a piece of cabbage weighing about
   ¾ pound
1 green pepper

2 onions which have been simmered in
   butter in covered pan for about 10 minutes
1 raw onion
2 heaping tablespoons peanut butter

Put all ingredients except the peanut butter
in food chopper and grind fine. Then take
the peanut butter and mix well with the
other ingredients. Season with salt to taste.
Serve on lettuce leaf with sliced tomatoes.
   —*The Jewish Examiner: Prize Kosher
   Recipe Book, Volume I*, 1937

CHAPTER NINE

Celia Steele's Modest Endeavor

BROILED CHICKEN DELUXE
Mrs. A.L. Karlik, Salisbury, Maryland

1 plump young DELMARVA broiler,
about 2½ pounds
½ lemon
2 teaspoons granulated sugar
¼ teaspoon black pepper
½ teaspoon paprika
½ cup melted butter
2 teaspoons salt

Split chicken in half. Clean and wipe as dry as possible. Chicken is easier to eat if joints are broken and wing tips removed. Rub entire surface of chicken with cut lemon, squeezing out some juice occasionally. Sprinkle with salt, pepper and paprika mixed. Coat with melted butter, then sprinkle with sugar. Lay chicken in broiler pan (without rack) and flatten pieces out. Set under broiler unit as far from heat as possible; heat there for 10 minutes to allow seasonings to penetrate chicken. Then move pan up so top surface of chicken is 4 inches from heat and continue broiling. Baste occasionally with melted butter and turn pieces to ensure even browning. A 2½ pound chicken takes about 35 minutes.

—1949 Contest Winner, Annual National
Chicken Cooking Contest

Celia Steele was a woman who did not put up with nonsense. Short and heavyset, with a shock of red hair and a fiery temper to match, she got up early and went to bed late. In charge of the modest home she had made in Delmarva, that patchwork peninsula of Delaware, Maryland, and Virginia that dangles into the Chesapeake Bay, she spent her days scrubbing the floors, mending the linens, cooking the meals, and washing the clothes.

Carrying on the long tradition of rural women before her, tending the household's chickens was Celia's domain. Each year she would send off for a new batch of fifty chicks from a nearby hatchery and wait patiently for her friendly United States Postal worker to deliver them to her door. After putting her new acquisitions into her sensible backyard coop, she went about refilling the waterers, spreading out enough kitchen scraps, and providing all the care her practical little hens needed to provide her family with eggs. Come late spring and early summer, Celia would sell whatever extra "springers" her flock produced to local chicken dealers eager to fuel the Kosher Wars still raging in New York. In exchange she earned her own pin money, which she spent on buttons, modest frocks, and other such practical things.

Tending to this small flock wasn't terribly difficult work, but Celia also didn't expect any help from her husband Wilmer. He was a captain at the nearby Coast Guard station and, like most American men, thought it almost sinful to enter the hen house. Still, Celia was grateful for his military career. Compared to their neighbors, who were largely subsistence produce farmers or dependent on their daily seafood catches from the Chesapeake, the Steeles' life together was comfortable. There was little luxury, mind you, but a sensible and practical existence was what Celia preferred. Unfortunately for her, a sensible and practical existence would be hard to come by after 1923.

According to poultry legend, in that year Celia's otherwise dependable hatchery man made some sort of mistake. Mrs. Steele's annual delivery of fifty chicks arrived instead as a whole fleet of corrugated crates filled with five hundred chirping balls of fluff. Stuck with four hundred and fifty extra birds, Celia set about practically and deliberately building them a larger hen house. She kept the size of her normal laying flock the same but treated all the extra unwanted arrivals, both male and female, as future spring chickens. After spending a few weeks getting nice and fat at the Steeles' home, the 387 birds still living were bought up by a dealer and sent to market a few weeks before everyone else's chickens. Celia's once-modest earnings were now an exorbitant sixty cents per pound, the equivalent of $8.60 today.

Newly flush with cash and equipped with bigger chicken facilities, the next year Celia doubled her hatchery man's mistake and ordered one thousand chicks. Within two years she was up to ten thousand. By 1926, with his home overrun with chickens and his wife getting close to out-earning him, Wilmer concluded that it might not be so bad to enter the hen house after all. He promptly and politely quit his job and what was once "her business" was now "our business." Together, by 1928, the pair was growing more than 25,000 birds on their property.

Word of the Steeles' financial success spread as rapidly as the chicken pox. Prosperity may have been an alien creature to the humble Methodist farmers of the Peninsula, but the chicken wasn't. Most families already kept small backyard flocks for eggs, which they readily multiplied following the Steeles' example. Much like Petaluma, Delmarva had a mild climate, good soil, ample timber, and easy access to urban areas, most notably New York City but also Washington, D.C. and Philadelphia. Just a short train distance from these population centers, the Delmarva birds arrived in these markets incredibly fresh, effectively eliminating any hold the Western shipper had on a city's dinner tables. As a result, the Delmarvan chicken businesses thrived. By 1925, the Peninsula produced 50,000 birds for shipment to nearby cities; by 1926, that number easily topped one million. "We made money like we could only dream," recalled one farmer. Raising broilers "isn't making money, it's having it given to you," declared another. To the men of Delmarva, "our business" had become "my business."

Although a rare treat well up to the 1920s, these so-called broiler chickens that the Delmarvans were championing are now the majority of chickens that reach our supper tables today. Also known as spring chickens or hothouse hens or squab broilers or springers, traditionally these were any chicken aged five to six weeks and weighing in anywhere from three quarters to two full pounds. The best way to eat a broiler is exactly as its name suggests: "picked up, plucked and trussed, split open and broiled much like a mackerel."

As a chicken grows older, fatter, and wiser, its name and use in cooking changes with it. Next comes the fryer, a bird of roughly the same age as the broiler but weighing in at a pound or so more. Today, a broiler and a fryer are considered the same thing, although a fryer's previous larger size made it more useful when cut up for frying. Next is the roaster, a much more mature chicken that enjoyed anywhere from eight to ten months of life upon the earth before gracing Christmas dinner tables. Roaster chickens, not surprisingly, are most often served roasted. And finally are the stewing fowls and old hens, those greying birds who had lived long chicken lives but no longer had any use but to flavor a good stew. While all chickens were urban luxuries, the broiler was the most coveted of all—it was widely believed that the young broilers "possess much more flavor than the mature chicken."

Another, much older recipe for broiled chicken, coming from the book Food and Cookery for the Sick and Convalescent. *This text was also written by Fannie Merritt Farmer, author of the famous* Boston Cooking-School Cook Book *(1896). All throughout the late nineteenth and early twentieth centuries, Fannie was a sought-after lecturer on the emerging science of nutrition, even training soon-to-be doctors on the subject at Harvard Medical School.*

BROILED CHICKEN

Order chicken split for broiling. Singe, wipe, sprinkle with salt, and place on a well-greased broiler. Broil twenty minutes over a clear fire, watching carefully and turning broiler so that all parts may be browned equally. The flesh side needs the longer exposure to the fire. The skin side cooks quickly and then is liable to burn. Remove to hot platter, spread with soft butter, and sprinkle with salt.

So much time and attention is required for broiling a chicken that the work is often simplified by placing chicken in a dripping-pan, skin side down, sprinkling with salt, dotting over with butter, and cooking fifteen minutes in a hot oven, then removing to broiler to finish the cooking.

—Fannie Merritt Farmer,
*Food and Cookery for the
Sick and Convalescent*, 1904

Although she's remembered as a poultry pioneer, Mrs. Steele certainly wasn't the first American to ever try to capitalize on the spring chicken. Almost in tandem with the rise of the massive artificial incubators and mammoth hatcheries at the turn of the century came flocks of poultry entrepreneurs eager to become winners solely through chicken dinners. In the spring and summer, when shipping prices weren't too high, these endeavors were incredibly profitable. But average prices and overall demand were far too low during the chicken glut, when the majority of broilers were sent to market, to make up for the complete inability of most farmers to raise chickens in the winter. For this reason, no nineteenth-century broiler farm managed to find long-term success. As a result, most Americans thought the raising of chickens for food "cannot be profitably conducted beyond a certain point." But these people didn't yet understand the power of cod liver oil.

Back at the very end of the nineteenth century, an intrepid Dutch doctor with the strong Dutch name of Christiaan Eijkman found himself on the island of Java studying beriberi, a deadly disease that causes fatigue, loss of feeling in the limbs, and heart failure. His methods were standard for his day: injecting cheap and readily reproducing chickens with strains of the disease, watching them become infected, and then systematically trying to cure the birds. Over the course of many months spent shooting up chickens to no productive conclusion, Eijkman gradually realized that the illness wasn't contagious like he thought. The birds weren't getting beriberi from anything he was doing; they were getting sick because of their food.

Throughout most of Eijkman's experiments, the

chickens were being fed hulled and polished military-grade white rice. The birds on this diet promptly became weakened, grew paralyzed, and died. But halfway through the trials, Eijkman's hospital got a new cook who thought it silly to waste military-grade rice on birds. The cook promptly switched the chicken's diet to locally grown whole rice with the hulls still on. When the chickens ate this new rice, they miraculously recovered from their sickness.

Eijkman would not know what the curative substance in brown rice was until 1912, when an intrepid Polish chemist with the proud Polish name of Casimir Funk became intrigued by the Dutch physician's work. After much trial and error in his laboratory, Funk eventually isolated the potent substance in rice bran—thiamine, also known as vitamin B1—that was curing beriberi. In the process he discovered the existence of vitamins themselves. For all his time spent injecting chickens with beriberi with no results, Eijkman would eventually win the Nobel Prize for Medicine. For all his time spent isolating the actual cure for beriberi and developing an entire new field of science, Funk received nothing.

The discovery of vitamins, not just B1 but the whole spectrum, was of course groundbreaking for everything that eats, but most crucially for Celia Steele's chickens. Vitamin research continued steadily from Funk's work, and by the early

1920s researchers at the University of Wisconsin discovered that vitamin D was essential to the diet of healthy chickens. Just like human children, baby chickens grown without adequate vitamin D develop rickets, or what the poultry industry called "leg weakness," a disease that renders the bird lame and unable to walk. Although easily remedied by sunlight, winter weather did not provide enough rays to keep the chickens healthy, hence the difficulty farmers were facing in raising young birds during the cold season. Cod liver oil, however, was a substance rich in vitamin D and could be added to a chicken's diet at any season. Within months, the fishy substance was part of almost every commercial chicken feed in the country.

Most experts agree that without the discovery of the importance of vitamin D to chickens the present-day poultry industry would not have developed. Never mind the fact that farmers had long known not to feed fish to livestock, as it imparts a "fishy" flavor to them. (It bothered King Henry III of England so much that in the thirteenth century he forbade his subjects to let their pigs feed "on fish or on hemp seeds, because of the particular flavor those substances give the meat.") The simple addition of cod liver oil into feed by 1925 allowed Celia and her comrades to grow their chickens in the winter, and, much later, wholly indoors. With the help of the noble codfish, one flock of broilers became two, which eventually became three, and then four, spread throughout the year so the birds would hit the markets when prices were favorable.

Aimed at taking advantage of these good prices, farmers now found themselves with over ten thousand birds at once, which quickly taught them what kind of diseases an enormous group of chickens was prone to. On the opposite coast, Petaluma had long battled chicken plagues in their ever-growing flocks. Through deadly trial and error, the ranchers had learned to replace all their hens after just two laying seasons to prevent avian tuberculosis, and were constantly cleaning and re-cleaning their colony houses to stop the spread of chicken bronchitis. Still, all of their efforts could not prevent an avian influenza from decimating twenty percent of their feathered livelihoods in the early 1920s.

Celia and her Delmarvan comrades were plagued by chicken disease as well as their flocks grew to ever greater numbers, but these east coast farmers also came along at a much better time in chicken medical history. The fateful year of 1879, when Lyman Byce invented his mechanical incubator, was also the year when scientist Louis Pasteur left his Parisian laboratory for an extended summer vacation. The year prior, one of Pasteur's veterinarian friends had sent the famed physician the lovely gift of the head of a rooster that had died from fowl cholera, a disease that had been decimating France's chicken stocks for the better part of the last century. Honored by such generosity, Pasteur and his team at the Pasteur Institute set about trying to understand the nature of this disease.

Once cultured from a dead chicken, particular strains of the fowl cholera pathogen were kept fresh by regularly infecting other birds, letting them weaken and die, and then culturing the disease again. After Pasteur left on holiday in July of that year, with the boss gone, experiments on fowl cholera didn't resume again until October, meaning this re-culturing process didn't happen regularly for months. Many samples had even been carelessly left out and exposed to the environment of the laboratory during this time by assistants eager to start their own summer vacations.

Upon resuming experimentation in the fall, the researchers assumed all their previous cultures had spoiled, but—waste not, want not—they attempted to revitalize some of the older strains by feeding them to a group of chickens. Although the birds did grow sick and weak, the creatures still managed to survive. Seeing such results, the scientists assumed that the cultures simply did not work anymore and collected a newer strain of the illness to infect the birds again. The results of this second round were startling; the chickens that had been infected with the July strain had somehow developed a resistance to the disease while those that had not quickly perished.

Pasteur was intrigued when he finally returned from his holiday in December, and his experiments continued to focus on the air-exposed cultures. Through trial and error, he eventually came to the idea of the "attenuated virus," according to which extended exposure to oxygen weakened the disease and, when injected into the chicken again, generated an immunity without killing its host. From this concept came the very first vaccines.

Overlooking the fact that Pasteur later tried (and failed) to kill all of Australia's invasive rabbit population by purposefully spreading chicken cholera, the scientist's discovery of the vaccine was an incredible breakthrough in medical science for both man and bird. Pasteur's methods would eventually help doctors to eradicate diseases that had been the scourge of humanity for centuries, everything from smallpox to polio to typhoid fever. Chicken doctors would eventually learn to do the same.

During the early years of Petaluma, these vaccines were still incredibly expensive. Even after the chicken cholera vaccine was developed in the 1880s, most people with chickens still dealt with the disease the old-fashioned way: by isolating, killing, and burning all infected chickens as soon as any illness was detected. By the end of the 1920s and early 1930s, however, commercial laboratories and experiment stations had developed cheaper and more effective vaccines that could be given to birds through a prick of a pin, a drop in their water, or a heavy spray over their shells before they even hatched.

Delmarva still did have its own host of disease problems—pullorum and chicken bronchitis were taking their toll, and a particularly nasty intestinal parasite called coccidiosis was spreading rapidly through flocks in the 1920s, but poultry resistance to illness was growing stronger. Knowing that "if chickens were not so susceptible to all manner of disease, great would be the poultry profit," groups started organizing massive, countrywide efforts to eradicate even those poultry illnesses that couldn't be vaccinated against. Beginning with the tentative "Manhattan Plan," a national program hatched by farmers in Manhattan, Kansas in 1925, and then the much more powerful, government-backed National Poultry Improvement Plan (NPIP) in 1934, chicken disease grew ever more manageable with each passing year.

It wouldn't be until 1935, however, that sick chickens would really be on the American mind. That June the Supreme Court laid down a unanimous and groundbreaking decision in the case between the A.L.A. Schechter Poultry Corp. and the United States government. The defendants in the case, a cohort of kosher chicken slaughterers from New York City, were accused of marketing "unfit chickens," falsifying records, selling to unlicensed dealers, paying below code wages, and making their employees work above code hours, among fourteen other crimes. All of these actions, claimed the suit, were in violation of the Live Poultry Code that President Franklin D. Roosevelt had recently made law under the auspices of the 1933 National Industrial Recovery Act (NIRA). The NIRA was a cornerstone of Roosevelt's New Deal and gave the president authority to regulate industry to help pull the nation out of the Great Depression. This authority apparently extended even to chickens.

Being accustomed to cockfights back in New York City, when presented with their charges, the butchers pushed back—they weren't at fault, President Roosevelt was. Congress and not the president was the only entity with the power to write laws, their lawyers argued, and Congress was overstepping its boundaries in the first place by attempting to regulate the Schechter's "in-state activities." Therefore, the National Industrial Recovery Act was unconstitutional.

The Schechters lost their original case, appealed, then lost again, and eventually landed in front of the Supreme Court. After hearing both sides, and spending an exorbitant amount of time amusing themselves with chicken jokes, all nine Justices eventually agreed with the boys from Brooklyn.

The NIRA was declared unconstitutional, and FDR's grand plans were destroyed. The country was shocked; it's safe to assume most Americans didn't really expect a couple of sick chickens to cripple the New Deal.

Few Delmarvans seemed to notice the hubbub the bird was causing down in Washington, however. After all, they had sick chickens of their own to tend to and their backyard flocks were growing by the week. By 1934 Delmarva was producing some seven million birds per year, and the work itself was backbreaking. Newly received chicks spent their first few weeks huddled for warmth around brooder stoves, which needed to be constantly stoked and refilled with coal. Hundred-pound bags of nutritionally advanced feed needed to be purchased, hauled, and spread around, water crocks refilled, and guards needed to be constantly vigilant for the threat of predators, both animal and human. When hungry neighbors didn't get into the chicken coops, particularly bad were the rats, which liked chicken just as much as anyone else and could munch their way through an entire flock of brooding chicks in one night. When the chicks became broilers and outgrew the brooders, they had to be moved into larger houses and constantly watered and fed. Temperature needed to be monitored and ventilation constantly adjusted; the droppings and sawdust on the floor had to be thoroughly cleaned before the next batch arrived to ensure the new birds had a healthy start.

In the early days, single families like the Steeles could manage a poultry farm by themselves, but as flocks grew so did the workload. Fortunately for Delmarva, its gravity in the chicken universe was growing so great that it was pulling other poultry-related industries to it. Driven by a large number of Jewish transplants, often with roots in the New York kosher trade, the peninsula sprouted hatcheries, processing plants, and feed factories. Chicken producers no longer had to call chicken dealers to come inspect their crops; a central poultry exchange had been set up, so great was the demand. Cheap labor followed in droves.

Of great importance in the early years of Delmarvan chicken were African American laborers. Driven from the South by abject poverty, violence, and racism, families made their way up the east coast as part of the Great Migration, and many stopped in Delmarva. There they made $2.50 per day as farm laborers or chicken catchers, a huge jump from the wages of $1.60 or less in many parts of the South. By the 1930s, blacks comprised nearly thirty percent of the Peninsula's population but almost none of them owned growing facilities themselves. Overt racism even among the Peninsula's god-fearing Methodists prevented African Americans from owning farmland, and Delaware continued to use a cat-o-nine-tails to publicly punish chicken thieves well into the 1940s.

Problems and all, prosperity had hatched in Delmarva at a time when financial assurance of any kind was hard to come by. With patience and dedication and humility, the farmers of Delmarva would continue to make their home the center of chickendom and, by 1936, two out of every three chickens in America were raised on the Peninsula. One witness of the feathered cornucopia couldn't help but declare that, "if the Delmarva Peninsula. . . . had its own flag, it probably would display a haughty rooster rampant over crossed drumsticks." Celia's modest endeavor had taken flight.

Even though it's a broiler, a Delmarva chicken could be roasted as well.

ROAST DELMARVA CHICKEN
Mrs. Ernest Schults, Bordentown, N.J.
(Senior Division)
1 3 lb. DELMARVA chicken, ready-to-cook
Lemon
¼ cup pork sausage
3 tablespoons chopped onion
¼ cup butter or margarine
½ teaspoon paprika
¾ teaspoon salt

Cream celery leaves
Rosemary, fresh or dried
1 tablespoon chicken or sausage fat
¼ tablespoon chopped celery
¼ tablespoon chopped parsley
4 cups bread crumbs
Milk

Rub skin of chicken with cut lemon, set aside to season. Prepare dressing: Cook sausage over low heat until golden brown, breaking it into small pieces as it cooks. Add butter or margarine and 2 tablespoons of the onion. Continue cooking until onion is softened, but not browned. Remove pan from heat, and add paprika, salt, celery, parsley, and bread crumbs. Add enough milk to give desired moistness. Stuff the body and neck cavities lightly; then truss. Rub skin with the chicken or sausage fat, then sprinkle with the celery leaves, crushed rosemary, and remaining onion. Wrap loosely in aluminum foil. Place on rack in open shallow pan. Roast in slow oven (325° F) one hour. Open foil and pull it away to expose chicken so it can brown. Brush with some of the cream. Continue roasting—basting with remaining cream until nicely brown and tender, one-half to one hour. To test, move leg up and down.

Joints should move easily or break. In serving, garnish with baked halves of oranges, and with watercress or parsley. 5 to 6 servings.

—1952 Contest Winner, Annual National Chicken Cooking Contest

An artist's rendering of the popular "Cochin-China" fowl from the Hen Fever, 1855.

Lithograph of a nineteenth-century poultry yard, 1869.

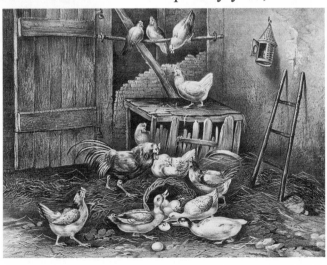

Uncle Sam Expects You
To Keep Hens and Raise Chickens

Two Hens in the Back Yard for Each Person in the House Will Keep a Family In Fresh Eggs

EVEN the smallest back yard has room for a flock large enough to supply the house with eggs. The cost of maintaining such a flock is small. Table and kitchen waste provide much of the feed for the hens. They require little attention—only a few minutes a day.

An interested child, old enough to take a little responsibility, can care for a few fowls as well as a grown person.

Every back yard in the United States should contribute its share to a bumper crop of poultry and eggs in 1918.

In Time of Peace a Profitable Recreation

In Time of War a Patriotic Duty

For information about methods of Back-Yard Poultry Keeping suited to your location and conditions, write

Your State Agricultural College

or

The United States Department of Agriculture
Washington, D. C.

"Uncle Sam expects you to keep hens
and raise chickens," 1917.

Mechanized slaughter facility, 1904.

RIGHT: Chicks with (above) and without (below) leg weakness, the disease that made it difficult to raise chickens in the winter, 1920.

BELOW: A young girl in Charleston feeds her chickens, 1921.

ABOVE: A poultry scientist working for the United States Department of Agriculture continues her work to rid America's chickens of parasites, 1930.

RIGHT: A farm family prepares chickens for canning, 1936.

ABOVE: Celia Steele vaccinating chickens, 1936.

BELOW: A broiler shed in Indiana capable of housing just 40 chickens, 1937.

ABOVE: A chicken vendor at a farmer's market
in Weatherford, Texas, 1939.

BELOW: The rolling hills of Petaluma, California,
dotted with chicken houses and Leghorn chickens, 1942.

A woman candles eggs at a factory in Petaluma to make sure no chicken embryos are developing inside, 1942.

A man places sheets of eggs into an incubator to be hatched, 1942.

A man determines the sex of chicks at a Petaluma hatchery, 1943.

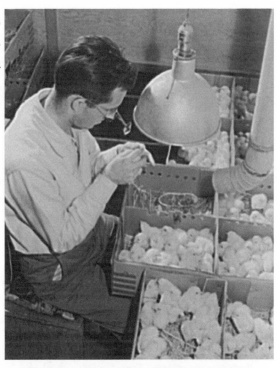

A flock of White Leghorns in a yard in Petaluma, California, 1942.

ABOVE: A live poultry inspector in New York City makes sure a chicken's crop hasn't been stuffed full of sand and corn, 1951.

BELOW: Poultry scientists inspect chicken carcasses for quality, 1960s.

ABOVE: A chicken carcass is being plucked
by machine, 1960s.

BELOW: Stages in chicken processing
from bird to cellophane, 1960s.

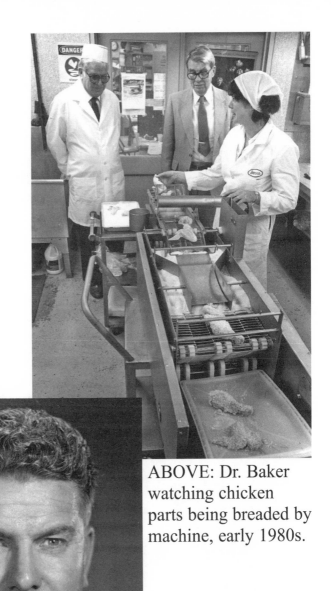

ABOVE: Dr. Baker watching chicken parts being breaded by machine, early 1980s.

LEFT: Dr. Robert Baker, 1963.

ABOVE: Two of Robert Baker's groundbreaking
value-added chicken products: Chickalona
and Chicken Bologna.

BELOW: Dr. Robert Baker's Chic-A-Links.

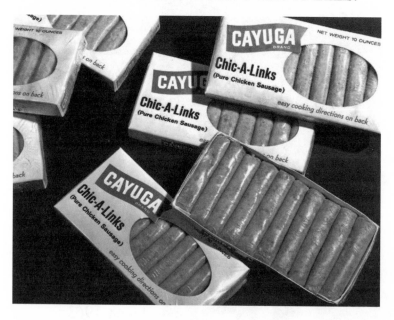

ABOVE: Dr. Robert Baker's Chicken Hash.

BELOW: Chicken Crispies in action in the late 1970s.

ABOVE AND BELOW: Lines of cooks grilling up Robert Baker's famous Cornell chicken at the annual Cornell University summer barbecue in 1953.

ABOVE AND BELOW: Broiler shed in the 1960s.

ABOVE: Young chicks in a poultry house
in Pennsylvania, 1960s.

BELOW: The inconspicuous outside
of a 1960s broiler shed.

Brahma hen   Brahma rooster

Buff Orpington female   Buff Orpington male

Buff Plymouth Rock female Buff Plymouth Rock male

Dominique hen   Dominique rooster

Silver Penciled Wyandotte
female

Silver Penciled Wyandotte
male

Silver-Gray Dorking female   Silver-Gray Dorking male

White Leghorn hen   White Leghorn rooster

CHAPTER TEN
They Saw in Hens a Way

Chicken Pilau is the Southern take on the international standby of chicken and rice. The name comes from the Persian rice pilaf, and is similar to a Southern Chicken Bog, which is simply rice cooked for house with chicken, and the Latin standby Arroz con Pollo.

CHICKEN PILAU

2 cups rice
¼ teaspoon pepper
2 quarts boiling water
1 onion chopped
1 stewing chicken (3½ lb.), cut in pieces
2 stalks celery, chopped
2 tomatoes, sliced
2 teaspoons salt
6 tablespoons butter

Drop rice into boiling water in large saucepan, add chicken and simmer, covered 1½ to 2 hours, or until chicken is almost done, adding salt and pepper after first hour of cooking. Brown onion, celery and tomatoes in butter; add to chicken and continue cooking ½ hour. Approximate yield: 6 portions.

—The New York Herald Tribune Home Institute, *America's Cook Book*, 1943

"Talking about chickens is a risky thing," mused celebrated American author E. B. White in 1944, thus introducing a passionate essay on the art of chicken keeping. "Be tidy. Be brave," he advised. "Elevate all laying house feeders and waterers twenty-two inches off the floor . . . Walk, don't run. Never carry any strange objects into the henhouse with you." There is an elegant cadence to White's words just as there was in the call of the hen and the independence a little flock could provide. Robert Frost heard it too, forty years before. "Aiken had worn the starched collar of servitude to dress long enough," opined the poet in 1903, "he wished to get back to loose clothes and the country, and he saw in hens a way."

In between the hopeful words of Frost and White unfortunately came the Great Depression. Times were undoubtedly tough for most Americans, particularly rural Americans, after the financial crash of 1929. The Dust Bowl that followed was covering agricultural livelihoods in a thick coat of financial ruin, and commodity prices dropped faster than telegrams could carry word of their decline to farmers, who were in turn watching the land dry up before their eyes. People in cities were growing hungry too, but work anywhere was scarcer than food. There was certainly not a "chicken for every pot," as the Republican Party had promised in its effort to get the great food aid organizer Herbert Hoover elected president in 1928. Skewers of city chicken were much more likely to grace American dinner tables at the time, and instead of reelection, the Republican Party was slapped with a host of lawsuits over this egregiously unfulfilled campaign promise.

Among the ranks of the struggling was a twenty-five-year-old man by the name of John W. Tyson. He was born on his family's farm in Missouri in 1906, and after he finished his agricultural studies the lanky youth had every intention of dying on that land as well. But the foolhardy speculation of Wall Street destroyed even the best-laid plans of the American farmer, and after the crash the Tyson family farm could no longer support John.

Hearing rumors of work in Fort Smith, Arkansas, the young man loaded his wife and his hopes into the back of a rickety pickup truck and headed south in 1930. But his money and gas didn't take the young couple as far as the promised land they were seeking, and the pair soon found themselves stranded in the small town of Springdale, Arkansas.

Like many areas in the American South, the

Depression hit Springdale hard. The soil had never been very fertile there and most who lived in the small town got by generation after generation on pitiful harvests of cotton. Fortunes (and land) were better just a bit west, where a lucky few managed to make ends meet through apple and apricot trees. Learning of higher produce prices in Kansas City and St. Louis, orchard owners were shipping their products across state lines. With a truck that still ran and eager to take any job he could, John Tyson became a produce driver.

At first business was good. Tyson's trips would take him far from his family for days at a time, but he would return with enough cash to keep a roof over their heads and food in their bellies. As the Depression wore on, however, pests and price collapses ate into the fruit business and fewer orchard owners were in need of Tyson's services.

As every penny grew harder to come by, Tyson began to catch glimpses of feathered opportunity among the apple trees. Since the end of the nineteenth century, many a poor Southerner had made decent side money off of chickens and their eggs. The problem had always been getting birds in sufficient quantities for these growers to make any sort of living out of it. With Delmarva demonstrating how money could at last be made off of broilers, with a minimal entry cost, the hardship of the Depression sweetened the poetic call of the hen. In place of cotton and fruit, chickens and chicken houses began to sprout up around Springdale.

Word spread that poultry was commanding a higher price outside of Arkansas, and with his produce shipping jobs running thin, John cashed in all his savings to buy a shipment of chickens. His rusty old pickup filled again, this time with feathered hope, he drove those birds across state lines and into greener financial pastures. Tyson's first trip earned him enough for a second trip and then a third. The gyrations of the broiler market sometimes rendered a shipment a loss even before Tyson completed it, but the intrepid youth won more often than he lost. In trucking chickens, it seemed, Tyson had found a way.

Being one of the few men shipping chickens, initially John Tyson had no trouble procuring Springdale birds, which he had now begun driving as far afield as Chicago, Memphis, and Nashville. But by 1935 Tyson's business was growing even faster than the chicken houses could be built. Wanting his ability to procure birds to be in line with his ability to ship them, Tyson soon bought a hatchery to supply growers with chicks. But Tyson's capacity to produce chicks soon outpaced his growers' financial abilities to purchase them. Tyson in turn began providing the jobless small sums of credit to buy the birds, and later the feed he also began to distribute. By the 1940s, John's holdings included a feed mill, a farm, and a whole fleet of commercial growing houses. Step by step, problem by problem, what is now the multibillion dollar empire known as Tyson Foods was born.

A similar fowl kingdom was hatching by the end of the 1930s in Gainesville, Georgia. There a young man by the name of Jesse Jewell found himself an actor in a similar series of unfortunate events. The Depression weighed heavily, Jewell's family feed business was slowly going under, and the poor citizenry of Gainesville were in desperate need of work, especially after a tornado leveled the town in 1936. They, too, saw chickens as their economic salvation. Much like Tyson, what initially started out as Jewell's feed and shipping operation eventually gained a hatchery, then a processing plant, then a feed mill, then a rendering plant. By the early 1950s, the now middle-aged Jesse Jewell would find himself presiding over the first vertically integrated chicken company in the world.

Fueled by desperation that was continually stoked by the dozens of feed dealers and chicken distributors who had emulated the likes of Tyson and Jewell, the incredible rise of the broiler industry in the American South was nothing short of an agricultural miracle. Queen Chicken had dethroned even King Cotton, and a region that was producing just eight million broilers in 1934 was pumping out an unprecedented 486 million by 1953. So prolific in its production, Gainesville would eventually overtake even Delmarva as the "Chicken Capital of the World," a title the small town still proudly holds today, commemorated by a giant chicken statue standing at the corner of Jesse Jewell Parkway.

A common chicken recipe people like to associate with the Great Depression is "Chicken and Dumplings," in which a cook adds flour to chicken broth to extend both ingredients farther for more meals. This dish is actually centuries old, coming more from the prosperity of a Sunday supper than from the financial hardship most associate with it. As this dish is generally made in a large pot, another name for "chicken and dumplings" is simply "chicken pot pie."

CHICKEN POT-PIE

Cut a good-sized chicken in small pieces. Put a small plate in the bottom of the kettle. Put the chicken in and cover it with hot water. Season high with butter, pepper, and salt. A half hour before serving, drop in small lumps of dough made like biscuit. A quart of flour makes enough dumplings for one large chicken. Cover closely; 20 or 25 minutes will generally cook them. Take out with a skimmer carefully, on platter, and if gravy is not thick enough, thicken it with a small spoon of flour and water, made smooth. Pour it over the chicken and dumplings.

—Mrs. F. E. Owens, *Mrs. Owens' Cook Book and Useful Household Hints*, 1903

Thanks to the innovations of Celia Steele and the work of Tyson, Jewell, and other entrepreneurs, by the end of the 1930s and beginning of the 1940s, broilers were available year round. Prices declined and chicken consumption shot up, far outstripping that of other meat birds like turkey and goose that once competed with chicken for space on American dinner plates. Instead of fighting each other in a limited market, New Yorkers were now "literally eating their way out of one of the greatest oversupplies of poultry and poultry products that have occurred in the industry." Afraid of what this glut might do to the much less violent but still lucrative chicken market, the New York municipal government started issuing guidelines instructing individuals formerly unable even to conceive of eating chicken on how to best take advantage of these low prices for the bird.

This chicken explosion could not have come at a better moment in American history. World War II would soon begin to rage, and as red meat supplies dwindled, the United States Government was in dire need of an alternative protein source. Turning to chicken wasn't its initial plan by any means. As with the First World War, the bird was firmly not part of the official government "Food for Defense" and "Food for Freedom" programs. Federal officials, making it clear that "armies don't eat chicken," still asked its citizens at home to substitute the bird for red meats so the latter could be given to the manly fighting men abroad.

But, by 1943, it appeared the Army did need that chicken after all. It was already consuming some 50,000,000 pounds of poultry annually, largely for its bimonthly Sunday chicken dinners and as soup at military hospitals, but even with strict rationing on the home front, the supplies of pork and beef the nation's warriors depended on were diminishing. Predicting an impending chicken shortage, the government issued a command that all stocks of already frozen poultry should be set aside for the troops. But this measure would not prove enough, and the army ate right through those supplies. Declaring next that chicken is "so important to the morale of all servicemen," later that year the War Food Administration announced that all of the ninety million broilers Delmarva was now producing annually must be set aside for the Army Quartermaster Corps.

The reason Delmarva was singled out to be the Army's exclusive chicken purveyor was because the federal government had noticed the patience and dedication and humility of the Peninsula's people in growing their birds. That is, policy-makers rightly believed that Celia Steele and her comrades were too honest and too hardworking to have ever smuggled moonshine during Prohibition a generation ago. The government's other options for procuring chickens for the troops were in the mountain regions of rural Georgia and Arkansas, where Jewell and Tyson had set up shop, which also happened to have once been a hotbed of illegal alcohol production. These states were riddled with backcountry routes and black market byways that had long made enforcing government mandates annoyingly difficult. Instead, in December of 1944, the National Guard drove into Delmarva, cut off all major roads, and began seizing chickens off of trucks headed in and out of the honest Peninsula, all the while declaring that the new official government stance was that "Chicken is for fighters first!"

Eaters of New York, who had grown accus-tomed to a steady oversupply of Delmarva's chicken on their tables since Tootsie Herbert's demise, were understandably disgruntled by this invasion. In almost every one of his weekly radio broadcasts at the end of the war, celebrated Mayor Fiorello La Guardia had to reassure his populace that he was doing everything he could to rectify the chicken problem. "I want to say to the armed forces," the Mayor announced, "that the people of the City of New York will take this willingly, no grousing or grouching about it, and that we do not consider it a big sacrifice to make when we know that this supply is going to the armed forces right on the battle front." He went on saying, "I hope that dealers will not embarrass our city by protesting." But of course the dealers did, and proceeded to ignore ceiling prices, boycott government enforcement, and eagerly took their products to the black market.

The invasion of Delmarva, which supplied some forty percent of the nation's chickens at the start of the war, was also a big blow for eaters across the country. After the government's voluntary "Share the Meat" campaign failed in 1942 and meat rationing became mandatory, chicken was one of the few animal proteins that remained un-rationed for the remainder of the war. Diners in restaurants enforcing a "meatless Tuesdays," flocked hungrily to their " 'meatless' chicken, which they seemed to prefer broiled, with a sort of gay gusto."

With government declarations pushing Americans toward the bird and Delmarva's millions of chickens now out of the picture, demand was ever growing but there were fewer and fewer chickens to be found. Although production increased from 413 million pounds in 1940 to an astounding 1.1 billion pounds annually by 1945, prices went up even more and the increasingly expensive bird was unavailable almost anywhere besides those unregulated black markets.

What then was the average American left to do? Many, besides protesting and grumbling, heard again that fateful call of the hen. "Chicken-minded but not a bit chicken-hearted," declared one wartime editorial, "America buys a box of chicks and prepares serenely to face the future till the Hitlers cease from troubling and the Tojos get the axe." It was the rise of the "Poultry for Freedom" movement, in which hen houses sprouted up where hen houses had long been forgotten, demand for incubators increased 2,000 percent, and hatcheries were so swamped with orders that they were months behind on deliveries. All across the fifty states, citizens both rich and poor were scrambling to get their hands on the bird. "The chicken situation is hectic," summarized the editor of *Cackle and Crow*. Unfortunately for commercial chicken producers, however, this frenzy would not last for long.

This is one way in which the army fed its soldiers chicken during World War II: chicken tamales, a popular dish from Mexico. Like most dishes Americans typically associate with Mexican cuisine, this recipe is not authentically Mexican. The dough that makes a traditional tamale is not made out of cornmeal and mashed potatoes but out of corn masa, *a dough produced by first soaking the corn kernels in lye and then mashing to make a paste. This process is called nixtamalization and it produces some delicious dough!*

NO. 391 CHICKEN OR TURKEY TAMALES
Yield: 100 servings, 4 to 4½ ounces each

Chicken or turkey, cooked, cubed
15 pounds (15 No. 56 dippers)
Salt
3 ounces (6 mess kit spoons)
Pepper
¼ ounce (1 mess kit spoon)
Chili powder
2 ounces (8 mess kit spoons)
Garlic, crushed
1 clove
Chicken stock
1 quart (1 No. 56 dipper)
Potatoes, mashed
5 pounds (2½ No. 56 dippers)
Cornmeal
1½ pounds (1½ mess kit cups)
Water (to make sufficient dough)
Fat (for frying)

Combine meat, salt, pepper, chili powder, garlic and chicken stock; mix well.

Prepare mashed potatoes. Mix mashed potatoes, corn meal, and flour together; add enough water to make a stiff dough.

Roll out dough ¼ inch thick. Cut into long strips, 2½ inches wide.

Place enough chicken mixture in center of each strip of dough to form a small core about ½ inch in diameter.

Moisten edges of dough and seal together. Cut rolled strips into pieces about 5 inches long.

Fry in deep hot fat (350°F) until biscuit dough is cooked.

—United States War Department,
Army Recipes, 1944

CHAPTER ELEVEN

A Chicken for Every Grill

CHICK-N-QUE SAUCE

Cue: To ensure delectable chicken every time, cook slowly over glowing coals (not flame) 12 or more inches from heat. Allow 1 to 1¼ hours total cooking time, turning chicken frequently and basting with sauce each time you turn.

½ cup Mazola Corn Oil
½ cup lemon juice or vinegar
¼ cup water
2 teaspoons salt
¼ teaspoon pepper
1 tablespoon sugar
1 teaspoon paprika
1 tablespoon minced onion

Mix all ingredients in a bowl and let stand about an hour to blend flavors. *To use as a marinade,* arrange chicken pieces in shallow baking dish. Pour sauce over all and let stand one hour or more. Turn chicken occasionally to season evenly. *To use as a basting sauce,* brush pieces with sauce before grilling. Enough for 3 broiler-fryer chickens.

—Chick-N-Que Cue Book: 15 Delicious Recipe 'n Menu Ideas from Mazola, 1960

O ne could taste the excitement in the air on that pleasant day in June 1948 as the "Chicken of Tomorrow" Queen waved her way through the streets of Georgetown, Delaware, the very heartland of the Delmarva Peninsula. While men, women, and children cheered the parade outside, poultry enthusiasts from all parts of Canada and the United States filled the gym at Georgetown High School, their hushed voices echoing off the bleachers as they weighed the merits of each of the some forty finalists in the "Chicken of Tomorrow" contest. This was it, the "world series of the billion-dollar broiler industry," a competition aimed at finding a better meat bird, one that was "broader breasted . . . with bigger drumsticks, plumper thighs, and layers of white meat."

The idea behind this competition came to the executives of the Great Atlantic & Pacific Tea Company (better known as the A&P) in 1946. The war was over, which meant rationing was too. Although at peak consumption just a few short years ago, by 1947 the chicken had "fallen far in popular favor since its wartime flight to glory as the result of a shortage of meat." With the fighting finished abroad, Americans wanted their red meat and they wanted it now. The slow pace at which both the government and the food industry were returning to normalcy aggravated already irritated consumers who had spent the past three years imprisoned by their ration books.

Using their constitutional rights as free citizens, the American people went to the polls in 1946 proclaiming, "No Meat—No Vote" in what became known as the "damn beefsteak election." "The only thing people will talk about is meat," bemoaned one congressman. Even President Truman was exasperated by the public's meaty obsession, firing off in a 1946 speech "You've deserted your President for a mess of pottage, a piece of beef, a side of bacon." But the people had spoken, with both their stomachs and their ballots, and with that election the Democratic Party lost its congressional majority for the first time in fourteen years.

Seeing that America's passion for red meat could topple governments was not heartening for the fledgling chicken industry. The wartime chicken boom had drawn record numbers of producers into the chicken business between 1940 and 1945, and in spite of rising farming costs, the value and number of the nation's chickens had grown more than 250% over the course of the war.

Servicemen fresh from the war were the largest group of new chicken farmers, aided in large part by government occupational programs, but it was becoming almost trendy to be involved with our feathered friend. The 1945 novel *The Egg and I*, a humorous account of the life of a chicken farmer, was a runaway success, which ballooned into an Oscar-nominated film and a series of TV spinoffs. Perhaps inspired by Prince Erik of Denmark, who renounced his throne, married a commoner, and then moved to California to become a chicken farmer in the 1920s, even celebrities got in on the act, including the husband of silver screen siren Marlene Dietrich, who moved out of Hollywood to become a chicken rancher. The bird's newfound superstar status was having an effect on production; despite declining prices, between 1946 and 1950, the volume of chickens produced in the United States more than doubled from 275 million to 616 million birds.

Although the pages of *The Egg and I* are filled with more than their fair share of humor, there was nothing funny when the protagonist asks, "Why in God's name does everyone want to get into the chicken business?" Yes, advances in poultry nutrition and disease control over the past half century had yielded incredible strides in the efficiency of production. Wholesalers, retailers, processors, feed distributors, and chicken farmers had also invested an immense amount of money into making chicken possible. But the bird was still a very tricky business, and with the end of rationing, chicken supply remained high while demand sharply declined, causing prices to drop to a point where the nation's now almost $3 billion chicken industry was immensely worried.

Besides revitalizing American's love for red meat, the prosperity after the Second World War also helped many citizens to achieve their dreams of home ownership. The late 1940s spawned the golden age of suburbia, and in every perfectly manicured lawn there appeared the latest in American culinary fixtures: the outdoor charcoal grill. More of a rudimentary open brazier than anything else, these popular contraptions had come a long way since the wooden *barabicu* frames the locals of the Caribbean were using to cook their meats when the Spanish first arrived in the sixteenth century. By the 1940s, an open pit blazing with fire had shrunk down to the at-home grill and manly beefcakes took great pleasure in inviting their friends and families over to witness their mastery of the charcoal flames.

Thanks to heavy efforts by advertisers, by mid-century the grill was declared a distinctly masculine domain, and as a result the American chicken was rarely celebrated in these beefy back-yard rituals. Investigating why their products were conspicuously absent from such flame-broiled affairs, chicken producers quickly concluded that the problem wasn't the chicken industry but rather the bird itself. Growers, warned Dewey Termohlen, the director of the US Department of

Agriculture's Poultry Branch, "faced the permanent loss of a large part of their market to the other types of meat unless they came up with a better type of bird."

Just prior to World War II, the American turkey industry had successfully increased demand for its product by starting to breed birds with wider breasts, and the chicken industry was eager to emulate it. What the government and growers alike wanted was a chicken that was "a sort of super-bird—more meaty, more juicy, more tender, and less bony than the chicken in last night's pot." They essentially wanted a chicken that could compete with the juicy steak or succulent sausage that was being blackened to a crisp by the intrepid weekend grill master.

As the country's largest purveyor of less-than-super birds, A&P food stores led the charge in improving the appeal of the American chicken. Alongside the USDA, ten prominent poultry organizations, and two poultry magazines, the chain announced in 1946 their "Chicken of Tomorrow" program and its $5,000 prize for the bird with the juiciest breasts. Hearing the call of cash, chicken farmers throughout the United States eagerly set about breeding and crossbreeding their plumpest and fastest-growing birds for the competition.

Although the industry may have been complaining about the lack of juiciness in their chickens, these birds the farmers were breeding and crossbreeding were actually already plumper and faster-growing than any other birds in chicken history. Even with the Hen Fever largely abated, poultry shows still raged on in the United States throughout the latter half of the nineteenth century. In 1873 there came the American Poultry Association (APA), which subsequently published its breeding bible, *The American Standard of Perfection*, a book that explicitly laid out the characteristics of true prizewinning chickens. There are dozens and dozens of required traits for each variety of bird. For a chicken to be considered a true White Leghorn, for example, its head must be moderate in length, its wings large and well folded, and its feathers must not be any color than white nor its legs any color other than yellow. To be a multipurpose Barred Plymouth Rock, by contrast, the bird's eyes must be full and prominent, its wattles moderately long and free from serrations, and its plumage must be grayish white.

This regulation of the same variation that had so inspired Darwin paved the way for the next generation of inheritance researchers. At the forefront was British biologist William Bateson. Recording his results from breeding chickens the same way nineteenth-century Augustinian friar Gregor Mendel did with his pea plants, crossing and recrossing individuals to reveal their dominant and recessive traits, Bateson was the first to demonstrate that such a relationship also existed in the inheritance of animals. His experiments became the building blocks of the entire field of genetics.

Among the first to embrace these discoveries were some of America's leading eugenicists, including Charles Davenport and Harry Laughlin, who themselves were fanatical chicken breeders. Together with others interested in maintaining the "purity" of the white American race through the power of genetics, they helped found the American Breeders' Association (ABA), the nation's first and premier eugenics group. The ABA's growing influence is what would eventually promote the passage of those racially charged laws that sterilized "genetically inferior" chicken thieves.

While many chicken farmers were indeed members of the American Breeders' Association, most more eagerly applied these genetic break-throughs to make money. Bateson's controlled breeding experiments demonstrated clearly that many primary chicken traits, such as overall body size and color, followed a generally predictable pattern in subsequent generations. The commercial applications of this were obvious.

It had long been known that the best eating, and the best egg laying abilities were incompatible in chickens. Petaluma had pushed heavily toward egg production with their Leghorns, resulting in birds that produce impeccable eggs while remaining scrawny on the supper table, while the large Brahma, that "King of Poultry," remained the most popular meat breed in the country until Delmarva started using the Delaware breed, a cross between those multipurpose Plymouth Rocks and a meaty variety called a New Hampshire, to build their feathered empire. The majority of small farmers, however, used birds that were decent at both and not the best at either. With the power of genetics on their side and the prosperity of Petaluma on their mind, the USDA in the early twentieth century first focused their efforts on producing the best egg layers as were physically possible.

The process was the application of survival of the fittest at its finest. Agricultural scientists organized huge laying competitions, and the hens that produced the greatest number of eggs within the year would be kept on to produce the next flock. (The other birds weren't as lucky.) Over time, these concerted efforts worked; while the laying production of a barnyard bird in the nineteenth century averaged just one hundred eggs per year, by the 1920s, that number reached an average of two hundred or more. These competitions have continued over the past century, and today the average "egg machine" lays 265 eggs per year.

The drive for egg-laying efficiency was mirrored

in other ways across the pond thanks to renowned British geneticist Reginald Crundall Punnett, a colleague of William Bateson and creator of the Punnett Square, a diagram that provides the statistical likelihood of certain inherited traits appearing in an offspring. (It haunts seventh grade biology classrooms the world over.) Building off of Bateson's work, Punnett developed techniques to breed different colored chickens according to sex. With the shortages of the First World War, these advances allowed egg producers to quickly identify and get rid of unproductive male chicks who would otherwise eat into valuable grain supplies. (Getting rid of these male birds, as it still does today for much of the commercial egg industry, typically involved throwing the live chicks straight from their shells into what is essentially a wood chipper.) Genetic perfection too was part of the National Poultry Improvement Plan of 1935, which aimed to control avian disease not only through management but also through breeding efforts.

All these programs to eliminate disease and produce more eggs were effective in their aims, but they didn't improve the quality of an American chicken dinner. This was where the Chicken of Tomorrow contest was meant to step in, and when farmers from around the country submitted their meaty birds for judging in 1946 and 1947, the industry's excitement was evident. In 1947, long before a winner was crowned, the USDA's Termohlen declared, "I believe that within five years, as a result of the Chicken of Tomorrow program, we will see a complete revolution in the production and marketing of poultry meat."

On that June afternoon in 1948, as the breeding competition reached its climax, newspaper head-lines throughout the country excitedly proclaimed the Red Cornish cross bird submitted by the Vantress Hatchery of Marysville, California the winner of the Chicken of Tomorrow contest. For the duration of the twelve weeks spent maturing in the controlled growing areas and then under the fluorescent lights of the assessment space, the hatchery's chickens excelled in health, appearance, weight gain, and meatiness. Presumably to the great delight of Delaware's Chicken of Tomorrow Queen, this champion boasted the desired "broad-breasted appearance" that the contest's originators so coveted and it dominated the field in both meat yield and efficiency.

The one unfortunate attribute of the Red Cornish, however, was that its feathers were red. To the detriment of a great many delicious things, what a food looks like to consumers really does matter. In a complete turnaround from decades of precedence, when it came to chicken, shoppers of the 1950s no longer wanted to see birds with those visible pinfeathers that used to be a sure sign of youth. Chickens with darker feathering necessarily had darker, more visible pinfeathers.

With this proverbial housewife in mind, farmers came to prefer a bird with white feathers, or at the very least with a light-colored skin. For most of chicken history, this preference would have been quite regrettable. As the Roman agriculturalist Columella warns in the first century A.D., white chickens are much more visible and therefore more likely to die gruesome deaths in the clutches of predators such as hawks and foxes. But, thanks to vitamin D and feed supplements, the chickens of the 1950s could live out their lives wholly inside, without once ever seeing the sky and the predators that circled in it. Instead, consumer demands, not nature, became a primary selecting force on the bird's evolution, which meant by 1955 there had been a strong trend toward a white bird.

The white bird that then became the chicken of choice was not the plumper, prize-winning Chicken of Tomorrow, but rather a cross between that bird and the chicken that came in second. This runner up was a White Plymouth Rock Cross developed by Henry Saglio of Arbor Acres Farms in Connecticut, a bird that happened to be white.

Today, Henry Saglio is considered the "Father of the Modern Poultry Industry," and for good reason. Born in 1909 in Connecticut, severe dyslexia pushed him out of school by age thirteen and an aversion to dirt farming—his parents' occupation—pushed him toward chicken breeding not long after. "The sun was too hot," he later explained, "I wanted to do something under cover." And so the young Saglio spent much of his youth inside the barn on his family's fruit and vegetable farm hatching chickens in a small coop he had fashioned out of a piano box.

Saglio's first clients were locals involved in the chicken business who had gripes with their birds. In fact, Henry's white bird that would come in second at the competition in Delaware started out simply as a response to a kosher butcher who complained that birds with red feathers were staining his final product, thus making them less appealing. Building off of his popular white chicken, over the years, Saglio would begin his breeding and crossbreeding experiments. Eventually the chickens would become more uniform in size (a fact that would appeal to Arbor Acre Farms' first major client, the Campbell Soup Company), and would mature in half the time, a trait later coveted by chicken farmers the world over.

In the following decades, a period that magazines dubbed "the era of the designer chicken," Henry Saglio would eventually rise to be one of the strongest elements of selection a modern chicken faced. Riding the lucrative waves of his Chicken of Tomorrow success, Saglio steadily built Arbor Acres from a small family farm into the world's leading poultry genetics company. In fact, as Saglio's son remarked, "there was once a point where if you ate a commercially produced chicken, there was an 8 out of 10 chance that it was from an Arbor Acres breeding stock."

The incredible success of the first Chicken of Tomorrow, albeit centered on the runner-ups, led A&P to host another round of the competition in 1951, this time in Arkansas, a rising star in the poultry-producing world thanks to John Tyson. This obviously meant there also had to be another round of the Miss Chicken of Tomorrow beauty pageant, a competition in which there were many great candidates of the human kind. This second series was as successful as the first in producing more productive chickens, which pushed A&P to further diversify their meaty holdings. They eventually aimed to produce a hog with less lard, which achieved moderate success. As their spokesman suggested, however, "there probably would not be a contest for the title of 'Miss Hog of Tomorrow.' "

After the competitions were over, the impact these advanced birds had on the market was indeed immediate and profound. By 1949, at least twenty million "bigger and better" chickens were estimated to have reached supermarket shelves and by 1950, approximately sixty-seven percent of all commercial broilers carried these improved bloodlines. "The day of the slick-hipped chick is over," declared the *Arkansas Agriculturalist* in

1951, "Now it's the era of the pleasantly plump, balloon breasted model built not on the lines suggested by Paris and New York fashion designers, but by the leaders of the Chicken of Tomorrow Program."

Americans were appreciative of these new, plumper, and juicier birds. "People think they're wonderful," claimed one Midwestern hatchery man. "Never tasted anything like them." Locavores be damned, these new chickens were such a hit that eaters across the country were willing to pay a premium price for these commercially raised broilers shipped out of the South or from Delmarva than for their neighbor's farm-raised chickens. American fowls had experienced a "wonderful" and "super colossal" transformation from "slender, slim-picking birds" to "today's meat-packed numbers." Now was the moment for a chicken for every grill.

By the mid 1950s, "Let's Have a Chick-N-Que" became the boastful rallying call of the proud broiler industry. Cosponsored with growing brands like Mazola corn oil, McIlhenny's Tabasco sauce, and Pepsi Cola, the chicken growers financed advertisements in magazines, on TV, and on the radio. President Dwight Eisenhower even met a broiler chicken to honor the great advertising campaign and it was believed that the "Chick-N-Que" would be the "outstanding barbeque promotion of the season."

Real barbecue fanatics might have taken issue with this declaration. For it to be barbecue, technically speaking, there needs to be wood smoke and it can only be a pig that's being cooked. (One of the earliest recorded definition of "barbecue" in the English language actually defines it simply as "a hog dressed whole.") Unversed in the hours of slow cooking employed by real Southern barbecue joints, at-home American cooks still ate the campaign up. Between the end of the World War II and 1957, coupled with the fondness for the new fatter and faster growing bird, US chicken consumption doubled to 31.5 pounds per person.

Barbecued chicken was becoming increasingly popular by the 1950s, and cookbooks tried to make it available even to those without an actual barbecue in their backyard.

OVEN-BUTTERED BARBECUED CHICKEN

2 chicken breasts (cut in half)
2 chicken legs
2 chicken thighs
½ cup Bisquick
1 tsp. salt
½ tsp. McCormick paprika
½ cup real butter (1 stick)

Rinse chicken in cold water and pat dry in a clean cloth. Mix Bisquick, salt, and paprika in a paper bag and shake chicken in mixture until thoroughly covered. Melt butter in baking pan in oven. Remove pan from oven and place chicken, skin side down, in melted butter. *Bake at 400° for 30 min.* Turn chicken and cover with barbecue sauce. *Bake another 15 to 30 min.* or until tender. Spoon sauce (below) over chicken pieces as served.

Barbecue Sauce:
Melt ¼ cup butter. Sauté 1 large onion, finely chopped, in butter. Add ¼ cup vinegar, 1 cup water, 1 tsp. McCormick dry mustard, ¼ cup Worcestershire sauce, few drops Tabasco sauce, 1 cup tomato catsup, ½ cup Stokely chili sauce, ½ cup lemon juice, 2 tsp. chili powder, 2 tsp. salt, ¼ cup brown sugar (packed). *Simmer ½ hr.*

—American Dairy Association,
Let's Eat Outdoors: Recipes and Ideas for Picnics, Barbecues, Patio Parties, Camping, mid 1950s

In spite of its rapid takeover of American grills, talking about chickens was still a risky thing in the 1940s, and raising them was even worse. The already volatile market was getting more difficult to manage as prices sunk lower with each newly hatched broiler chick. Realizing full well that raising chickens alone was still very much a hazardous enterprise, by the beginning of the 1950s new growers were hesitant to join in. But the vertically integrated companies, with their fleets of feed mills and hatcheries, still had products to sell. In an effort to convince more people to grow chickens, these large operations agreed to shoulder all of the economic risk involved in a very risky industry. The broilers, hatched and owned by the companies, were contracted out to small growers, who in turn were supplied with feed and expertise in raising them. Once nice and fat, the company would come by to truck the birds back to their own slaughterhouse. The growers owned nothing in the process but their own labor, and thus risked nothing if the chicken market dropped without warning.

To protect themselves in turn, large chicken operations starting with Jesse Jewell began imposing standards in quality, uniformity, and feed as part of what is now known as the contract system of chicken farming. Fair enough in principle, harder in practice when, almost overnight, farmers that had been scrambling along with three thousand birds now found themselves responsible for twenty or even forty thousand chickens at once.

The easiest way to achieve dominion over a

massive flock of chickens, growers soon learned, was to completely control every aspect of their short and feathered lives, from temperature to ventilation to food. Proof that this could actually be achieved came from the egg industry. Farmers had long known that a hen's egg production is tied to daylight: when the sun rises, a bird takes its cue from Mother Nature and lays an egg. This doesn't happen every day, but a good layer can produce four or five eggs in a single week. As soon as electricity became widely available to America's farmers, the intrepid farmhand realized that turning on the lights in the hen house in the middle of the night would convince the biddies that another day has passed and the birds would attempt to lay a second egg. With the discovery of vitamin D came the realization that farmers could make more money by keeping laying hens wholly inside, experiencing endless short and artificial days.

The move indoors transformed hen houses almost overnight into egg factories, equipped with automatic ventilation, temperature control, devices that self-turned the eggs, and increasingly effective heating and lighting. No longer did one need a mild climate, good soil, and ample timber to raise chickens, and so these massive hen houses started springing up throughout the country, effectively eliminating Petaluma's control over the egg industry. Soon the highly efficient and even more controversial "Battery System" was developed, where chickens are kept in small, slanted wire cages that allow their waste to be dropped and help their eggs roll to the front for easy pickup. In spaces that were increasingly calibrated like rocket ships, laying operations reached "factory proportions" just in time for the country's financial hardship. While the purchase of most foods decreased during the Great Depression, the consumption of these cheap and mass-produced eggs skyrocketed.

And what worked for the egg could also definitely work for the chicken. By the end of the 1940s, almost all of the broilers in the United States were raised in complete confinement, a practice that was incredibly effective in achieving its aims of efficiently producing very cheap meat. By 1955 the average time required to raise one thousand birds to maturity was just forty-eight man hours, as opposed to the average of two hundred and fifty in 1940.

Even though the hefty genes of the Chicken of Tomorrow meant that these same birds now grew to the same size in two weeks less time, feeding these rapidly ballooning indoor broilers still amounted to roughly half the cost of producing a chicken. Poultry growers obviously wanted to change that, and agricultural experiment stations agreed. Since the days of Eijkman and his beriberi birds, researchers had been slowly but surely ticking off all the boxes of a chicken's nutritional requirements: vitamin B1, vitamin D, calcium, vitamin K, vitamin E, pantothenic acid, choline. By the beginning of World War II, science knew more about the nutritional requirement of the chicken than that of any other animal on the planet, humans included, and the bird's food reflected this.

Among these essential vitamins was B12. What was probably just seconds after it was first isolated in 1948, researchers found that the vitamin was indeed important to the development of *Gallus gallus domesticus* and growers immediately started dousing their chicken feed with it. By 1950, there were two main B12 supplements available in the market, but chickens fed one of the two grew exponentially fatter faster than chickens fed the other. Nobody knew why.

The production of vitamin B12, like the egg, had reached factory proportions in the two short years since its isolation. For centuries an incurable and deadly disease known as pernicious anemia had ravaged the world, killing off everyone from telephone inventor Alexander Graham Bell to sharpshooter Annie Oakley. In 1934 a man with a brave palate and the lovely surname of George Whipple had the inkling that force-feeding patients raw liver would help stem the disease, which it did, miraculously so. When the liver was eaten in concentrated form, pernicious anemia was even cured. Although the treatment would eventually win Mr. Whipple and his colleagues a Nobel Prize in 1934, the actual reason raw liver cured pernicious anemia was unknown. It wasn't until 1948, when a talented female chemist by the name of Mary Shorb managed to identify B12 as the curative substance. (She made this breakthrough while working in a poultry science laboratory in Maryland no less.)

To cheaply mass-produce the vitamin, chemists started extracting it from the microorganism-soaked residues that were by then the common byproducts of the production of commercial antibiotics. After the vitamins hit the feed market, chicken growers quickly discovered the company that was more lax in their separation of the B12 from the antibiotic residues produced more effective supplements. Further scientific investigation ensued and researchers found that while B12 was indeed essential to a happy chicken, the antibiotic residues affixed to them were veritable chicken Miracle-Gro. When fed antibiotics, the birds required less feed, grew fatter faster, and the mortality rate dropped sharply. Farmers were ecstatic—the discovery was heralded as "the Biggest Feeding News in 40 years!"—and within the next two decades every single commercially produced chicken in the United States was supplemented with antibiotics.

All these vitamins and the antibiotics were in

turn mixed in with a newly developed combination of corn and soybeans. The corn, heavily supported financially by the US government, was a cheap source of carbohydrates while the soy gave the chickens the protein they required to grow quickly. It was a perfect nutritional cocktail that maximized chicken growth. Put into experimentation, chicks fed this feed gained almost six times as much weight in the same time period as their brothers and sisters in the same brood who were fed older versions of chicken feed.

With perfectly calibrated hen houses and feed rations that also helped prevent the birds from growing sick, farmers could cram the now even faster-growing birds into the same spaces as before. Not a creature inclined to behave, this practice in turn exacerbated the chickens' innate behavior that industry analysts called "feather pulling, feather eating, and cannibalism," which increased in correlation to their ever-tighter quarters.

As anyone who keeps their own chickens can inform you, when groups of chickens get together they have a tendency to peck at each other to establish a social hierarchy within their flock. This is a literal pecking order. At its best, this behavior results in some chickens becoming battered and bruised, which makes them look bad and tends to reduce their quality when being sold;

at its worst, chickens will literally peck each other to death and a farmer can lose up to twenty-five percent of his or her flock as a result. Behavior learned from watching other chickens do it, overcrowding, poor nutrition, and even boredom exacerbate this vice, which isn't helped by the fact that chickens go wild at the sight of blood. Compounding these factors, by the 1950s nearly all chicken producers started to keep the birds in enormous flocks that are particularly difficult for a chicken to socially navigate, and thus these frenzied attempts to establish pecking orders only increased.

A very fashionable solution for this fowl problem was chicken eyewear. First patented in 1903, the popularity for these glasses for chickens rose and fell often over the course of the twentieth century, with the frames gaining a daring rose tint and a swivel contraption by the 1950s. This rose coloring "effectively cause[s] red to disappear, thereby reducing cannibalism" and also thereby makes the birds more fabulous. According to a salesman from the National Farm Equipment Company of Brooklyn, one of the nation's largest purveyor of chicken sunglasses, by 1955 his company sold two to three million pairs of these glasses a year to America's egg layers and meat birds.

But glasses can be difficult to maintain in proper working order, especially when worn by chickens that don't really enjoy wearing glasses. The next stage in the saga of chicken eyewear was therefore chicken contact lenses. Now an infamous case study at Harvard Business School, the story goes that in the sixties a medical supply salesman was inspired to make vision-impairing lenses for birds after meeting several chickens with cataracts who behaved much less violently than their well-seeing compatriots. Although his company, Vision Control, Inc., did its small part to reduce the plague of chicken murders sweeping the nation, the state of polymer and lens technologies were not advanced enough and the company fell into financial ruin.

But some ideas cannot be crushed by mere bankruptcy; the dream of providing lenses to all of America's hens was carried on by the son of one of Vision Control, Inc.'s founders, a young Mr. Randall Wise. Wise, a Harvard Business School graduate himself and former nautical shipping consultant, used the millions he made from selling his software company to establish Animalens, Inc. in 1989. Like his father's corporation, Animalens, Inc. was in the chicken contact lens business, a concept that Wise claimed would "add up to a quadrupling of chicken-ranch profit margins."

While the arguments for the lenses were promising, the lenses themselves made the already miserable life of a modern chicken much more depressing. Instead of pecking at each other (success!), the hens were now pecking at the air, rubbing their eyes repeatedly on their wings, and suffering from corneal ulcers and ruptured eyes. With almost no ranchers purchasing these tiny red pieces of plastic, the $24 million company Wise envisioned instead became public enemy number one of America's chicken rights groups and eventually folded.

Although so-called "chicken peepers" are still in use today on some farms, a more practical solution farmers developed to combat feather pulling and cannibalism is to simply cut off part or all of the bird's beak. No beak means less death and destruction when chickens violently peck at each other. This practice is the most commonly utilized means of controlling feather pulling today, with chicks being debeaked with a hot knife almost immediately after hatching.

Even with all the advances in be-spectaling, finessed feed, and indoor chicken ranches, however, the industry itself could not seem to shake its intense cycles of boom and bust. Chicken had always been a highly perishable commodity, but now it was also mass-produced. For other consumer goods, like appliances or cars, the production line can just be shut off when supply is too high. Not the same for chickens. Once you start raising them you can't stop, and, as one chicken man quipped, "If you don't sell them, you smell them."

Before, when chicken was just a source of pin money, it didn't make or break a farm if birds didn't sell, and most chicken owners were prepared for the high possibility of low prices. But thanks to the massive buildup of technology and money and science, by the mid 1950s chicken was now big business. When prices were high, poultry producers would throw more eggs into hatcheries, send more chicks to broiler houses, and pump out more edible birds. But when profits vanished, instead of cutting back production like in most industries, the producers, with their multimillion-dollar hatcheries and slaughterhouses and processing facilities, were afraid of losing market share and kept cranking out chickens at ever cheaper prices. If they weren't going to make a lot of money on each bird, they might as well live like the New York kosher kings and make a little money on a lot of birds.

These price storms destroyed many a feathered dream even before it hatched. Those called to the broiler, now realizing that answering that call required the incredible outlay of cash to keep up with the latest developments in feed, disease controls, marketing practices, chicks, feeding, and management, were going bankrupt faster than their chickens could grow.

Independent dealers operating outside of contract-growing arrangements with bigger firms were the first to go under. Next went the smaller vertical operations. When prices went too low to make any profits, large chicken producers held back on production, weathering the price storms with the bare-bones cushion their greater size and broad expanse over the chicken industry afforded them. Smaller firms and growers could not do the same and quickly folded, soon to be gobbled up by the business-savvy owners of bigger chicken companies. When prices went back up, larger firms ramped up production again, bolstered anew by their now larger market share.

By the mid 1960s, ninety percent of all commercial broilers were coming out of large, vertically integrated firms that were increasingly powerful, flexible, and hungry, in the words of John Tyson's son Don, "to control the center of the plate of the American people." But, as these big chicken conglomerates soon learned, it would take a whole lot more than just cheap chicken to keep Americans satisfied.

If you would like Tyson to control the center of your plate tonight, here's a recipe from their 1984 cookbook entitled Chicken Just for You!

CHICKEN CELESTE
6 fresh Tyson Breast or Thigh Steaks
¼ cup all-purpose flour
½ teaspoon salt

¼ teaspoon paprika
⅛ teaspoon pepper
1 small onion, finely chopped (¼ cup)
2 tablespoons cooking oil
½ cup dairy sour cream
¼ cup mayonnaise or salad dressing
2 tablespoons dry sherry
2 tablespoons water
Snipped parsley

Combine flour, salt, paprika, and pepper. Rinse steaks; pat dry. Coat steaks with flour mixture. In a large skillet cook steaks and onion in hot oil over medium heat about 15 minutes or just till tender, turning once. Transfer to a warm serving platter; keep warm. Drain fat from skillet.

In a bowl combine sour cream, mayonnaise or salad dressing, sherry, and water; stir till smooth. Add to the skillet and heat over low heat; *do not boil*. Pour over steaks; sprinkle with parsley. Makes 6 servings.

Total Time: 25 minutes

—Tyson's Chicken,
Chicken Just for You!, 1984

CHAPTER TWELVE
A Nugget Worth More Than Gold

CHICKEN CRISPIES
Basic Formula for Chicken Crispies
Made From Mechanically Deboned
Spent Layer Meat*

Ingredient	Percent
Mechanically Deboned Spent Layer Meat	85.00
Bread Crumbs, Dry	8.00
Fresh Onion, Chopped	6.20
Chicken Seasoning**	0.45
Salt	0.35
Batter and Breading	As Needed

All ingredients were mixed using a Hobart K50 mixer with the flat paddle, for 1 min on low speed (#1). After shaping in approximately 9 gm (⅓ oz.) balls, using a

---

* Formula variations and additions were made by adjusting the percent of chicken.
** Chicken Seasoning was a commercial blend composed of salt (45%), extractives or onion and celery, and turmeric.

hand shaper, they were battered and breaded using batter mix and Gourmet Japanese Crumbs (Modern Maid Food Products, Inc., Garden City, NY).

After freezing overnight at –10°F (–23°C) on a tray covered with foil, they were sealed in polyethylene bags for storage at the same temperature. They were deep fried at 375°F for 2 minutes before serving to a taste panel of 8 people who had had much experience in evaluating chicken products.

—Robert Baker, *Miscellaneous Bulletin No. 110*, 1981

By 1955, the chicken industry had hit the billion-bird mark and showed no signs of stopping. The big, vertically integrated chicken producers had become so good at their jobs that what was once the most expensive thing in the butcher's case was now the cheapest. Supermarket shelves were overflowing. With the lowest chicken prices they had ever seen, people were buying up the bird in record quantities; by the end of the decade the bird became the second most sold item in grocery stores, overtaking pork and lagging only behind beef in popularity.

And the birds kept getting cheaper. In their attempts to simultaneously master the tumultuous chicken market and keep prices affordable, producers were slowly but surely losing control over production. Suddenly there was too much chicken. Retailers started advertising chickens at "price specials" to attract people to their stores and to get rid of the surplus, but to no avail. Prices were in free fall and in 1959 the industry experienced what the United States Department of Agriculture termed the "Broiler Depression."

Unsure of how to recover, chicken producers held an official meeting of the newly formed National Broiler Council to blame the supermarkets and their "price specials" for the chicken industry's predicament. Marketing executives on the grocery side fired back, "If chicken weren't so abundant, we couldn't sell them so cheap." The government tried to step in on this mounting cockfight, helping the industry force massive quantities of chicken on Europe, but prices just weren't stabilizing. Big Chicken was doing its part to lessen supply, hatching fewer chicks and slaughtering fewer birds, but the industry also needed American eaters to eat through more of the surplus. The problem was that American eaters didn't want to. Because chicken was so cheap, more people were eating it, but after about once a week they lost their appetite.

Once a week was nowhere near enough to eat through the hundreds of thousands of pounds of excess chicken the companies were churning out daily. At the behest of the chicken producers, with questionnaires in hand and the fledging commercial broiler industry on the line, intrepid consumer reporters went into the wilds of supermarkets to see what people really thought of the bird. What they discovered was a sort of "lobster effect"—that all chicken ever really seemed to have going for it was that it was at one point expensive. Surveys found that "many housewives," like their forbearers, "do not consider chicken to be a meat" and to many a drop in price meant a drop in status. Where before, "Chicken used to be prized as a Sunday dinner," now it was just another cheap item in the butcher's case that "apparently has not fully achieved the status and prestige of a meat item."

Not only did consumers consider chicken to be cheap in the worst sense of the word, they also found the bird boring. The red meat industry had just experienced a processing renaissance and when browsing the deli case in the 1960s, shoppers saw before them a bounty of beef and pork shaped into patties, ground into sausages, and cut into roasts, steaks, and ribs. For chicken, the opposite was true. Where before you could buy Plymouth Rock broilers, Jersey Giant fryers, and New Hampshire roasters, the efficiency of commercial broiler production meant chicken now only came in a three ways: cut up chicken, halved chicken, and whole chicken. What resulted was what surveyors called "chicken fatigue," consumers believing that chicken was a "one size fits all" product that "gets tiresome if eaten more than once a week."

This wasn't good. Scientists and farmers and the government had spent so much time and money making chicken affordable and accessible to the American people only to find that after there were literally multiple chickens for every pot, no one really wanted them. "Consumers must be taught to think of broilers as a fine quality, delicious and nutritious meal," the industry declared, and they launched an all-out attempt "to give chicken full status as a meat product." The multibillion-dollar question was how.

The answer would come, piping hot and golden delicious, from the food science laboratories at Cornell University. In 1949, the school's Department of Animal Sciences added to their faculty a young man by the name of Robert Baker. Teaching at Cornell had long been Baker's dream, one he had had even before he started his bachelor's at the university in 1939. Although he majored in fruit agriculture, having tended a hearty flock of Rhode Island Red chickens in his youth, he felt an immediate attraction to the poultry classes. When asked why he made the switch from fruits to birds, he replied, "I guess I fell in love with chickens. . . . I thought the future was brighter in chickens than in fruit." And thanks to him, it would be.

Although he wanted to stay on at Cornell, he

was advised to take some time away from the university, and upon graduation started working as a poultry extension agent in the South, helping struggling farmers to better grow their birds. It was in this capacity that he later returned to his beloved Cornell. As an assistant professor in poultry extension, Baker was charged with teaching farmers how to raise their flocks in the most efficient and profitable manner possible.

Baker quickly saw the limits of the growing side of the chicken equation; the farmers he was working with around Ithaca, N.Y. were keeping up with the latest in feed and housing technologies but were still falling behind. Having grown up on a struggling apple orchard in upstate New York during the Depression, Baker knew all too well the difficulties these farmers were facing. He had lived them. There had to be a way to help chicken growers not only sell more birds but also make even more money off of each one.

This was the United States of America, and so something deep-fried would obviously have to be the solution. In the 1950s, convenience products were the fastest growing facet of food sales in the United States. Wanting to maintain the standard of the two-car garage, more American women began to work outside the home. Although she still enjoyed cooking, a homemaker was also increasingly pressed for time. Not wanting to be considered a bad wife, she still made most dinners from scratch but little shortcuts started creeping into her kitchen. As their husbands were in their backyards grilling their meats, the wives were enjoying powdered drinks and baking with boxed cake mixes and heating up frozen fish sticks. People were not only eager to buy more of these "convenience" foods as the years progressed but were also willing to pay a higher price for them. Beef and pork had already discovered the wonder of these value-added foods and were reaping the benefits. Chicken in its three forms was being left behind.

Foreseeing the revolutionary possibility of processed chicken, Baker decided that value-added poultry products would be his life's work. He went on to receive his doctorate in food sciences from Purdue University in 1956 and by 1959 had set up a state-of-the-art poultry-products technology lab in the basement of a building at Cornell. On any given day, under the florescent lights of the windowless room, dozens of food science students would scurry between lab benches and food-prep tables with beakers and baking sheets in hand and food-safety-grade paper hats secured to their eager young heads. A delicious hybrid of serious scientists and intrepid line cooks, Dr. Baker's team spent their semesters mincing and molding and measuring every facet of the chicken and the egg.

One of the early accomplishments to come out

of that basement was the original Chicken Crispie, a bite-sized piece of chicken, coated in batter, and deep-fried. Nothing like it had ever been cooked up before because no one had yet figured out how to keep ground meats together without a skin, nor had they developed a batter that could withstand the dramatic temperature shifts of both freezing and frying. By mixing the chicken with salt and vinegar to draw out moisture and then throwing it in with pulverized grains and a binder of milk powder, the Crispie was able to stick together. The batter ended up as a coating of eggs and cereal that was flash frozen at −10°F. After many variations, Baker and his colleagues managed to find a way to keep the batter on the nugget even during frying.

This process, down to the packaging and costs of the Crispies, which could also be called "chicken sticks" if shaped correctly, Baker shared freely and widely in a *Cornell Bulletin* in 1963. These innovations would eventually resonate with all corners of the chicken world, most importantly at the drive-through window.

The year 1977 was a bad one for fast food giant McDonald's. Ever since owner Ray Kroc opened the doors of the hamburger joint's first outpost in 1955, its golden arches beckoned suburbanites looking for a quick, tasty, and affordable bite. Within three years the rapidly multiplying chain had already sold its 100 millionth hamburger and would soon move comfortably into the billions. Its whole history up until 1977 had been one smooth saga of high sales and fat profits.

But as McDonald's and other fast food companies were whipping up their speedy fare, the eating public also started hearing unsettling rumors about their favorite foods. Although cardiovascular disease had really started scaring people at the beginning of the twentieth century, by the 1950s it seemed to be reaching almost epidemic proportions in America. Twice as many people died of heart attacks and stroke at this time than they did of all cancers combined. Previously considered a disease that only affected the old, autopsies of soldiers killed in action during the Korean War were revealing that these otherwise vigorous young men were showing early signs of cardiovascular disease.

It's now known that there are a great many risk factors that cause the buildup of plaque in the arteries that leads to heart disease—the big one for the golden age of suburbia being smoking—but all throughout the 1950s, the scientific community was increasingly muttering words like "cholesterol," "saturated fat," "heart disease," and "death" in the same breath. Words are easy enough to shrug off while dining on all-beef patties, but in 1961 what were long written off as rumors were published as an authoritative report by the American Heart Association. This report linked heart disease to a type of fat known as cholesterol. The culprits identified as having the most cholesterol? Beef and pork.

The news that these meats could be bad for you was very confusing to the red-blooded, beef-eating citizens of the United States. For the past four hundred years, red meat had paid their taxes, beefed-up their warriors, nourished their laborers, and even unseated their elected leaders. It had long been considered the most nourishing of all foods, one that was sanctioned by both chemistry and Uncle Sam, America's original celebrity meatpacker. What's more, industrial pork and beef producers had recently started to emulate the broiler industry's factory farm techniques, and by the 1960s, the nation's meaty bounty had grown to the point that all Americans could at last enjoy their favorite red meats morning, noon, and night. But the Heart Association's evidence was compelling enough in a country increasingly sensitive to changes in the science of nutrition. One scientific discovery upended the nation's entire culinary history and an estimated twenty-two percent of American families changed their diet because of the report.

The scientific literature linking not just cholesterol but also saturated fats to heart disease and stroke only continued to mount over the coming years, as did the sickness and death of increasingly younger men. Concerned for the arteries of their taxpayers, who were still smoking away and were now eating close to one hundred pounds of beef a year, in 1977 the US government stepped in and announced its dietary goals for the nation. For the first time, the bureaucracy no longer had to be concerned about its people having enough of certain foods but rather had to contend with the fact that the eating public now had too much of some. As a result, the government explicitly and loudly called for people to "decrease consumption of meat and increase consumption of poultry and fish."

McDonald's was understandably horrified. Although their menu had expanded over the years, the restaurant chain was still a hamburger joint at its core, and the US government had just told people to eat fewer hamburgers. Ever more people were listening to these nutritional messages, and sales for McDonald's fell off dramatically. The company, now expanded to 6,000 stores across four continents, desperately sought a way to stay relevant in the rapidly shifting eating environment. Heeding the bureaucracy's advice, people were flocking steadily over to the now cheap and abundant "white meat" chicken. So, in chickens too, McDonald's saw a way.

The restaurant chain had tried and failed to add chicken items to their menu many times before, but in the late 1970s they now had the services of

Chef Rene Arend, who had once cooked dinner for the Queen of England. Charged with saving the company, his first attempt at a chicken dish was a deep fried potpie. This failed in testing. Next came fried chicken, which, although delicious, could not compete in the already heavily saturated fried chicken market, which included the growing fast food powerhouse Kentucky Fried Chicken (KFC).

Apparently giving up already on the difficult bird, Ray Kroc then asked Arend to shift his focus to making a bite-sized onion ring, an onion nugget. But the chairman of the McDonald's board, Fred Turner, had his heart set on chicken. "Why not a chicken nugget?" he casually quipped to the chef as they passed each other one morning in the corporate hallway. The very same day Arend cut up chicken into tiny chunks, battered it, and threw it in the deep-fryer. This he called the Chicken McNugget, and it was love at first bite.

Instantly the company formed an elite and secretive McNugget SWAT team to produce their new poultry product. For the perfect bite-sized chicken chunks they called on processor Keystone Foods, which already provided McDonald's its frozen hamburgers. For the perfect batter to coat these chunks, the chain turned to its friends at fish-stick maker Gorton's, which had already helped the chain with their hit Filet-O-Fish. The sauces they left up to Arend. Although McDonald's has no record of direct contact with Baker, the famous poultry scientist's innovations undoubtedly influenced how the McNugget's binding and batter were processed and perfected.

Just five months after this casual hallway conversation with Arend, a prototype nugget hit stores in Tennessee for a blind test, and the product broke all previous sales records. Knowing full well how much Americans were now embracing chicken, from the moment every franchisee heard about the success of the nuggets in testing, they wanted them. In less than half a year, McDonald's tacked together a new multimillion-dollar factory dedicated just to these nuggets, and called in the big guns at Tyson Foods to help them ensure a steady supply. Tyson in turn developed a custom breed of chicken for the nuggets, "Mr. McDonald," that had an even larger breast than the Chicken of Tomorrow. The instant they debuted in 1983 Chicken McNuggets were a global phenomenon. Within months, the bite-size chicken pieces made McDonald's, a hamburger restaurant, the second biggest retailer of chicken on the planet, trailing behind only KFC.

Although his nuggets would eventually change dinner the world over, for Dr. Baker back in his Cornell laboratory, the Chicken Crispie was just the beginning. From the 1960s onward, Robert Baker would consistently be one of the most innovative individuals in all of chickendom. When a vague idea for new and presumably marketable chicken product popped into his mind, Baker would immediately subject it to a battery of rigorous culinary and taste tests. Once taken home and approved by his wife, the product was packaged and sent off to markets in upstate New York. Advertising campaigns were implemented and consumer purchases were carefully monitored over the course of a few weeks. A true scientist to the core, each step of the way was meticulously recorded and revised: How can the packaging be improved? How long can the product remain in storage? What are the effects of different cooking times? How can the product's formulations be tastier? How likely will this product contain disease? How can it be made simply more appealing?

One of the primary goals of Baker's food work was efficiency. Everyone knew very well how to market a chicken breast, what supermarkets called "the Cadillac of the chicken," but fewer knew what to do with the necks and backs and other undesirable little bits. Like food reformers before him, Baker knew that these generally discarded parts tasted just as good and were just as nourishing. Find a way to use all this otherwise wasted food and one could feed the world while putting more money in farmers' pockets.

When Baker started his work, the world of

industrial chicken slaughter had already come a very long way. A processing facility a century previous was usually a dark warehouse on the outskirts of a city, where lines of men, typically disadvantaged immigrants desperate for work, would stand holding knives until a bird, squawking and struggling and hanging by its feet from a long chain, would pass by. Once slaughtered, another line of workers would rip out the bird's feathers and throw its body on top of a box filled with ice. At the time, in the early twentieth century, this was "the most rapid method ever introduced for killing chickens," capable of preparing up to 10,000 birds for the market in a single day.

This system remained relatively unchanged until 1942, when a processing plant received government approval for "on-line evisceration," presumably to increase the speed at which chicken was reaching the hungry army during the Second World War. This meant that the answer to the second "Great Chicken Question" of the nineteenth century, whether chickens should be sold with their insides intact or not, was firmly revised and the guts could now be legally removed by machine. From there, innovators went to town. Soon birds could not only be processed and picked, but they could be eviscerated, sanitized, cooled, and packed all with the push of a button.

By the end of the 1960s, almost all of the nation's chickens were going through these advanced processing plants, which were now officially "ptomaine free" thanks to mandatory government inspections implemented in 1959. The same uniformity that made these broilers so boring to eat made them really easy to process, meaning plants could now slaughter, disembowel, and cut up some 150,000 birds per week. Chicken processors like Holly Farms started making big profits when they started selling cut up chicken, the first real fruits of industrial slaughter, in the early 1960s, but Baker pushed it even further. His revolutionary chicken products in mind, he helped set up machines to debone and mince and chop chicken in every which way to suit his experimental needs. And from the little bits were born chicken sticks, and also chicken bologna, chicken hot dogs, and chicken burgers.

In the field of taste, Baker was less of an innovator. Food is perishable, making its flavor a characteristic that does not easily stand the test of time. It's hard to know exactly what a chicken tasted like when prepared by a Gordonsville waiter-carrier during the Civil War, or a kosher housewife at the turn of the century, but by the time Baker went to work, it was safe to assume that chickens were starting to taste radically different than they ever had before.

Setting aside the impact of cooking, the inherent flavor of any meat comes largely from the animal's genetics as well as its lifestyle. The life of a broiler in the 1950s and 1960s was dramatically different from the days their colonial ancestors spent being finished on beer or milk or bread. The birds didn't peck in the yards for insects or eat green foods or roost in trees or gobble up butcher scraps from the kitchen. In their permanent fattening coops, chickens now sat basically immobile and grew grotesquely rotund by chowing down on perfectly calibrated vitamin mixes conveyed to them on beds of corn and soybeans.

For much of history, nobody would have complained about eating corn-fed chickens—even in the colonial era they thought it produced flesh that "was the sweetest of all others"—but now there was really only one type of corn-fed chicken to eat. The diversity of breeds that had induced awe at the Boston Poultry Show had been whittled down to just a handful of absurdly fat Chickens of Tomorrow. People as early as the 1850s were already complaining about how farmers switching to a more rugged bird were producing "dry, stringy, tough and tasteless" fare akin to "a shriveled-up fossil of a spread eagle;" who knows how these same chicken connoisseurs would have reacted to the uniformly plumper breasts, juicer thighs, and layers of white meat never before seen, or tasted, on a bird.

Although some food scientists were genuinely worried by this sudden shift in the meaning of "tastes like chicken," systematically testing the differences in flavor between "old" and "new" type chickens, Baker wasn't overly concerned. The poultry pioneer firmly believed "there's no flavor to chicken" and this was perfectly all right for his purposes. As your friendly-neighborhood food scientist can confirm, the primary way humans distinguish between meats is by the flavor and texture of the fat. With the right processing Baker believed he could use chicken to replicate any other meat product out on the market. There was no threat of the new chicken's poor flavor reputation sabotaging, say, a chicken sausage when it was cheaper but still tasted and looked exactly like one made out of beef or pork or even lamb. After cholesterol scared the pant sizes off of people, the equalization of flavor would actually give chicken the upper hand. Same great taste, half the fat!

Always for convenience and efficiency until the end, and definitely not one to mince words as he minced chicken, when asked about the flavor issue Baker was blunt. "Some people say the flavor used to be better," he quipped. "I grew up on a farm. We'd chop the head off the chicken and it would bounce around the yard and lay there for a while before we picked it up; then we'd scoop it into a pail and it would lie in the house a bit before my mother would get around to cooking it. Probably it did taste different. But do you want to put up with that to get the taste?"

Eschewing nuanced palates for commercial creativity, Baker created some fifty-plus value-added items to get Americans to eat more chicken and eggs over the course of his career. From the chicken's egg he created extra egg-ariffic French toast, egg-white pizza crusts, and frozen omelets. From there he moved to the bird and from the mind of Robert W. Baker came "Bake and Serve" Chicken Loaf, Chicken Chunk Roll, Chicken Hash, Chickalona, Chicken Chunkalona, Chicken Sticks, Chicken Bologna, Chic-a-Links, Chicken Franks, Chicken Salami, Chicken Chili, Chicken Steak, Chicken Ham, and Poulet Supreme, among many others.

ROBERT BAKER'S CHIC-A-LINKS
Manufacturing Process
1. Remove and freeze skin from the carcasses.
2. Debone the breasts and thighs, being sure to remove breast tendons and knee caps.
3. Cook the remainder of the carcass.
4. Grind separately, through a ⅛-inch plate, the deboned cooked chicken meat, the frozen skin, and the hearts and gizzards.
5. Grind enough fat through a ⅛-inch plate to bring the analysis of the finished product to a 15-20 percent fat level.

6. Weigh all ingredients into a silent cutter or a high-speed mixer, and chop at lowest speed only long enough to mix all ingredients, and to chop the raw skinless meat into small particles. (Over-chopping will raise the temperature of the product, and make for an emulsion that results in a rubbery product.)
7. Stuff into edible casings and link to the desired size. Temperature at time of stuffing should be 45°F or below, to avoid "greasing out" and/or discoloration of the product.
8. Package and refrigerate, or store frozen at 0°F or below, until ready for marketing.

Ingredients and Projected Ingredient Costs for Chicken Sausage

Item	Unit	Amount (dollars/lb.)	Unit Cost	Total Cost
Raw Skinless meat	Lbs.	45	0.63	28.35
Cooked meat	Lbs.	10	0.45	4.5
Skin	Lbs.	10	0.10	1.00
Gizzards and hearts	Lbs.	25	0.17	4.25
Chicken fat	Lbs.	10	0.25	2.50
Salt	Lbs.	2.5	0.015	0.04
Seasoning	Ozs.	6	1.00	0.38
Total (approx.)	Lbs.	102.9		41.02

Ingredient cost: per 100 pounds   39.86
Per pound   0.40
Per 10 oz. package   0.25
—Robert Baker, *New Marketable Poultry and Egg Products*, March 1967

With some products, like the Chicken Crispies, Baker had ready-made hits. They were made from the parts of the chicken not being used, and the convenience of them for consumers, combined with the low production costs, made them fly off the shelves. Almost as soon as his laboratory published their findings on chicken burgers in the 1970s, Tyson started marketing chicken-breast burger patties, which were soon being slung by the likes of the popular fast food chain Burger King. With others, like the gelatinous sausages filled with whole hard-boiled eggs that he named the "Hard-Cooked Egg Roll," Baker had some very firm misses. Most of the time in between, the intrepid food scientist was developing products so new that consumers had no idea what they were. A regular on the chicken-industry speaking circuit, Baker had no problem describing his creations to the eating public. Chicken loaf? "That's like meat loaf." Chic-A-Links? "Looks and tastes like pork sausage." Chickalona? "That's chicken baloney that's white."

After being a loss leader well into the 1970s, chicken consumption increased after companies got their hands on Baker's inventions and began churning out chickens as burgers and hot dogs and sticks. Now, instead of being viewed as a daunting culinary task, chicken was now increasingly seen as the most convenient and saleable meat available at the grocery store and by the 1980s, more than forty percent of all chicken sold was processed in some way. Robert Baker was chicken's new Louis Pasteur and singlehandedly cured the nation's "chicken fatigue."

Hand in hand with Baker's profitable products came innovations in marketing from the chicken producers themselves. In 1971, Frank Perdue, CEO of Delmarva-based Perdue Farms, went on national television to boldly declare, "It takes a tough man to make a tender chicken." The spot would quickly become one of the most memorable catchphrases in the history of advertising. The women who had minded most of America's chickens in the nation's history probably rolled over in their graves a bit when this particular campaign aired, but "If Frank Perdue didn't look and sound like chicken, he wouldn't be in the commercial," explained his advertising firm. Not only was Perdue Farms the second-largest chicken purveyor in the country at this time, many thought Frank looked quite a bit like a chicken himself.

In a commodity market comprising largely the same robust chickens, all fed the same feed, housed in the same houses, and now cut up in almost identical manners thanks to Dr. Baker, there needed to be something to distinguish one chicken from another. By claiming he was the toughest man for the job, Frank Perdue pioneered the concept of a branded bird. The company's advertisements would continue to point out what made Perdue birds superior to the competition: their golden color, their healthy diet, and the fact that Perdue's birds were "given pure well water to drink." To "eat as good as my chickens," Perdue explains, "you'll just have to eat my chickens." In 1967, Perdue's annual sales were a respectable $35 million. Within a year of his "tough man" campaign, the company's sales had ballooned to $80 million. Those kinds of increases attracted the attention of rival chicken companies. By 1990, seventy-five percent of all chicken sold in the United States were branded, which also meant they could be sold at a higher price.

Perdue Farms is still clucking along happily with over 19,000 employees and over $6 billion in annual sales, but what happened to the man behind the chicken industry's multibillion-dollar products, the professor who was poultry's saving grace? Nothing. A modest academic through and through, Robert Baker gave away all of his results and innovations for free. He stayed at his beloved Cornell and worked tirelessly to the end of his career trying to help farmers to use science to increase their margins and to feed the world in the process. Day after day, with a white laboratory coat over his clean-cut suits, and his horn-rimmed glasses perched on his nose, Baker would spend hours in his laboratory puzzling over the latest questions plaguing poultry science. Every aspect of the chicken, from egg to plate, was important to Baker. His experiments varied widely, ranging from the microbiology of eggs, the impact of the length of storage on the flavor of chickens, to the increasing prevalence of salmonella on farms.

People came to regard him as a poultry savant, a chicken Thomas Edison. He knew so much about the chicken industry that he became the unofficial advice columnist for the poultry world. Growers wanting to know why their birds were going bald sent him feather samples, and processors encountering troubles in frying nuggets sent him the failed greasy fried bits. Word of Baker's skills spread abroad, and foreign governments, impressed by his ideas, flew him across oceans to consult with their chicken farmers.

The brilliant poultry scientist passed away in 2006, but a little taste of his spirit can still be had every September at the New York State Fair. As they have for the past sixty plus years, his family still runs the legendary Baker's Chicken Coop. The modest shack is one of the most popular vendors at the fair, serving up thousands of pounds of

Robert Baker's famous Cornell Chicken Barbecue to attendees willing to stand in long lines for it in the waning summer heat.

A patty or gelatinous log Cornell Chicken Barbecue is not. This is real chicken barbeque, the likes of which a Chick-N-Que's disciple could only aspire to. Back in the 1940s, long before his nuggets conquered the globe and still just involved in poultry extension work, Baker was challenged to create a tasty chicken dish for the visiting governor of New York. Unafraid of cross-disciplinary work, Robert Baker grabbed some kids from the engineering school and together they built a cinder block grill with a set of wire racks on top. The chickens, cut in half and slathered in Baker's tangy, homemade barbecue sauce, were set on the racks and charcoal-roasted to perfection.

Over the next few years, Baker would pile his children into the car and drive them around the state demonstrating to eaters the wonders of barbecued chicken. Although the technique at the time was cutting-edge in the increasingly popular field of chicken barbecue, it was really the sauce that turned "Barbecue Bob" into a minor celebrity in upstate New York. At one point his recipe was the most popular barbecue sauce in the country and was undoubtedly tangy enough to convince Cornell that Robert Baker might know a thing or two about chicken.

CORNELL BARBECUE SAUCE
(FOR 10 HALVES)

1 cup cooking oil
2 cups cider vinegar
3 tablespoons salt
1 tablespoon poultry seasoning
½ teaspoon pepper
1 egg

Beat the egg, then add the oil and beat again. Add other ingredients and stir. The recipe can be varied to suit individuals. Leftover sauce can be stored in a glass jar in the refrigerator for several weeks.

To barbecue broilers, place the halves over the fire after the flame is gone. Turn the halves every 5 to 10 minutes, depending on the heat from the fire. The chicken should be basted with a fiber brush at each turning. Baste lightly at first, and heavily near the end of cooking.

Cooking time is about 1 hour, depending on the amount of heat and on the size of the broiler. To test doneness, pull the wing away from the body. If the meat in this area splits easily and there is no red color in the joint, the chicken is done.

—Robert Baker,
"Cornell Chicken Barbecue"

CHAPTER THIRTEEN

The Tale of the Colonel and the General

The author of this recipe purportedly learned it in the kitchens of the dish's original creator, Taiwanese chef Peng Chang-Kuei.

GENERAL TSO'S CHICKEN

4 boneless chicken thighs
  (about ¾ lb/350 g)
6-10 small dried red chilies
Cooking oil, for deep-frying
2 tsp finely chopped ginger
2 tsp finely chopped garlic
2 tsp sesame oil
1 tbsp thinly sliced spring onion greens
  (optional)

For the marinade/batter:
2 tsp light soy sauce
½ tsp dark soy sauce
1 egg yolk
2 tbsp potato flour
2 tsp cooking oil

For the sauce:
1 tbsp tomato puree mixed with 1 tbsp
  water
½ tsp potato flour
½ tsp dark soy sauce
1½ tsp light soy sauce
1 tbsp rice vinegar
3 tbsp chicken stock or water

Unfold the chicken thighs and lay them, skin side down, on a chopping board. (If some parts are very thick, lay your knife flat and slice them across in half, parallel to the board.) Use a sharp knife to make a few shallow criss-cross cuts into the meat; this will help the flavors to penetrate. Then cut each thigh into 1½–1¾ (3–4 cm) slices, an uneven ⅛ in (½ cm) or so in thickness. Place the slices in a bowl.

For the marinade, add the soy sauce and egg yolk to the chicken and mix well. Then stir in the potato flour, and lastly the oil. Set aside while you prepare the other ingredients.

Combine the sauce ingredients in a small bowl. Use a pair of scissors to snip the chilies into ¾ in (2 cm) sections, discarding seeds as far as possible.

Heat a wok over a high flame. Pour in the deep-frying oil and heat to 350–400°F

(180–200°C). Add the chicken and fry until crisp and golden. (If you are deep-frying in a wok with a relatively small volume of oil, fry the chicken in a couple of batches.) Remove the chicken with a slotted spoon and set aside. Pour the oil into a heatproof container and clean the wok if necessary.

Return the wok to a high flame. Add 2–3 tbsp cooking oil and the chilies and stir-fry briefly until they are fragrant and just changing color (do not burn them). Toss in the ginger and garlic and stir-fry for a few seconds more, until you can smell their aromas. Then add the sauce and stir as it thickens. Return the chicken to the wok and stir vigorously to coat the pieces in sauce. Stir in the sesame oil, then serve, with a scattering of spring onion greens if desired.

—Fuschia Dunlop,
Every Grain of Rice: Simple Chinese Home Cooking, 2013

Every year on December 24th the people of Japan cheer, "Kurisumasu ni wa kentakki!" then hop into their efficient cars and drive to KFC. There they are greeted by a statue of the brand's patriarch, Colonel Sanders, in a Santa suit, and are directed to the end of the long line of other people also waiting to pick up their "Christmas Party

Barrels." These come with fried chicken, salad, and a Christmas cake, and cost the equivalent of $40. Most have been ordered two months in advance. It's not a real Japanese Christmas unless you spend it with the Colonel.

Having the birth of Jesus Christ associated with your product is the kind of national tradition corporate dreams are made of; KFC Japan's sales double in December every year because of it. Given that less than one percent of the Japanese population is Christian, it's also quite an unusual one. According to KFC, the custom began in the early 1970s after a distraught expat wandered into one of their stores on Christmas Eve. She was apparently unable to find a turkey in all of Japan and thought fried chicken would be the next best thing. A savvy manager picked up on the potential of this idea and, with a little advertising, the tradition took off from there.

The bigwigs at KFC in Japan attribute their yuletide success to a concept known as *omotenashi*, a spirit of selfless hospitality they feel the chain and the Colonel embody. Translated into American, it means KFC serves up some good old Southern hospitality. Translated further into big-budget national television spots, it also means that most Japanese think Americans eat chicken on Christmas and that Christmas means chicken to the Japanese. (Most Japanese also aren't familiar with eating turkey.)

The fact that he is the embodiment of Father Christmas to an entire foreign nation would probably have pleased Harland Sanders, Kentucky Fried Chicken's colorful founder. He was a man who had lived a great many lives even before donning his iconic white suit and going door to door to sell people his "secret recipe" fried chicken. After quitting school at the age of twelve because he didn't like math, Sanders worked on a farm, joined the army, started a ferry company, and sold Michelin tires. In between, he was an insurance salesman, a railway fireman, and, despite having no formal medical training, delivered poor people's babies. He was a lawyer for a little while too, but had to stop practicing because he punched one of his clients. He also shot a man but got off because the other guy started it.

Most importantly, Sanders knew his way around a kitchen, and although originally from Indiana, eventually started serving up home-cooked food out of the back of a gas station in Kentucky. After selling this operation to pay off his debts, in 1952, at the age of 62, he managed to license his famous chicken recipe to a store in Utah. This became the first Kentucky Fried Chicken and by the 1960s the restaurant was the flagship of the largest food-service chain in the entire United States. By the 1970s KFC would be the biggest user of chicken on the entire planet.

Like the chicken it fries, KFC owes much of its success to its incredible ability to adapt. This is particularly true at KFC China, the crown jewel in the Colonel's global empire. The first Kentucky Fried Chicken in China opened its doors at 9:30 A.M. on November 12, 1987 just outside Beijing's Tiananmen Square. It readily multiplied to a constellation of 5,000 stores spread across the whole of the Middle Kingdom in a matter of years. (By contrast, there are only roughly 4,000 KFCs currently in operation in the United States.)

The Chinese love KFC, and the majority of the chain's most profitable stores are in the booming Asian superpower. Its loyal customers are drawn not just by the restaurant's finger-licking good food but also by its knack at integrating the American cliché of fried chicken with Chinese flavors. Under the aura of the Colonel's mischievous smile and Western *je ne sais quoi*, loyal Chinese KFC fans enjoy fried chicken *mapo duofu*, a riff on a traditional spicy Sichuan tofu dish, or bite into a variation of a Peking duck wrap updated with fried chicken and named the "Dragon Twister." Environmentalists back in Kentucky, where the secret blend of eleven herbs and spices is still kept underground under eleven layers of lock and key, hope that one day soon this menu might include the Asian carp population rapidly crowding American waterways. If the Chinese start gobbling it up as Kentucky Fried

Whitefish, they might eat the United States out of a very big invasive species problem.

Just as the Chinese grew accustomed to the Colonel, Americans back at home were learning to love the General. The great nineteenth-century scholar-warrior General Zuo Zongtang is a popular figure in China. Raised on a farm in the province of Hunan, he failed his civil service exam seven times, united his nation, and presided over the Taiping Rebellion, the bloodiest civil war in world history. Twenty million people died and a legacy worth naming take-out after was born.

The life of the real Zuo Zongtang, or as Americans know him, General Tso, bears no relation whatsoever to the chicken dish that has since made the statesman a household name. That connection was made in the 1970s when one Chef Peng and one Chef Wang, formerly of Taiwan but by then of New York City, both aimed to make a "House Specialty" that would be worthy of the name of a fiery Hunanese military leader. Chef Peng's General Tso's Chicken was a dish of dark meat seasoned heavily with soy, garlic, and vinegar. Chef Wang's General Ching's Chicken, Ching being a mentor of General Tso, was crispy-coated and meant to appeal to Americans. Somewhere along the way, General Ching's chicken absconded with the name General Tso's chicken but retained its crunchy shell and cloying sweetness.

The fable of the colonel and the general has not always been a happy one, however. When people in the United States had their first taste of Chinese food in San Francisco in the 1850s, they were suspicious. It was delicious no doubt, and fed the hungry forty-niners well, but the Chinese were a new people with a strange language, long braids, and a proclivity for what Americans believed were bizarre foods. The Chinese, like the prospectors, were first drawn to this country by the prosperity of the Gold Rush, but as gold finds started to decline and jobs became scarce, labor groups blamed the Chinese. Widespread xenophobia did the rest.

"Do the Chinese eat rats?" asked the *New York Times* earnestly in 1888. This was a great American fear at the time, especially as the Chinese and their restaurants spread out further and further from the San Francisco Bay with each new wave of immigration. "Yes," was the publication's answer, as proven by American drawings of Chinese men peddling racks of rodents that appeared often in geography classes. The students in these classes would in turn do their part to mine the fear. *"Chink, Chink, Chinaman,"* went the racist nineteenth-century children's jump rope rhyme, *"eats dead rats; eats them up like gingersnaps."*

This "coolie diet," as Americans came to call it made the Chinese, and the Japanese and "Hindoos" for that matter, an "inoffensive" people. Inoffensive was not good. "You can not work a man who must have beef and bread, and would prefer beef, alongside a man who can live on rice," declared Senator James G. Blaine in an 1879 speech before Congress. "In all such struggles," he continued, "the result is not to bring up the man who lives on rice to the beef-and-bread standard, but it is to bring down the beef-and-bread man to the rice standard." Senator Blaine would go on to have a tremendous political career that would involve losing a presidential election and winning a fight against the "Pratomagno Chicken," the then-reigning Italian boxing champion. One of Blaine's proudest achievements was being an early supporter of the Chinese Exclusion Act of 1882, which would prohibit any further waves of "inoffensive" Chinese immigrants from coming into the country for the next sixty years. It would not be well until the 1970s, after Chinese immigration to the United States resumed and President Nixon's famous visit to China normalized relations between the two nations, that Chinese food would regain its rightful status as one of America's favorite cuisines.

Another delicious Chinese-American recipe from 1969 by Fu Pei Mei, one of Taiwan's most famous early television chefs and a woman many considered to be the "Julia Child of Chinese Cuisine."

SAUTEED CHICKEN
CHENG-TU STYLE

Ingredients:

½ Chicken (about 1½ lbs.)

2 t. Salt

2 T. Shredded green onion

1 t. Sugar

½ T. Shredded ginger

½ T. Brown vinegar

½ T. Shredded garlic

1 T. Wine

2 T. Shredded celery

2 T. Hot soybean paste

1 T. Shredded red hot pepper

2 t. Cornstarch (make paste)

1 t. Brown peppercorn

2 t. Cold water (make paste)

½ c. Lard or peanut oil

Procedure:

1. Chop the chicken with bone and skin into 1″ square pieces.
2. Heat the oil boiling hot. Saute the chicken pieces for about 2 minutes, (only half cooked), add peppercorn, stir thoroughly. Add red pepper and hot soybean paste, stir 2 more minutes.
3. Add wine, ginger, garlic, sugar, vinegar, salt and 1 C. hot water. Cover and simmer for 5 minutes.

4. Stir in the cornstarch paste until thickened. Add shredded celery and green onion. Mix well and serve.

NOTE: Chengtu is a big city in the western part of China.

—Fu Pei Mei, *Pei Mei's Chinese Cook Book*, 1969

Across the oceans, being so brightly lit and so recognizably American is not always as effective a marketing plan as "Christmas with Kentucky," or as delicious as a heaping plate of General Tso's. KFC faces a different kind of threat as it has braved new countries in recent decades, a danger that has involved arson and bombings in outposts as far-flung as Indonesia, Chile, Pakistan, Peru, and Lebanon. In Cairo, amid the turmoil of the "Arab Spring" in 2011, protestors chanted, "No Kentucky! No Kentucky! No Kentucky!" to criticize what they saw as flawed in US foreign policy toward Egypt. To many abroad, it seems, Colonel Sanders is the modern Uncle Sam.

There are over 18,000 KFC outlets in 115 countries and territories worldwide. All of these serve up the Colonel's world-famous fried chicken. Conversely, there are now over 45,000 Chinese restaurants in the United States alone, more than all the KFCs, McDonald's, and Pizza

Huts combined. And without any sort of formal collusion, almost all of them serve a variation of General Tso's famous chicken. Take this dish back to China and the Chinese will look at you funny. This is not Chinese food, they will say, this is American food. Where the chicken is concerned, adaptation has always been key.

Almost a decade before KFCs were gracing food courts the world over, chicken from the United States had begun to dominate the globe's dinner plates. With the Broiler Depression of 1959 hurting the chicken industry, the US government set its sights on Europe. The continent seemed like a good place for America to sell all of its cheap chicken, particularly given the French appetite for the bird and the fact that European fowls remained relatively expensive. By 1960, American poultry producers were sending millions of pounds of frozen chicken to the Common Market each week, and by 1962 American chicken totally dominated the low-end European poultry palate.

Although chicken was affordable and consumption was on the rise, Europe was not happy. Cuisine is thicker than blood on that continent, and the flood of cheap chicken was drowning out local chicken producers and European birds. The French were particularly up in arms, confusing the by-then standard antibiotics in American chicken feed for growth hormones and declaring that these were a major threat to the virility of their own Gallic cocks.

The Common Market's response to this influx was a reasonable one—the imposition of a tariff on imports of the bird. Naturally, the United States responded to this tax with a threat to immediately remove its military support from NATO, and then set about imposing an even larger duty on the import of light trucks, among other goods, that European producers like Volkswagen dominated.

The tariff on light trucks has since been declared one of the stupidest taxes in US history, one scholars argue directly caused the downfall of the American auto industry by insulating car makers from foreign competition for sixty years. Big money in cowboy-friendly pickup trucks meant little innovation in other sectors of automobile production. As oil prices soared, the efficient cars the Japanese were driving to pick up their Christmas Buckets finally came to the United States in the 1980s and 1990s. Americans were impressed, and local automakers were doomed. Thanks in part to frozen chicken, Detroit is now a shadow of its former self. The "Chicken Tax" is still in place today.

Such trade wars over inexpensive American chicken would continue for decades. Some places, like Japan and rapidly urbanizing Nigeria, were very excited about the bird. Hungry after political upheaval in the 1980s, the Egyptians too gladly took boatloads of low-priced American chicken, pushing up fowl consumption in the Middle Eastern nation by forty percent in just two years. But other countries had to be force fed, like India, where the arrival of American chicken sparked protests and brought about huge tariffs by the Indian government. Further trade skirmishes occurred between Europe and the United States over access to the hungry Middle East in the 1980s, which reignited when Brazil started getting involved in the international game of chicken in the 1990s, and started again in recent years with the United States and African governments getting into a massive cockfight over access to growing sub-Saharan chicken markets.

For the better part of the past twenty-five years, the chicken trade has been one of the most reliable barometers for the state of US-Russian relations. Russia received its first taste of American chicken in 1991 after the fall of the Soviet Union. The downfall of its longtime Cold War enemy was pleasing to the United States, and it donated food aid in the form of chicken legs. Unoffended by the fact that these were the parts of the bird Americans themselves weren't eating, hungry Russians celebrated the gifts as "Bush Legs," honoring then-President George H. W. Bush.

Aid gradually gave way to trade, and in the free

market these new chicken parts didn't go down quite as easily. Like in the rest of Europe, a huge influx of cheap American chicken took a toll on domestic Russian chicken production, and President Boris Yeltsin threatened to wholly cut off US chicken imports before the impending Russian elections in 1996. American President Bill Clinton, whose political career has received substantial support from Tyson Foods in his home state of Arkansas, convinced Yeltsin to back down at the 1996 Sinai talks. The meeting was aimed at countering global terrorism, but ended up including large portions dedicated to the trade of our fowl friend.

When the United States raised steel tariffs in 2002, Russians banned US chicken. In 2003, George W. Bush aided Russia in joining the World Trade Organization, and Russians started importing poultry again. When Russians went to war in the country of Georgia in 2008, they blamed the United States for instigating the conflict, and banned US chicken. When relations normalized, so did the chicken trade. Although Russia is steadily becoming self-sufficient in poultry production, such a political posturing erupted yet again in 2015 over Russia's involvement in Crimea in the Ukraine.

Russia often justifies these bans over concerns that the birds are a threat to human health, findings bolstered by Russia's so-called "Chicken

Napoleons," veterinarians with military-style ranks sent to the United States to inspect and "list or delist" American chicken-processing plants. Russian leader Vladimir Putin allegedly once tried to confirm the American chicken conspiracy with President George W. Bush, quipping in a brief and private poultry summit, "I know you have separate plants for chickens for America and chickens for Russia." Aghast at such a rumor, Bush blushed, "Vladimir, you're wrong."

Beyond causing political turmoil, Russia's constant back-and-forth with the bird often disturbs the delicate global balance of America's chicken exports. Americans have their overwhelming preference for white meat, which stays at home, while places like China and Russia enjoy the darker cuts of the bird and thus receive the US's dark chicken meat. The leftover viscera winds its way to South Africa to be made into pet food, and the feathers are turned into cheap down coats and fertilizer in Indonesia. The United States used to send the wings to China along with the dark-meat legs, but the development of the Buffalo Chicken Wing in the 1960s was such a momentous event for American cuisine that it singlehandedly changed the structure of the global chicken trade. Now US producers keep most of the wings at home, and in its place, the Chinese now receive some 330,000 pounds of giant

American "chicken paws," the bird's feet. These the Chinese snack on lightly cooked with a cold beer.

This is the original Buffalo Chicken Wing Recipe, developed in Buffalo, New York.

ANCHOR BAR'S
BUFFALO CHICKEN WINGS

Peanut oil, for frying
4 lb. chicken wings (about 40), separated into 2 pieces, wing tips removed, rinsed
12 tbsp. margarine
1 c. hot sauce, preferably Frank's RedHot Original Cayenne Pepper Sauce
1⅓ c. chunky blue cheese dressing
4 ribs celery, halved lengthwise, then cut crosswise into 3" sticks

1. Heat oven to 200°. Pour oil to a depth of 2″ in a 6-qt. Dutch oven, and heat over medium heat until a deep-fry thermometer reads 350°. Dry wings thoroughly with paper towels, and working in batches, fry wings until golden brown, about 12 minutes. Transfer wings to a wire rack set over a baking sheet, and place in oven to keep warm until all wings are fried.
2. Heat margarine in a 12″ deep-sided

skillet over medium heat; stir in hot sauce until smooth. Add wings, and toss until completely coated. Serve wings in a large bowl with dressing and celery on the side.

Americans have a lot of excuses as to why they don't like the dark meat—it's tough, it's dirty, it tastes bad. A lot of it too probably stems from the fact that the dark meat of a leg clearly comes from an animal while with a chicken breast, a cut and shrink wrapped slab of protein, it is much easier to camouflage the fact that it came from a living being.

The reason the chicken has different colors of meat in the first place has to do with a protein called myoglobin. Myoglobin's main job is to deliver oxygen to muscles, so the more a muscle is used the more myoglobin it has. Dark meats are generally "slow-twitch" muscles, meaning they are used for longer activities such as standing and walking. Chickens spend their days running around on their two legs, and so these particular muscles require more energy, meaning they have a darker hue due to the larger concentration of myoglobin. In contrast, the chest muscles of a chicken are meant to help the bird fly and, save for very rare emergencies, are rarely used. These are "fast-twitch" muscles, designed for quick bursts of activity, and thus have less myoglobin and are much lighter in color. Myoglobin also accounts for the difference between red and white meat; animals considered to be "red meat" animals typically have muscles with higher levels of myoglobin. (In terms of nutrition, the white meat of a chicken tends to have a lower calorie and fat content, while the bird's dark meat has higher levels of essential vitamins and minerals, including a spectrum of B vitamins, zinc, and iron. Overall, however, these differences are negligible.)

Knowing that such an American preference for light meat in chicken was but superficial, "Barbecue Bob" Baker did his best to try to shift the balance of eating to something more sustainable for the whole bird. His Cornell laboratories developed a fleet of dark-meat-only chicken hamburgers and hot dogs, but even when coated in breading, Americans kept thinking of these products as dirty and wouldn't buy them.

The proclivity of Western culture toward certain parts of the bird struck other people as strange as well, including avid picnicker and prime minister of England Winston Churchill. Writing an essay entitled "Fifty Years Hence" in 1931, when he was still a member of the lower house of the British Parliament, Churchill paints a world in which the extra chicken parts have all but disappeared. Using laboratories, he predicts, "we shall escape the absurdity of growing a whole chicken in order to eat the breast or wing, by growing these parts separately under a suitable medium." The man who led Great Britain through its darkest hour was predicting what scientists now call "in-vitro meat," animal proteins grown in a laboratory. The idea is so promising for today's Chicken of Tomorrow that animal rights group People for the Ethical Treatment of Animals (PETA) has offered a $1 million award to whoever develops a viable source of lab-grown chicken. Despite extending the deadline twice, no one has yet claimed the prize.

For real chickens, over the past few decades, global chicken consumption has skyrocketed. In regions of sub-Saharan Africa, Latin America, and Asia that face risks from food insecurity, chicken's economic appeal as an increasingly cheap protein source has been undeniable. As the developing world almost doubled its total meat consumption between the 1970s and the mid 1990s, the largest portion of that increase came from chicken.

In places where too much food was much more of a threat to human lives than too little, chicken's popularity rose astronomically as well. Although developed countries saw very little increase in their total meat eating in those same decades, nine-tenths of what growth they did experience came in the form of poultry. In addition to chicken being relatively low-priced and convenient, the

Western world was largely drawn by the same dietary fears that spurred the chicken revolution in the United States. By the early 1990s, England, Germany, and much of what became the European Union counted their calories as avidly as Americans did.

Although it's hard to get an exact dollar amount for the value of the entire global chicken trade, as of 2015 it involved over 59.2 million tons of chicken meat, and is conservatively worth hundreds of billions of dollars. In the 1950s and the 1960s, the United States completely dominated this lucrative international market. Come the 1970s, however, with demand rising globally, domestic chicken industries began to blossom abroad, a development also spurred on largely by American interests.

While chicken growing heavyweights like Perdue and Tyson have strong incentives for chicken production to remain under their control in the United States, independent poultry genetics companies have incentive for as many people as possible to buy their enhanced varieties of the bird. Today there are four major firms that provide the vast majority of the genes of the 50 billion chickens that exist at any given time on planet earth. Two of those companies got their start when Mr. Henry Saglio came in second in the Chicken of Tomorrow Contest in 1948.

Although his fabled white bird and the growth

of his company Arbor Acres Farms brought a man known as the "Father of the Modern Poultry Industry" much financial success, Henry Saglio's stated mission in life was to use his gifts at fowl breeding to make chicken affordable to poor people. Such a noble goal resonated strongly with Nelson Rockefeller, grandson of the oil tycoon John D. Rockefeller Sr. and son of the financier John D. Rockefeller Jr. Besides being very rich and later becoming a very successful politician, this youngest Rockefeller was also well known for being a vehement anticommunist. His hatred for all things Marxist was so deep in fact that he once destroyed a priceless mural that renowned Mexican painter Diego Rivera had created in Rockefeller Center because it included a portrait of Lenin.

When it came to combating the Red Scourge abroad, Rockefeller firmly believed that "it is hard to be a Communist with a full belly." Nelson had spent much of the early 1940s in Latin America as President Franklin D. Roosevelt's Coordinator of Inter-American Affairs, where he used economic development projects as a tool to combat the rising influence of Nazism in the region. When his government gig ended in 1946, Rockefeller founded the International Basic Economy Corporation (IBEC) and continued on with the same work. Tapping his family's vast resources and creating partnerships with corporations interested in doing business with Latin America, IBEC began setting up dairies, mechanized farms, food processors, wholesalers, supermarkets, and the like. By the 1960s, IBEC had spread beyond Latin American to Asia and Africa and established some 119 subsidiaries in 33 countries across the globe.

In 1964, IBEC purchased Saglio's Arbor Acres breeding farm and the pair promptly went about fulfilling the mission of feeding all the world's poor—and potential socialists—with poultry and eggs. Despite the fact that at this point the bird itself was increasingly too fat to physically fly, thanks to Rockefeller's efforts, the American chicken started to migrate abroad in prolific numbers. With the world's most talented chicken breeder at its side, IBEC helped to expand the operations of Arbor Acres into twenty-one countries, including Brazil, Thailand, and China, whose farmers readily gobbled up these plump and fast-growing birds. Today almost fifty percent of all Chinese chickens are descended from American Arbor Acres breeding stock. Even when separated by oceans, General Tso's and Colonel Sanders's chickens are very likely cousins.

CHAPTER FOURTEEN
The Modern Chicken

TARRAGON AND LEMON ROAST CHICKEN

This recipe was Epicurious.com's most popular recipe in 2015.

Yield: 4 Servings

Ingredients:
4 pounds skin-on, bone-in chicken pieces
1 tablespoon extra-virgin olive oil
Sea salt and cracked black pepper
10 small sprigs tarragon
1 tablespoon finely grated lemon zest
3 cloves garlic, sliced
2 fennel bulbs, trimmed and sliced
½ cup dry white wine
½ cup chicken stock
Lemon wedges, to serve

Preparation:
Preheat oven to 350°F. Heat a heavy ovenproof casserole dish on a stovetop over high heat. Score the chicken skin at regular intervals, drizzle with the oil, sprinkle with salt and pepper and toss to

coat. Add to the dish and cook for 6–8 minutes on each side or until well browned. Remove from the pan and set aside. Add the tarragon, lemon zest, garlic and fennel to the dish and cook for 2–3 minutes or until golden. Return the chicken to the dish with the wine and stock and bring to a simmer.

Transfer to the oven and roast for 20–25 minutes or until the chicken is just cooked through. Serve with the lemon wedges.
—Donna Hay, *The New Easy*, 2015

T he modern chicken really is an incredible piece of technology. Give today's broiler twelve pounds of food and it will turn out six pounds of edible chicken in just over seven weeks. This is a remarkable 1.92 feed conversion ratio and it's unheard of anywhere else in animal agriculture. The Chicken of Tomorrow wouldn't even have reached three pounds in that same time. Give Celia Steele's birds seven weeks and they would have been just one pound and barely half way done growing.

This modern bird, which "eats like a fashion model but puts on weight like a New York Giants defensive lineman," is no dunghill fowl. It struts around its chicken farm under monikers like Cobb 500, Ross 50, and Hubbard F15, basking in the fact that its scientifically advanced pedigrees make it the most efficient meat-making machine on the planet.

The modern chicken's natural habitat, the broiler house, is a model of efficiency that mirrors that of the bird. Lighting and temperature are optimized to fit a broiler's needs and can be controlled with the flick of a switch. Rows of florescent water-nipples dangle from the ceiling while yards upon yards of metal feeding troughs line the floors, which themselves are covered with wood shavings, sawdust, and other absorbent materials. An average of 25,000 or more birds now live in a single broiler shed at a time, which itself averages between 20,000 and 36,000 square feet in size. With all the trimmings, a state-of-the-art chicken house can cost upward of $300,000 to build.

A day in the life of a broiler chicken, at its most fundamental level, is a study in the art of sitting. Revel in a fowl's glory long enough and maybe the bird will get thirsty. Gingerly, the chicken will get up and hobble over to a fluorescent-colored water-nipple. Once rehydrated, it will sit back down. A few minutes later, maybe the chicken becomes peckish for some ultra-enriching fuel. Once properly refilled with all of its essential vitamins and minerals at a nearby feed trough, the bird will return to the newspaper-sized space of floor that has been allocated for its brief existence. The same set of thrilling events happened with the chicken yesterday and will also happen again tomorrow, and the next day and the day after that until the bird's seven weeks of growth are complete.

Even in its technologically advanced, albeit largely reclined form, the modern chicken is still quite skittish. To prevent a panic from spreading among the birds in their tight quarters, growers keep the lights dim in their windowless broiler sheds. Closely packed, the fowls still peck at each other with their trimmed beaks and an average of eighteen in any given flock will die each day, be it from attacks by other chickens or disease or stress. The birds' close proximity to each other is made even worse by the chicken's newly gargantuan form, which is most likely the cause of all the sitting. Walking around is simply too difficult. If humans grew as fat as fast as a modern chicken, a 6.6 pound human baby would reach 660 pounds in just two months. To compensate, today's chickens have been bred with much bigger feet, but sometimes their incredible growth outpaces even the capacity of their lungs and skeletons, and the birds quickly expire.

But the broiler house is just one of a few stops in the short and efficient life of a modern broiler chicken. First, a breeder company supplies a breeder farm with breeder chicks. These chicks become chickens and eventually produce hatching eggs that are sent to the hatchery. The hatchery hatches the chicks and sends them to grow at the grow-out house. When the broilers are grown, they get sent to a processing plant, where they are slaughtered, processed, and sanitized, and then packed, cooled, and shipped to whoever wants to eat chicken.

Thanks to the steady march of capitalism at the dinner plate and beyond, the thousands of chicken ranchers that used to dot the horizon of the American dream have today been whittled down to less than fifty highly specialized integrated chicken companies, who also own the feed mills and often times the many distribution channels the modern chicken needs. The meaty tendrils of these massive corporations have expanded and multiplied. As of 2010, Tyson Foods owned thirty-six hatcheries, thirty feed mills, thirty-three slaughter plants, another twenty-two plants used for additional processing and cooking, and thousands of trucks and trailers for shipping. The company now also produces twenty-four percent of the nation's beef and seventeen percent of its pork.

Ninety percent of all growers, as chicken farmers are now called, work for these integrators. The labor is done largely under the same contract-farming arrangements that can trace their roots back to the hardships of the Great Depression. In many ways, these contracts are still beneficial to both growers and integrators—an integrator has the labor it needs to raise its chickens and the grower is protected from the strong likelihood that that same chicken will not make him or her any money at all. These contracts vary from firm to firm but are mostly made on a flock-by-flock basis, with the average grower raising four to five flocks per year. The integrator drops off the baby chicks, along with feed and expertise, and then returns seven weeks later to bring the birds to meet their maker.

A straightforward concept, but growers complain often of complications. Contract renewals can come with stipulations to quickly modernize broiler houses before the next batch of chicks, but the equipment upgrades required to make the modern chicken as plump as efficiently as possible can run tens of thousands of dollars. In keeping up with the times, growers can fall behind in paying back the monstrous mountains of debt it took to build the chicken house in the first place. A new grower has, on average, just under $5 of debt for each square foot of housing they own, which can add up, in some instances, to well over half a million dollars.

Payment too is less certain as more integrators begin to use what is known as the "tournament system." The chicken companies will start each flock with an average price they are willing to pay for a pound of chicken, generally five cents. After the birds are rounded up from the growing shed, each farmer's flock is tabulated and ranked according to a formula relying heavily on each bird's feed efficiency. Growers who receive a better score are ranked higher and earn more money per pound. Growers with a relatively worse performance are ranked lower and can receive up to fifty percent less for their birds. Individual performance thus matters less than comparative performance. Even if all the growers raise exorbitantly fat chickens, half will still make less.

Those who defend this system say that keeping a price floor for growers protects them from the vagaries of a sudden fowl plague or a hike in feed prices. From a purely economic view, this system is ingenious as well, solving the eternal conundrum of incentivizing workers to upgrade their equipment and to maintain quality standards even when they are not being constantly supervised. Many growers argue back simply that the tournament is unfair. The primary determinant of their incomes, they say, is the quality of chicks received from the integrator, a step in the chicken process over which the growers have no control. A handful of growers even claim that they have been blacklisted, their complaints about their treatment causing the companies to continually send them poor quality birds and keep their farm at the bottom of the tournament rankings.

Some chicken farmers are perfectly happy with

the modern chicken farming system, tournaments and all. Many others are not. Their high levels of debt can make them vulnerable and the relative geographic isolation of chicken companies can leave growers with limited options for better deals. Many contracts too stipulate that growers cannot speak about their integrators or that growers cannot know the terms of their contract until they have taken out a massive loan to build expensive broiler houses. Growers have attempted to organize, to ensure themselves a minimum pay, to get recompense if treated poorly, but they are competing against a handful of huge chicken producers that dominate the lucrative business of "white meat" now worth over $48 billion annually. Laws to protect chicken growers have continually stalled in Congress, although legislation has been recently introduced that promises to improve the growers' situation. As that bill waits for votes, the tournament system is spreading to pork.

Even with the incredible advances in science and technology that have made the modern chicken industry possible, it's hard to imagine that if Prince Erik of Denmark gallivanted off into the sunset with a woman he loved more than a throne in this day and age he would still want to become a chicken farmer. According to one survey of the broiler industry, a typical grower in 1995, "had been raising chicken for fifteen years, owned three poultry houses, remained deeply in debt, and earned perhaps $12,000 a year." Unfortunately, not much has changed in the time since. Today, the median-income poultry farmer owns between three and five chicken houses, produces some 483,600 broilers each year, and lives below the poverty line. "Rural poor" is a term commonly used to describe them and their situation. In their efforts to provide the country with ample supplies of cheap and healthy meat, chicken growers spend their days living in steep debt, repairing expensive equipment, and refilling feed troughs in a state-of-the art chicken house that is filled with the most advanced chicken technology in world history and burns with clouds of ammonia.

The ammonia comes from the chicken waste, which is its own source of problems. Farmers long knew diseases like fowl cholera were spread through chicken feces, so they did their best to make sure their birds did not live in one area for too long. Today, thanks to the past century's advances in fowl medicine, it is industry standard that growers only change the litter of their houses when they change each flock. In its seven-week life, a chicken will produce an average of eleven pounds of manure, which means the over 8.6 billion efficient meat birds produced in the United States annually are also efficiently making some 95 billion pounds of waste each year.

As the chicken industry is a highly effectual

one, all this chicken waste ends up in a myriad of places. Many growers sell it as a potent fertilizer to fruit or vegetable farmers, and as the excrement is protein rich, it often also ends up as food for beef cattle and fish. The feces is most often used on farms bordering major chicken-producing areas, but its overuse can be harmful; the high concentrations of runoff from chicken fertilizer used by non-poultry farmers in Delmarva are being blamed for "dead zones" in the Chesapeake Bay, areas where marine life no longer thrives.

Another place almost guaranteed to contain chicken feces is, unfortunately for eaters everywhere, chicken meat itself. Independent surveys have found *E. coli*, a bug spread almost exclusively through contact with poop, to be present in 92% of poultry samples tested in ordinary retail markets; government surveys have put that number at 99%.

Medical researchers are growing increasingly worried that this already nasty bug, along with scores of other illnesses one can still catch from eating chicken, are becoming harder to treat thanks to their increasing antibiotic resistance. The cause of such resistance: modern chickens themselves eating too many of those essential growth-promoting antibiotics. Although a number of chicken producers have already announced plans to reduce their usage of antibiotics "also used in humans," today seventy percent of all antibiotics produced in the United States are still given to livestock and poultry in their feed.

The way these infectious bugs get into the meat in the first place is largely at the slaughterhouse, where guts get ripped and the fowl contents of intestines leak. It is against a chicken company's economic interests to sell tainted foods to the public, thus causing illness, scandal, and the US government to interfere with their production, and so dead birds are often chilled in chlorine baths as a means to disinfect their carcasses. Still, preventing the spread of disease in even the cleanest slaughter facilities is a difficult task, and some consumer reports have found that up to 97% of chickens found in supermarkets to be contaminated with harmful bacteria. To prevent the spread of fowl-borne illnesses, the government and chicken producers alike advise consumers to not wash raw chicken (the splashing of water can spread the germs), and instead to thoroughly and properly cook the bird. (Let's hope Americans are better cooks in this century!)

Aside from having to work with the contents of chicken intestines, the employees of these processing plants have their own gripes about their dealings with the modern bird, as advanced and efficient as our feathered friend may be. Pay is low for eight- to ten-hour shifts spent shackling chickens by their legs and sending them off to an electrocution bath, where the birds are stunned and prepared for slaughter. In subsequent rooms that smell of wet feathers, the bird's throats are then sliced and their carcasses bled. What was once a chicken is then whisked away to be scalded, plucked, and then chopped and molded in every which way.

What is deadly for a modern chicken is dangerous, too, for a human. A system that once only produced ten thousand birds a day running at full speed now can churn out an incredible 12,000 BPH, an industry abbreviation for "birds per hour." Accidental "neighbor cuts" are common, and one in six poultry slaughterhouse workers gets severely injured or sick on the job each year. Like growers, these groups have long been marginalized, frequently minority women or new immigrants with little power or recourse to protect their rights.

Animal-rights groups and consumers alike voice concerns over the chicken's well-being during its journey from egg to plate, attacking the modern bird's gargantuan growth, the broiler house's tight growing conditions, and the lack of government oversight in the standards of humane chicken slaughter. To some, the technologically advanced modern broiler is "grotesque" and a "monster;" the practices of the chicken and egg industries akin to "a race to the bottom;" the chicken's life one of complete "suffering" from being used as simply a "means to our ends." Surveying the modern bird's condition, both as a laying hen and a broiler bird, the animal rights group People for the Ethical Treatment of Animals claims, "chickens are arguably the most abused animals on the planet."

For better and for worse, this is the system that produces the vast majority of the 160 million servings of cheap and convenient chicken the people of the United States are devouring each and every day. It is the product of centuries of hungry striving to at last have a chicken in every pot, and in world history no other field of food production has been such a focus of such profound scientific and technological advancement. As a result, the cost of chicken has grown only half as fast as the rest of the consumer price index; in the past fifty years, the price of a pound of chicken in supermarkets has only gone up four cents. And yet, in spite of the tremendous amount of capital that has gone into building the modern bird, these four cents are roughly what an integrator makes in profit, and even more than what a grower might have received for making that same pound of food.

Fueled by the spread of genetically advanced broilers and rising global demand for chicken meat, this same factory farm system is starting to spread across the globe as entrepreneurs continue to hear the chicken's irresistible siren song. Large integrators with generic names like the New

Hope Group in China and LDC Groupe in France, and the CP Group in Thailand are steadily expanding their production capacity, and today the top fifteen chicken firms worldwide each produce over half a billion broilers annually.

Outside of the United States, the two countries that grow the most chickens are China and Brazil. Chicken in Portuguese is *frango* and early European explorers of the country's steamy jungles and glowing beaches recorded that native Brazilians were deathly afraid of the first crowing *frangos* they encountered on European ships. Despite that slow start, today Brazil's broiler industry stretches squawking and chirping from the Amazon to Rio Grande do Sul and is led by JBS, the biggest chicken company on the planet, which singlehandedly produces 3.3 billion birds a year. Although the world too knows them as beef-eaters, Brazilians today consume fifty percent more chicken than they did just ten years ago.

Thanks to its burgeoning domestic broiler industry, Chinese chicken consumption too has grown tremendously over recent decades. While the average Chinese person ate only twenty pounds of chicken in 2015, there are over 1.3 billion of these average Chinese people, which makes the country one of the biggest growing markets for chicken meat. Together the United States, Brazil, and China produce fifty percent of all exported chickens on the planet. The Japanese, for their part, are the world's biggest per capita importers.

One of the biggest fears associated with this global expansion of the industrial chicken farm is the increased likelihood of a deadly avian flu pandemic wiping out off a vast chunk of humanity. It has happened before. The Hong Kong Flu killed almost a million worldwide in 1968, and the Asian Flu up to four million in 1958, but both of these outbreaks paled in comparison to the devastation wrought by Spanish Influenza in 1918. Up to fifty million people died worldwide in a single year, making the disease more devastating than the bubonic plague or the battlefields of a World War. All of these were illnesses that humans caught from birds.

Wild birds are the primary source of all influenza viruses in chickens, and subsequently humans, and there are two basic subsets of influenza in birds: low pathogenic strains (LPAI) and highly pathogenic strains (HPAI). Infected with low pathogenic strains, chickens experience mild illnesses, such as "ruffled feathers or a drop in egg production." On a very rare occasion, a chicken flock will be infected with a low pathogenic version of a dangerous H5 or H7 strain of influenza, which can mutate and become highly pathogenic. If a chicken catches one of these nasty strains, death is imminent and often grotesque. A bird's comb and wattle start to swell, its head turns blue, and its entire body starts to hemorrhage. Understandably, egg production and growth virtually stop as the bird's organs begin to leak blood and essentially liquefy. When a researcher encountered a fowl plague in Pennsylvania in 1983, he described the feathered victims as "bloody Jell-O."

At the very least, these highly virulent diseases are economically devastating. It took almost a full year to control the 1983 outbreak in Pennsylvania, culminating in the slaughter of over seventeen million birds and costing farmers and the government more than $60 million. That was the worst bird flu outbreak in US history up until 2015, when the rapid spread of an H5N2 strain among American laying flocks resulted in the USDA culling nearly forty-eight million birds. Egg prices in some parts of the country skyrocketed to nearly $3.00 per dozen that year, a level high enough to ruffle a few proverbial feathers among the just recovering common murre population of the Farallones.

But the human cost of avian influenza can be much higher. In 1997, eighteen people fell ill and six died from H5N1 in Hong Kong, the same strain of influenza that had turned Pennsylvania's birds into Jell-O. In 2003, so soon after, cases of avian influenza were again reported in people in Hong Kong; an even more virulent strain appeared among birds in Vietnam, Cambodia, Thailand, and Indonesia. In 2006, human deaths from the disease were reported in places as disparate as Turkey, China, Indonesia, and Iraq. Every year since, more birds and more humans have died from avian influenza.

The spread of these diseases globally has been blamed on migratory wild birds, which are indeed influenza carriers that cross oceans and continents, and on backyard poultry flocks, which commingle with wild birds and bring back diseases to humans. As a result, containment methods in recent global outbreaks have focused on the culling of wild birds and the banning of outdoor poultry raising in at-risk countries.

But intensive chicken farming methods, however technologically advanced they may be, compound these deadly risks. One slip in biosecurity, and an entire industrial flock can become infected. Modern broiler houses, with their dark, moist, and cramped conditions, perfectly designed to efficiently grow the modern bird are also conveniently "designed like a disease incubator." And with birds packed body-to-body, living their entire lives in a steadily growing layer of chicken excrement, viruses can mutate into a virulent strain and spread rapidly. The genetic diversity that helps wild birds and backyard flocks withstand epidemics is virtually nonexistent in a modern broiler house. Naturally prone to get sick and die, modern birds are now bred mainly to get twice as juicy and meaty in half the time, not to survive deadly plagues.

The industrial chicken system has become a highly interdependent and global one, so the spread of a pandemic across borders over chicken trade routes can be rapid. If chicks in a hatchery in Thailand become infected, or a wild duck gets into a feed mill in China, the global commerce of these companies can infect poultry in Cambodia, Vietnam, and Indonesia.

Even for countries such as the United States, with an established Department of Agriculture primed to leap in to control potential outbreaks of influenza, the battle to stop its spread among birds is long and costly. Monitoring must be intensive, specimens sampled, vaccinations developed, culls organized, and actions swift. In Southeast Asia, where poultry production has increased sixfold since 1980, these regulatory systems are virtually nonexistent; many do not find it coincidental that the region has been the source of all major avian influenza outbreaks in recent memory. With little regulation, wild ducks come into contact with domestic ducks and geese, which commingle with humans and outdoor chickens, who in turn find their way to intensively farmed chickens, whose parts come into contact with more humans and more feed and more wild birds.

Even for viruses, adaptation has always been

key, and novel strains of avian influenza are discovered every year. While the modern chicken, for its part, just sits and waits, virologists are on high alert, knowing full well that while there are many winners when it comes to affordable chicken dinners, there is always the unfortunate potential for a large number of losers as well.

The End and the Beginning

The fact that pork branded itself the "Other White Meat" in 1987 is an homage to one of the most dramatic eating revolutions of our time. Completely disregarding five hundred years of its own Western culinary history, pig producers thought pretending their product was like chicken would save it from the poor reputations of saturated fat and cholesterol. For its part, the campaign did work, and by 1994 pork consumption had actually increased by twenty percent.

Beef too attempted to put up a similar fight against its popular decline after centuries of dominating the American plate. While the Senate was drafting their 1977 declaration of dietary recommendations for the US population, cattlemen lobbied hard to get the wording "eat less meat" changed instead to "increase consumption of lean meat." When that failed, they channeled their inner ancient Briton and promoted their national "Beef Gives Strength" advertising campaign. When that failed too, they slapped "Support Beef—Run Over a Chicken" bumper stickers to the back of their trucks, and presumably roamed the country looking for any chickens that had made the unfortunate decision to cross the road.

In centuries past, sociologists used to be able to tell how rich a neighborhood was by the number of animal bones in the street. By the 1980s in the United States, the opposite was true. The chicken and its giant boneless-skinless breasts were taking over, and not just on low-fat, calorie-counting dinner plates. Banquet halls, school lunchrooms, and institutional cafeterias were all switching heavily to serving chicken, seeing the bird as more universally popular for their clientele, not to mention much cheaper and easier to prepare. By 1985 chicken was more popular than pork; by 1992 the bird was more popular than beef.

And the chicken industry itself wasn't silent during its precipitous rise in the nation's eating favor. Keying onto the bird's newfound health food status as a "white meat," television advertisements starting in the 1970s featured plot lines like two overweight individuals eyeing the red meat freezer as Frank Perdue, the tough and tender man himself, cries out "Come on folks, shape up! Start eating my chickens!" Despite being relatively low in fat to begin with, poultry producers in the 1990s also started breeding and processing even lower-fat chickens, meaning they could now legally label their products "low-fat chicken" and sell them at higher margins.

Although chicken was increasingly everyone's favorite entrée, the same couldn't be said for the egg. This once great thinking food that powered the country through the Great Depression was now stuck in the same sinking ship as beef and pork, largely because of its high cholesterol content. Always concerned about his hen men, Robert Baker tried to give egg consumption a boost, inventing an egg-white pizza crust and perfecting an egg-white icebox merengue in the 1980s, but to no avail.

To make matters worse, starting in the late 1970s, a particularly nasty strain of the food-borne illness salmonella, *S. Enteritidis*, was becoming increasingly prevalent on egg farms. (This occurred thanks in large part to the success veterinarians were having in eradicating another strain of salmonella, one that happened to be *S. Enteritidis*'s biggest rival.) In 1987, an outbreak of the illness killed dozens at a hospital in New York, and the widely publicized tragedy was blamed on the raw eggs in the cafeteria's mayonnaise. Although studies at that time found that only 1 in every 2 million eggs in the United States contained the bacteria, going forward, consumers would forever link eating raw eggs with the disease.

The whole irony of this switch to chicken and away from eggs for health reasons, however, was that the chicken Americans were increasingly choosing was often unhealthier for them than red meat. Chicken McNuggets have twice as much fat per ounce than a McDonald's cheeseburger, but the demand for these and other fast-food chicken dishes was so great that by 1990 it pushed up chicken prices throughout the entire United States. Inside the home, according to Gallup polls in the 1980s, the majority of Americans were choosing chicken for dinner but they preferred to eat it fried over any other preparation, and sixteen percent of the other chicken they were buying was in a further processed, often much more fatty, form (as compared with a whole chicken).

With frozen dinners and deep-fried chicken bites increasingly dominating menus, calls yet again erupted against the poor-quality of American cookery. The phrase "tastes like chicken" appeared to hold no value to anyone anymore, bemoaned food reformers and high-minded chefs alike. Despite mounting concerns about how "conventional" chickens were being raised, so pumped up with antibiotics and living through a factory farm nightmare, Americans were still gobbling these birds up day and night.

A century after the glory days of Lyman Byce, in the mid 1980s Petaluma yet again proved it had the pulse of the nation's chicken needs and came out with "Rocky the Range Chicken," a bird raised without antibiotics, on vegetarian feed, and with access to an outdoor running space. These were not avian statues, their producer declared, but real chickens with real chicken flavor, something epicures and chefs were willing to pay high premiums for.

With such hype around Rocky, a newspaper conducted an informal blind taste-test to see if it was true about the bird's better taste. In their survey, four out of six guests actually preferred the ordinary chicken. One guest claimed that the industrial farm–raised fowl tasted "like a bird that flies around. It tastes happier." Renowned chef Wolfgang Puck, who served Rocky the Range Chicken at his own world-famous Los Angeles eatery Spago, volunteered for the blind tasting as well and, much to his surprise, preferred the ordinary chicken. His response: "I definitely think we should find out why they charge so much money."

Scientists have been replicating these anecdotal studies in more formal laboratory settings for decades, studying consumer taste preferences for birds of different breeds, raised under industrial versus free-range systems, and fed a variety of differing diets. Most American tests, by and large, have come to conclusions epicures and factory-farm opponents alike might find unsettling.

One 1959 study compared flavor preference between the era's commercially raised broilers and a diversity of other breeds that were termed "1930-type slow-growing birds grown under simulated 1930 conditions." The researchers' conclusion—"the modern bird has as much 'chicken flavor' as the old style bird." (Although an important issue to eaters, there is unfortunately a lack of more modern studies addressing the same subject.) Comparisons over environmental conditions, as articulated by one 2008 study of commercial broilers, have found as well that "meat from birds produced in the standard system was most preferred, and that from organic systems the least preferred." When it came to what the chickens ate, like at America's founding, controlled studies have consistently found that corn still produces the sweetest meat of all.

The jury's still out on whether or not the breed has a marked impact on a chicken's taste. Studies comparing consumer preferences between fast-growing commercial broilers and indigenous chicken breeds in South Africa and South Korea have found consumers largely prefer eating commercial broilers while competing studies in China and Japan have found the opposite to be true, that people find native birds far more enjoyable to eat than plumper foreign invaders. Americans, by and large, don't seem to notice a big difference in flavor between commercial and noncommercial chicken breeds, and when they do, they prefer to dine on the meat from industrial broilers.

These fowl preferences can, in large part, be attributed directly to the culture from which they come. Unlike the Chinese and the Japanese, and the majority of the rest of the world for that matter, the people of the United States generally don't like to eat the parts of the bird that actually have the most chicken flavor, like the legs and the "chicken oysters." (These "oysters" are the abdominal fat pads that flank a chicken's back bone and accumulate all the essential oils and flavors of a chicken's rich life. The French call them *sot-l'y-laisse*, which roughly translates to, "the fool leaves it there;" the majority of Americans, however, are probably concerned when they hear that a chicken has oysters.)

The most popular part of the bird in the United States today is still undoubtedly the "Cadillac of the chicken," the breast. Even free-range, organic chickens rarely fly, thus rarely using the muscles in their chest, and therefore developing little flavor on that cut of meat. So it makes sense that eaters can't really detect a difference in flavor among the breasts of different types of birds, conventional or otherwise, because none of them have much flavor to begin with. The preference for industrially produced broilers thus probably comes less from actual taste but rather from the meat's texture. People loved these plump broiler breasts the moment they were first made widely available in the early 1950s, a time before the complete domination of intensive farming methods and perfectly calibrated chicken feeds, and it seems not much has changed in the decades since.

Whether one likes them or not, these plump

broiler breasts are now what dominate dinner plates across the United States almost every night of the week. Where before no Americans bought chicken because it was too expensive, then no one bought chicken because it was too cheap, today, people buy chicken regardless of price. It is one of the few items in the contemporary grocery store that is almost completely price inelastic, meaning there is no corresponding change in demand when the price goes up or down.

Instead social and ethical issues are increasingly beating out price and even taste in importance as hungry Americans choose their chickens and many eaters across the country are ever more willing to shell out a few extra dollars per pound on a bird that provides them with peace of mind along with a scrumptious dinner. Capitalists to their feathered cores, big chicken companies are aware of this shift, and in recent years "antibiotic-free" has become the new rallying cry of the broiler industry, grocers, and chicken-slinging chains alike. Although sick chickens will continue to receive these essential medicines in the future (as veterinarians recommend), major poultry producers like Tyson and Perdue are now marketing birds under labels like "No Antibiotics Ever" and aim to end the practice of routinely dousing chicken feed with growth-promoting antibiotics by the end of this decade. Although such changes are no doubt beneficial to both man and bird in the long run, antibiotic-free chickens also happen to comprise the fastest growing segment of poultry sales today; such birds also command higher prices (and fatter margins) than conventional chickens in the grocery store.

But the chicken-labeling bonanza has not stopped there. What started with the "cage-free" movement in egg production in the early 2000s, a label that entailed eggs do not come from hens kept in battery cages, has subsequently hatched into "organic" chickens, "free-range" fowls, "hormone-free" birds, and even eggs coming from hens raised on "100% vegetarian feed." Each of these labels promises consumers a more ethically raised bird, and in turn result in pricier chickens on supermarket shelves.

Like the shift away from antibiotics, these changes in industry practices do hold the potential to benefit the health of both birds and humans,but the dangers of even these chickens, just like in the late nineteenth century, "lie in misrepresentation." For a bird to be considered "free-range," for instance, a "producer must demonstrate . . . that the poultry has been allowed access to the outside." Although such a term may conjure up glorious images of rolling hills and bucolic fields, "outside" can have a myriad of meanings (many parking lots are outside), and "access" does not necessarily mean a bird has ever made its way to this fabled "outside." "Hormone-free" too is simply an industry marketing ploy, as using hormones in chicken production is actually illegal in the United States, while "100% vegetarian feed" is in fact a practice that is harmful to naturally omnivorous chickens.

Such steps, as off-kilter as some may be, are good indications that today's Chicken of Tomorrow will not necessarily be just the fattest bird selling for the cheapest price. Some take this shift toward "organic" production models as a sign that the bird of the future will be the bird of the past, those slow-growing Heritage Breeds from the Hen Fever, and that small farming methods will be the sustainable solution to feeding the world's growing population.

But science and technology have long played a key role in the rise of America's favorite bird, and there's no reason to believe that their continued application cannot promote those same food production systems consumers and epicures alike are willing to spend a few extra dollars on. Through intensively mapping the chicken's genome, for example, researchers are attempting to create more drought-resistant birds to help small farmers across the globe to better withstand the effects of climate change while poultry scientists continue to test and retest the best possible chicken feeds used even in "organic" or "free-range" systems.

And the bird continues to push scientific boundaries even beyond the farm and the dinner plate. Groups of medical researchers are utilizing advanced procedures in gene editing, removing or adding certain genes for particular characteristics straight into a chicken's DNA itself, to create genetically modified birds that produce life-saving medicines for humans in their eggs while collaborations between geneticists and paleontologists have even produced chickens with the legs or snout of a dinosaur, meaning that perhaps someday soon the world will actually know the real flavor of a sharp-toothed and short-armed *Tyrannosaurus rex*.

Whether it will be a certified organic Buff Orpington or a hybrid drought-resistant fowl or a genetically modified "farmeceutical," today's Chicken of Tomorrow still owes much to the chicken of yesterday. The bird was the subject of wars, of parades, of great questions, and of even more important answers; the focus of doctors and lawyers and scientists, of accidental entrepreneurs and even more desperate laborers. On its path, the chicken has suffered from the deepest human indifference and has been the focus of the greatest of national praise. All the while, no matter where Americans found themselves, for richer and poorer, once only in sickness and now also in health, and in amounts both large and small, people still ate chicken. One can't help but think that maybe what chicken tasted like didn't really matter that much after all.

Recipe Citations

CHAPTER ONE: THE EARLY BIRD

"A Chicken Pie," Amelia Simmons, *American Cookery, or the art of dressing viands, fish, poultry, and vegetables, and the best modes of making pastes, puffs, pies, tarts, puddings, custards, and preserves, and all kinds of cakes, from the imperial plum to plain cake: Adapted to this country, and all grades of life*, (Hartford, Conn.: Printed for Simeon Butler, Northampton, 1798), 23.

"Conchiclatus Pullus" (Stuffed Chicken), *Apicius: Cookery and Dining in Imperial Rome*, edited and translated by Joseph Dommers Vehling (New York: Dover Publications, Inc., 1977), 135.

"A Sweet Chicken Pie," Susannah Carter, *The Frugal Housewife, or Complete Woman Cook;. Also the Making of English Wines* (New York: G & R Waite, 1803), 136–7.

CHAPTER TWO: A HEALING BROTH

Soup of Any Kind of Old Fowl, from Mrs. Mary Randolph, *The Virginia Housewife or, Methodical Cook* (Baltimore, Md.: Published by John Plaskitt, 1824), 19.

Chykenns in Cawdel, from The Chief Master

Cooks of King Richard II, *The Forme of Cury*, c. 1390, 33.

"Eggs," William Andrus Alcott, *The Young House-Keeper; or, Thoughts on Food and Cookery* (Boston: Waite, Pierce & Co., 1946), 284, 277.

CHAPTER THREE:
THE GENERAL CHICKEN MERCHANTS

Southern Fried Chicken, from *Union Recorder*, Milledgeville, Georgia, August 9, 1887.

Fried Chickens, from Mrs. Mary Randolph, *The Virginia Housewife or, Methodical Cook* (Baltimore, Md.: Published by John Plaskitt, 1824), 75.

Maryland Fried Chicken, New York Herald Tribune Home Institute, *America's Cook Book* (New York: Scribner's Sons, 1943), 294.

"Chicken Gumbo," *What Mrs. Fisher Knows About Old Southern Cooking, Soups, Pickles, Preserves, Etc.* (San Francisco: Women's Co-Operative Printing Office, 420, 424 & 430 Montgomery Street, 1881), 151.

CHAPTER FOUR:
OF CHICKEN AND CHAMPAGNE

"Chicken Salad, American Style," from, Charles Ranhofer, *The Epicurean: A Complete Treatise of Analytical and Practical Studies on the Culinary Art Including Table and Wine Service, How to Prepare and Cook Dishes, an*

Index for Marketing, a Great Variety of Bills of Fare for Breakfasts, Luncheons, Dinners, Suppers, Ambigus, Buffets, etc. and a Selection of Interesting Bills of Fare of Delmonico's, from 1862 to 1894. Making a Franco-American Culinary Encyclopedia (New York: 1894), 1020.

"To Make Chicken Croquettes," *New York Times*, August 28, 1881.

"Whole Chickens Curried," *Mrs. Putnam's Receipt Book and Young Housekeeper's Assistant* (Boston: Ticknor, Reed, and Fields, 1849), 49.

"Mr. Demorest's Chicken Fricassee," *Jane Cunningham Croly, Jennie June's American Cookery Book* (New York: The American News Co., 1870), 86.

CHAPTER FIVE:
THE POOR MAN'S CHICKEN

"Veal Birds," Fannie Merritt Farmer, *The Boston Cooking-School Cook Book* (Boston: Little, Brown and Company, 1896), 204.

"Cod Sounds to Look Like Small Chickens," Mary Eliza Rundell, *A New System of Domestic Cookery, Former Upon Principles of Economy, and Adapted to the Use of Private Families* (Philadelphia: Benjamin C. Buzby, 1807), 9.

"To Make Artificial Coxcombs," Richard Bradley, *The Country Housewife and Lady's Director* (London: D. Browne, 1732), 79.

"City Chicken," Mrs. Mary Morton, "Household Hints," *Washington Reporter*, November 27, 1926.

CHAPTER SIX: AMERICA'S EGG BASKET

"Spanish Omelet," *Los Angeles Times Cookbook No. 2* (Los Angeles: Times-Mirror, Co., 1905), 7.

"Oeufs à La Christophe Colomb," François Tanty, *La Cuisinier François* (Chicago: Baldwin, Ross & Co, 1893), 67.

"Chocolate Souffle," Maria Parloa, *Chocolate and Cocoa Recipes* (Dorchester, Mass.: Walter Baker & Co, Ltd., 1909), 18.

CHAPTER SEVEN:
CALORIES AND CONSTITUENTS

"Chicken Gelatin," *Good Housekeeping*, August 1917.

"Tomato Gumbo Soup," C. Houston Goudiss and Alberta M. Goudiss, *Foods That Will Win The War and How to Cook Them* (New York: The Forecast Publishing Co., 1918), 115.

"Casserole of Chicken and Rice," Mrs. Ida Bailey Allen, *Woman's World Calendar Cookbook* (Chicago: Woman's World Magazine Co, Inc., 1922), 24.

CHAPTER EIGHT:
THE KOSHER CHICKEN WARS

"Roast Chicken," Florence Kreisler Greenbaum, *The International Jewish Cookbook* (New York: Bloch Publishing Co., 1919), 92.

"Giblet Pudding," in Mrs. Esther Levy, *Jewish Cookery Book on Principles of Economy, Adapted for Jewish Housekeepers, with the addition of many useful medicinal recipes, and other valuable information relative to housekeeping and domestic management*, Originally published in Philadelphia in 1871 (Cambridge, Mass.: Applewood Books, 1988), 57.

"Imitation Chicken Liver," *The Jewish Examiner: Prize Kosher Recipe Book, Volume I*, Edited by "Balabusta" Woman's Page Editor of *The Jewish Examiner* (Brooklyn, NY: The Judea Publishing Corporation, 1937), 20.

CHAPTER NINE:
CELIA STEELE'S MODEST ENDEAVOUR

"Broiler Deluxe Chicken," in *23rd Annual National Chicken Cooking Contest Recipes* (Ocean City, Md.: National Chicken Council, 1971), 55.

"Broiled Chicken," Fannie Merritt Farmer, *Food and Cookery For the Sick and Convalescent* (Boston: Little, Brown and Company, 1904), 145.

"Roast Delmarva Chicken," *23rd Annual National Chicken Cooking Contest Recipes* (Ocean City, Md.: National Chicken Council, 1971), 57.

CHAPTER TEN:
THEY SAW IN HENS A WAY

"Chicken Pilau," New York Herald Tribune Home Institute, *America's Cook Book* (New York: Scribner's Sons, 1943), 307.

"Chicken Pot Pie," *Mrs. Owens' Cookbook and Useful Household Hints* (Chicago: F.E. Owens, 1903), 75.

"Chicken or Turkey Tamales," United States War Department, *Army Recipes* (Washington, D.C.: United States Government Printing Office, 1944), 131.

CHAPTER ELEVEN:
A CHICKEN FOR EVERY GRILL

Chick-N-Que Sauce, *Chick-N-Que Cue Book: 15 Delicious Recipe 'n Menu Ideas from Mazola*, 1960, 1.

"Oven Buttered Barbecued Chicken," *Let's Eat Outdoors: Recipes and Ideas for Picnics, Barbecues, Patio Parties, Camping*, no publication date, est. mid 1950s, 7.

"Chicken Celeste," Tyson's Chicken, *Chicken Just for You* (Des Moines, Iowa: Meredith Publishing Services, 1984), 25.

CHAPTER TWELVE:
A NUGGET WORTH MORE THAN GOLD

"Chicken Crispies," in Robert C. Baker and June M. Darfler, "Minced Chicken: Chicken Crispies," Miscellaneous Bulletin No 110, An Extension Publication of the New York State College of Agriculture and Life Sciences, A Statutory College of the State University, at Cornell University, Ithaca, N.Y., 1981.

"Chick-a-Links," in R. C. Baker, L. B. Darrah, R. J. Benedict, June Darfler, "New Marketable Poultry and Egg Products 18. Chicken Sausage," Departments of Agricultural Economics and Poultry Husbandry Cornell University Agricultural Experiment Station New York State College of Agriculture, A Unit of the State University of New York Cornell University, Ithaca, N.Y., March 1967, A.E. Res. 215.

"Cornell Barbecue Sauce," in "Cornell Chicken Barbecue," Robert Baker Papers, Folder 1.

CHAPTER THIRTEEN:
THE TALE OF THE COLONEL
AND THE GENERAL

General Tso's Chicken, Fuschia Dunlop, *Every Grain of Rice: Simple Chinese Home Cooking* (New York: W.W. Norton & Company, 2013), 12.

Sauteed Chicken Cheng-Tu Style, Fu *Pei Mei,*

Pei Mei's Chinese Cook Book (Cheng & Tsui, 1969), 133.

Buffalo Chicken Wings, From *Saveur*, October 18, 2013. Available online at: http://www .saveur.com/article/Recipes/Buffalo-Wings

CHAPTER FOURTEEN:
THE MODERN CHICKEN

Tarragon and Lemon Roast Chicken, Donna Hay, *The New Easy* (New York: HarperCollins, 2015), available online at: http://www .epicurious.com/recipes/food/views/tarragon- and-lemon-roast-chicken-56390090.

Photography Permissions

An Artist's Rendering of the popular "Cochin-China" Fowl from the Hen Fever, 1855. George P. Burnham, *The History of the Hen Fever: a Humorous Record.* Boston: J. French & Company, 1855, 18.

Lithograph of a Nineteenth Century Poultry Yard, 1869. Library of Congress, Prints & Photographs Division, FSA/OWI Collection, reproduction number, LC-DIG-pga-04977.

Mechanized Slaughter Facility, 1904. Ferdinand Ellsworth Cary, *The Complete Library of Universal Knowledge* (Chicago, 1904).

"Uncle Sam Expects You to Keep Hens and Raise Chickens," 1917. United States Department of Agriculture, "Uncle Sam Expects You to Keep Hens and Raise Chicken," *Poultry Tribune* 21, no. 1, September 1917, 54.

Chicks with and without Leg Weakness, the disease that made it difficult to raise chickens in the winter, 1920. Hart, E.B., J.G. Halpin, and H. Steenbock, "Use of Synthetic Diets in the Growth of Baby Chicks: A Study of Leg Weakness in Chickens," *Journal of Biological Chemistry*, no. 43 (June 1920), Appendix I.

A Young Girl in Charleston Feeds Her Chickens, 1921. Library of Congress, Prints & Photographs Division, FSA/OWI Collection, reproduction number, LC-DIG-nclc-04443.

A Poultry Scientist Working for the United States Department of Agriculture Continues Her Work to Rid America's Chickens of Parasites, 1930. Library of Congress, Prints & Photographs Division, FSA/OWI Collection, reproduction number, LC-DIG-hec-14523.

A Farm Family Prepares Chickens for Canning, 1936. Library of Congress, Prints & Photographs Division, FSA/OWI Collection, reproduction number, LC-DIG-fsa-8b29985.

Celia Steele Vaccinating Chickens, 1936. Reproduced with permission from the Delaware Public Archives.

A Broiler Shed in Indiana Capable of Housing Just 40 Chickens, 1937. Library of Congress, Prints & Photographs Division, FSA/OWI Collection, reproduction number, LC-USF-341-T-010513-B.

A Chicken Vendor at a Farmer's Market in Weatherford, Texas, 1939. Library of Congress, Prints & Photographs Division, FSA/OWI Collection, reproduction number, LC-USF33-012280-M1.

The Rolling Hills of Petaluma, California Dotted with Chicken Houses and Leghorn Chickens, 1942. Library of Congress, Prints & Photographs Division, FSA/OWI Collection, reproduction number, LC-USF34-071306-D.

A Woman Candles Eggs At a Factory in Petaluma to Make Sure No Chicken Embryos are Developing Inside, 1942. Library of Congress, Prints & Photographs Division, FSA/OWI Collection, reproduction number, LC-USF34-071275-D.

A Man Places Sheets of Eggs into an Incubator to Be Hatched, 1942. Library of Congress, Prints & Photographs Division, FSA/OWI Collection, reproduction number, LC-USF34-071306-D071322-D.

A Man Determines the Sex of Chicks At a Petaluma Hatchery, 1943. Library of Congress, Prints & Photographs Division, FSA/OWI Collection, reproduction number, LC-USF34-071322-D.

A Flock of White Leghorns in a Yard in Petaluma, California, 1942. Library of Congress, Prints & Photographs Division, FSA/OWI Collection, reproduction number, LC-USF34-071324-D.

A Live Poultry Inspector in New York City Makes Sure a Chicken's Crop Hasn't Been Stuffed Full of Sand and Corn, 1951. Library of Congress, Prints & Photographs Division, FSA/OWI Collection, reproduction number, LC-DIG-ppmsca-12730.

Poultry Scientists Inspect Chicken Carcasses for Quality, 1960s. Reproduced with Permission from Cornell University, Rare and Manuscript Collections.

Chicken Carcass Being Plucked By Machine, 1960s. Reproduced with Permission from Cornell University, Rare and Manuscript Collections.

Stages in Chicken Processing from Bird to Cellophane, 1960s. Reproduced with Permission from Cornell University, Rare and Manuscript Collections.

Dr. Robert Baker, 1963. Reproduced with Permission from Cornell University, Rare and Manuscript Collections.

Dr. Baker Watching Chicken Parts Being Breaded by Machine, Early 1980s. Reproduced with Permission from Cornell University, Rare and Manuscript Collections.

Two of Robert Baker's Groundbreaking Value-Added Chicken Products: Chickalona and Chicken Bologna. Reproduced with Permission from Cornell University, Rare and Manuscript Collections.

Dr. Robert Baker's Chic-A-Links. Reproduced with Permission from Cornell University, Rare and Manuscript Collections.

Dr. Robert Baker's Chicken Hash. Reproduced with Permission from Cornell University, Rare and Manuscript Collections.

Chicken Crispies in Action in the Late 1970s. Reproduced with Permission from Cornell University, Rare and Manuscript Collections.

Lines of Cooks Grilling Up Robert Baker's Famous Cornell Chicken at the Annual

Cornell University Summer Barbecue in 1953. Both images reproduced with Permission from Cornell University, Rare and Manuscript Collections.

Broiler Shed in the 1960s. Both images reproduced with Permission from Cornell University, Rare and Manuscript Collections.

Young Chicks in a Poultry House in Pennsylvania, 1960s. Reproduced with Permission from Cornell University, Rare and Manuscript Collections.

The Inconspicuous Outside of a 1960s Broiler Shed. Reproduced with Permission from Cornell University, Rare and Manuscript Collections.

Brahma Hen. American Poultry Association, *The American Standard of Perfection: a Complete Description of All Recognized Varieties of Fowls* (Rochester, NY: American Poultry Association, 1906).

Brahma Rooster. American Poultry Association, *The American Standard of Perfection: a Complete Description of All Recognized Varieties of Fowls* (Rochester, NY: American Poultry Association, 1906).

Buff Orpington Female. American Poultry Association, *The American Standard of Perfection: a Complete Description of All Recognized Varieties of Fowls* (Rochester, NY: American Poultry Association, 1906).

Buff Orpington Male. American Poultry Association, *The American Standard of Perfection: a Complete Description of All Recognized Varieties of Fowls* (Rochester, NY: American Poultry Association, 1906).

Buff Plymouth Rock Female. American Poultry Association, *The American Standard of Perfection: a Complete Description of All Recognized Varieties of Fowls* (Rochester, NY: American Poultry Association, 1906).

Buff Plymouth Rock Male. American Poultry Association, *The American Standard of Perfection: a Complete Description of All Recognized Varieties of Fowls* (Rochester, NY: American Poultry Association, 1906).

Dominique Hen. American Poultry Association, *The American Standard of Perfection: a Complete Description of All Recognized Varieties of Fowls* (Rochester, NY: American Poultry Association, 1906).

Dominique Rooster. American Poultry Association, *The American Standard of Perfection: A Complete Description of All Recognized Varieties of Fowls* (Rochester, NY: American Poultry Association, 1906).

Silver Penciled Wyandotte Female. American Poultry Association, *The American Standard of Perfection: A Complete Description of All Recognized Varieties of Fowls* (Rochester, NY: American Poultry Association, 1906).

Silver Penciled Wyandotte Male. American Poultry Association, *The American Standard of Perfection: A Complete Description of All Recognized Varieties of Fowls* (Rochester, NY: American Poultry Association, 1906).

Silver-Gray Dorking Female. American Poultry Association, *The American Standard of Perfection: A Complete Description of All Recognized Varieties of Fowls* (Rochester, NY: American Poultry Association, 1906).

Silver-Gray Dorking Male. American Poultry Association, *The American Standard of Perfection: A Complete Description of All Recognized Varieties of Fowls* (Rochester, NY: American Poultry Association, 1906).

White Leghorn Hen. American Poultry Association, *The American Standard of Perfection: A Complete Description of All Recognized Varieties of Fowls* (Rochester, NY: American Poultry Association, 1906).

White Leghorn Rooster. American Poultry Association, *The American Standard of Perfection: A Complete Description of All Recognized Varieties of Fowls* (Rochester, NY: American Poultry Association, 1906).

Bibliography

DATABASES, COLLECTIONS, & WEBSITES

Feeding America: The Historic American Cookbook Project at Michigan State University

Food and Agriculture Organization (www.fao.org)

Google News

Google Newspaper Archive

HEARTH Home Economics Archive at Cornell University

James W. Gwin Poultry Collection at the National Agricultural Library

JSTOR

Library of Congress Digital Newspaper Archive

National Institute of Health

Schlesinger Library Cookbook Collection

The Robert Baker Papers at the Cornell University Rare Manuscripts Collection

Wattagg.net

PERIODICALS AND NEWSPAPERS

Good Housekeeping

National Geographic Magazine

Poultry Science

The Chicago Tribune

The New York Times

The Wall Street Journal

The Washington Post
TIME Magazine

OTHER PRIMARY & SECONDARY SOURCES

"60,000 Eggs a Day." *Journal of Photography of the George Eastman House* 4, no. 4 (April 1955).

"Antibiotics now Proved in Hog and Poultry Ratios, They're the Biggest Feeding News in 40 Years!" *Successful Farming* 49, no. 3 (March 1951).

"Dangerous Contaminated Chicken." *Consumer Reports*, updated January 2014. www.consumer reports.org. 22 March 2016.

"Easter" *The Oxford Companion to Food and Drink*, ed. Andrew F. Smith. New York: Oxford University Press, 2007.

"Editorial." *Everybody's Poultry Magazine*. Hanover, PA: Everybody's Poultry Magazine Publishing Company, 1917.

"Egyptian Egg Oven." *The Penny Magazine of the Society for the Diffusion of Useful Knowledge, Volume 2*. London: Charles Knight, 1833.

"History of Sussex County: Celia Steele & the Broiler Industry." www.sussexcountyde.gov. January 17, 2012.

"Housewives Should Buy Chickens Undrawn." *American Food Journal* (January 1915).

"Massachusetts Correspondence." *American Food Journal* (January 1915).

"Mr. Blaine's Health." *LIFE Magazine.* Volume 11, 1888.

"Petaluma Pioneer, Samuel A. Nay, Dies." *San Francisco Call*, February 1912.

"The Chicken First." *American Food Journal* 13, no. 4 (April 1918).

"The Cult of the McRib." *MAXIM.* 3 February 2009.

"The Egg Reporter—B. Baff Murdered." *Poultry Processing and Marketing.* Watt Publishing Company, 1914, Vol. 20.

"To Kill and Bleed Poultry." *American Food Journal*, February 1914.

"UPC Pressure Pays!" *Poultry Press*, Spring 1996. www.upc-online.org. 12 March 2014.

"Weighing Chickens with Sand." *American Food Journal*, February 1914.

"Weighing Chickens with Sand." *American Food Journal.* February 1915.

"Wonderful Growth of Poultry Industry." *Reliable Poultry Journal.* Quincy, Illinois, Reliable Poultry Journal Publishing, Co.,1899.

Ackerknecht, Erwin H. "The End of Greek Diet." *Bulletin of the History of Medicine* 45, no. 3 (1971): 242–249.

Adler, Jerry and Andrew Lawler. "How the Chicken Conquered the World." *Smithsonian Magazine.* June 2012.

Agricultural Experiment Stations of Alabama, Arkansas, Georgia, Louisiana, Mississippi, North Carolina, South Carolina, Tennessee, Texas, and Virginia, and Agricultural Marketing Service. "Financing Production and Marketing of Broilers in the South." *Southern Cooperative Series Bulletin* 38 (June 1954).

Ahrens, Richard A. "Mary Shaw Shorb (1907–1990)." *The Journal of Nutrition* 123, (1993): 791–796.

Albala, Ken. "Ovophilia in Renaissance Cuisine." *Eggs in Cookery: Proceedings of the Oxford Syposium of Food and Cookery*, ed. Richard Hosking. 2007.

Alcott, William A. "Vegetarianism in the United States." *Vegetarian Advocate*, April 1850.

—————. *The Physiology of Marriage.* Boston: J.P. Jewett, 1856.

—————. *The Vegetable Diet: As Sanctioned by Medical Men, and by Experience in All Ages.* Boston: Marsh, Capen, & Lyon, 1838.

—————. *The Young Woman's Guide to Excellence.* Boston: Waite, Pierce, & Company, 1845.

Aldrovandi, Ulisse. *Aldrovandi on Chickens: The Ornithology of Ulisse Aldrovandi (1600), Volume II, Book XIV*, trans. L.R. Lind. Norman, Okla.: University of Oklahoma Press, 1968.

Alexander, Dennis J. "A Review of Avian Influenza in Different Bird Species." *Veterinary Microbiology* 74 (May 2000): 3–13.

Alvarado, C. Z., E. Wenger, and S.F. O'Keefe. "Consumer Perceptions of Meat Quality and Shelf-Life in Commercially Raised Broilers Compared to Organic Free Range Broilers." VXIIth European Symposium on the Quality of Poultry Meat, Doorwerth, The Netherlands, 23–26 May 2005, 257–261.

American Egg Board. "History of Egg Production." www.aeb.org. 21 August 2015.

American Federation of Labor. *Some Reasons for Chinese Exclusion: Meat v. Rice; American Manhood against Asiatic Coolieism, Which Shall Survive?* Washington, D.C.: Government Printing Office, 1902.

American Poultry Association. *The American Standard of Perfection, illustrated. A Complete Description of All Recognized Varieties of Fowls.* Boston, 1910.

Anderson, Virginia de John. *Creatures of Empire: How Domesticated Animals Transformed Early America.* Oxford: Oxford University Press, 2004.

—————. "King Philip's Herds: Indians, Colonists, and the Problem of Livestock in Early New England." *William and Mary Quarterly* 3, no. 51 (October 1994).

Arumugam, Nadia. "The Dark Side of the Bird." *Slate*. 16 January 2011.

Atwater, Wilber O. "Percentages and Costs of Nutrients in Foods." *Proceedings of the American Association for the Advancement of Science* 33 (1884).

—————. "The Chemistry of Foods and Nutrition. I. The Composition of Our Bodies and of Our Food." *Century Magazine* 34 (1887).

Baker, Michael. "How 'Barbecue Bob' Baker Transformed Chicken." *Ezra: Cornell's Quarterly Magazine* 4, no. 4 (Summer 2012).

Baker, Peter. "The Seduction of George W. Bush." *Foreign Policy*, 6 November 2013.

Bass, Jonathan S. "How 'Bout a Hand for the Hog'; The Enduring Nature of the Swine As a Cultural Symbol in the South." *Southern Cultures* 1, no. 3 (Spring 1995).

Bateson, W., and E.R. Saunders. "Experiments with Poultry." *Report to the Evolution Committee of the Royal Society, vol. 1.* London, 1902.

Batra, Rajeev, John G. Myers, and David A. Aaker. *Advertising Management, Fifth Edition.* Delhi, India: Pearson Education, 2006.

Beard, James. *American Cookery.* Boston: Little, Brown, and Company, 1972.

Beecher, Lyman. *The Autobiography, Correspondence, etc., of Lyman Beecher, D.D.* New York: Harper & Brothers, 1866.

Belasco, Warren. *Meals to Come: A History of the Future of Food.* Berkeley: University of California Press, 2006.

Bentley, Amy. "American Abundance Examined: David M. Potter's *People of Plenty* and the Study of Food." www.steinhardt.nyu.edu, 16 November 2011.

Berry, Wendell. "The Pleasures of Eating." *The Art of the Commonplace: The Agrarian Essays of Wendell Berry*, ed. Norman Wirzba, 520–528. Berkeley, Calif.: Counterpoint Press, 2002.

Blaine, James G. *James G. Blaine: A Sketch of his Life*, ed. Charles Wolcott Balestier. New York: R. Worthington, 1884.

Blavatsky, Helena Petrovna. *Isis Unveiled.* New York: J.W. Bouton, 1892.

Bodely, John. *The Power of Scale: A Global History Approach.* Armonk, N.Y.: M.E. Sharpe, Inc., 2003.

Boyd, William and Michael Watts. "Agro-Industrial Just-In-Time: The Chicken Industry and Postwar American Capitalism." *Globalising Food: Agrarian Questions and Global Restructuring*, eds. David Goodman and Michael Watts. Routledge: London, 1997.

Boyd, William. "Making Meat: Science, Technology, and American Poultry Production." *Technology and Culture* 42, no. 2 (October 2001): 631–664.

Bratley, Hazel. "Have You Had Your Eggs Today." *Timely Poultry Topic, Volume 2*, Louisiana State University and Agricultural and Mechanical College Division of Agricultural Extension, 1914.

Braudel, Fernand. *Capitalism and Material Life, 1400–1800*. Glasgow: Fontana/William Collins, 1975.

Bright, William. *American Indian Linguistics and Literature*. Berlin: Walter de Gruyter & Co, 1984.

Brillat-Savarin, Jean Anthelme. *The Physiology of Taste, or Meditations on Transcendental Gastronomy*, trans. M.F.K. Fisher. New York: Harper Books, 2011.

Brock, H. William. *Justus von Liebig: The Chemical Gatekeeper*. Cambridge: Cambridge University Press, 2002.

Brogi, Alessandro. *Confronting America: the Cold War Between the United States and the Communists in France and Italy*. Chapel Hill: University of North Carolina Press, 2011.

Brookings, Florence E. "Helping a Community to Conserve." *Journal of Home Economics* 9, no. 5 (May 1917).

Brown, S.N., G.R. Nute, A. Baker, S.I. Hughes, and P.D. Warriss. "Aspects of Meat and Eating Quality of Broiler Chickens Reared Under Standard, Maize-Fed, Free-Range, or Organic

Systems." *British Poultry Science* 49, no. 2 (2008): 118–124.

Brumberg, Joan Jacobs. *Fasting Girls: The History of Anorexia Nervosa*. New York: Plume, 1989.

Buchan, William. *Domestic Medicine: or, a Treatise on the Prevention and Cure of Diseases by Regimen and Simple Medicines. With an Appendix, Containing a Dispensatory for the Use of Private Practitioners, Eleventh Edition*. London: A. Strahan, 1790.

Bugos, Glenn E. "Intellectual Property Protection in the American Chicken-Breeding Industry." *Business History Review* 66, no.1 (Spring 1992): 127–168.

Bulliet, Richard. *Hunters, Herders, and Hamburgers: The Past and Future of Animal-Human Relationships*. New York: Columbia University Press, 2005.

Burnham, George P. *The History of Hen Fever: A Humorous Record*. Boston: James French and Company, 1855.

Cansler, Clay. "Where's the Beef?" *Chemical Heritage Magazine* (Fall 2013/Winter 2014).

Carpenter, Kenneth J. "The Life and Times of Wilbur O. Atwater (1844–1907)." *Journal of Nutrition* (1994): 1707S–1714S.

Carpenter, Kenneth J. and Barbara Sutherland. "Eijkman's Contribution to the Discovery of Vitamins." *The Journal of Nutrition* 125, no. 2 (February 1995): 155–163.

Carter, Donna K. "Preventing Avian Influenza in Backyard Poultry Flocks." North Carolina State University Department of Poultry Science, www.ces.ncsu.edu, 18 February 2016.

Cary, Ferdinand Ellsworth. *The Complete Library of Universal Knowledge.* Chicago, 1904.

Chandonnet, Ann. *Gold Rush Grub: From Turpentine Stew to Hoochinoo.* Fairbanks, Ak.: University of Alaska Press, 2006.

Charles, Dan. "Tyson Foods to Stop Giving Chickens Antibiotics Used by Humans." *National Public Radio*, www.npr.org, 18 April 2015.

——————. "The System Supplying America's Chickens Pits Farmer Vs Famer." *National Public Radio*, 20 February 2014.

Chen, Yong. *Chop Suey, USA: The Story of Chinese Food in America.* New York: Columbia University Press, 2014.

Cheyne, George. *Essay on Regimen.* London: C. Rivington, 1740.

Cheyne, George. *The English Malady.* London: G. Strahan, 1733.

Chinese American Restaurant Association. "About." www.ca-ra.com, 15 February 2016.

Columbus, Christopher. *The Log of Christopher Columbus*, trans. Robert H. Fuson. Camden, Maine: International Marine Publishing Company, 1987.

Churchill, Winston. "Fifty Years Hence." *Strand Magazine*, December 1931.

Clark, Thomas D. *Gold Rush Diary: Being the Journal of Elisha Douglas Perkins on the Overland Trail in the Spring and Summer of 1849*. University Press of Kentucky, 2015.

Cleland, Robert F. "Cattle on a Thousand Hills." *Green Versus Gold: Sources in California's Environmental History*, ed. Carolyn Merchant. Washington, D.C.: Island Press, 1998.

Coghan, Thomas. *The Haven of Health*. London: Printed by Anne Griffin, for Roger Ball, 1636.

Columella, L. *Junius Moderatus. Of Husbandry in Twelve Books and His Book Concerning Trees*. London: A. Millar, 1745.

Comenius, J.A. Cited in Steven Shapin, "Vegetarianism: Meat, Mind, and Morality." *History of Science* (16 October 2010): 153.

Conlin, Joseph. *Bacon, Beans and Galantines: Food and Foodways on the Western Mining Frontier*. Reno, Nev.: University of Nevada Press, 1987.

Cook, Doug. "White Meat Versus Dark Meat: Is there a Difference Nutritionally?" *Chicken Producers of Alberta*, www.chicken.ab.ca, 26 March 2016.

Crawford, John. *On the Relation of the Domesticated Animals to Civilisation*.

Crews, Ed. "Once Popular and Socially Acceptable:

Cockfighting." *Colonial Williamsburg Journal* (Autumn 2008).

Critchley, David. *The Origin of Organized Crime in America: The New York City Mafia, 1891–1930*. New York: Routledge, 2009.

Crockett, Albert S. "Hearty Eaters." *Saturday Evening Post*, 26 October 1929.

Cronon, William. *Changes in the Land: Indians, Colonists, and the Ecology of New England*. New York: Douglas & McIntyre, Ltd., 1983.

——————. *Nature's Metropolis*. New York: W.W. Norton and Co., 1991.

Crosby, Alfred W. *The Columbian Exchange: Biological and Cultural Consequences of 1492*. Westport, Conn., 1972.

Curtis, Grant M. "Use of Artificial Light to Increase Winter Egg Production." Quincy, Ill.: Reliable Poultry Journal Publishing Company, 1920.

Dahl, Arthur L. "Interesting." *Sunset: The Magazine of the Pacific and of All the Far West*, July–December 1920.

Darwin, Charles. *The Variation of Animals and Plants Under Domestication, vol. 1*. New York: Cambridge University Press, 2010.

——————. *The Variation of Animals and Plants Under Domestication, vol. 2*. New York: D. Appleton and Company, 1898.

Davies, Pete. "The Plague in Waiting." *The Guardian*, 7 August 1999.

Davis, William C. *A Taste for War: The Culinary History of the Blue and the Gray.* Mechanicsburg, Pa.: Stackpole Books, 2003.

de Reamur, Rene. *The Art of Hatching and Bringing Up Domestic Fowl.* London: C. Davis, 1750.

Defoe, Daniel. "The True-Born Englishman." *The Works of Daniel Defoe*, eds. George Chalmers and Sir John Scot Keltie. Edinburgh: William P. Nimmo, 1870.

Delgado, Christopher L. "Rising Consumption of Meat and Milk in Developing Countries Has Created a New Food Revolution." *The Journal of Nutrition* 133, no. 11 (1 November 2003): 3907S–3910S.

Derry, Margaret E. *Breeding Animals, 1750–2010.* Toronto, Ont.: University of Toronto Press, 2015.

Deutsch, Larry L., ed. *Industry Studies, 3rd Edition.* Armonk, N.Y.: M.E, Sharpe, Inc., 2002.

Dixon, Rev. Edmund Saul. *A Treatise on the History and Management of Ornamental and Domestic Poultry, Second Edition.* Philadelphia: E.H. Butler and Co., 1851.

Donovan, Robert J. *Conflict and Crisis: the Presidency of Harry S. Truman.* New York: W.W. Norton Co., 1977.

Doughty, Robin W. "San Francisco's Nineteenth Century Egg Basket: The Farallons."

Geographical Review 61, no. 4 (October 1971): 554–572.

Dubner, Stephen J. "Beef or Chicken? A Look at U.S. Meat Trends in the Last Century." 9 December 2010. www.freakonomics.com. 26 September 2011.

Dyck, John H., and Kenneth E. Nelson. "Structure of the Global Markets for Meat." United States Department of Agriculture, Economic Research Service, Market and Trade Economics Division. *Agriculture Information Bulletin No. 785.*

Dyubele, N.L., V. Muchenje, T.T. Nkukwana, and M. Chimonyo. "Consumer Sensory Characteristics of Broiler and Indigenous Chickens: A South African Example." *Food Quality and Preference* 21, no. 7 (October 2010): 815–819.

Ebos, W.F., R.H. Holmes, and J. Beyer. "Coronary Disease Amongst United States Soldiers Killed in Action in Korea." *Journal of the American Medical Association* 152 (1953): 1090–1093.

Elias, Norbert. *The Civilizing Process.* Oxford: Malden-Blackwell Publishers, 1994.

Elyot, Thomas. *The Castle of Health.* London, 1539.

Entis, Laura. "Will the Worst Bird Flu Outbreak in US History Finally Make Us Reconsider Factory Farming Chicken?" *The Guardian*, 14 July 2015.

Eveleigh, David. " 'Put Down to a Clear Bright Fire': The English Tradition of Open-Fire Roasting." *Folk Life* 19 (1990–91).

Evelyn, John. *Acetaria: A Discourse of Sallets.* London: Printed for B. Tooke at the Middle-Temple Gate in Fleetstreet, 1699.

Fanatico, Anne. "Organic Poultry Production in the United States." ATTRA—National Sustainable Agriculture Information Service, 2008.

Farber, Steven A. "U.S. Scientists' Role in the Eugenics Movement (1907–1939): A Contemporary Perspective." *Zebrafish* 5, no. 4 (December 2008): 243–245.

Farmer, Fannie Mae. *Boston Booking School Cookbook.* Boston: Little, Brown, & Company, 1896.

Fessenden, Thomas Green. *The New England Farmer* 6 (1828).

Fichera, Sebastian. *Italy on the Pacific: San Francisco's Italian Americans.* New York: Palgrave MacMillan, 2011.

Fletcher, Horace. *Fletcherism: What Is It? Or, How I Became Young At 60.* 1913.

Foer, Jonathan Safran. *Eating Animals.* New York: Little, Brown and Company, 2009.

Food and Drug Administration, Department of Health and Human Services. "Summary Report on Antimicrobials Sold or Distributed for Use in Food-Producing Animals." www.fda.gov, 24 February 2016.

Fraser, Steve. *The Age of Acquiescence: The Life and Death of American Resistance to Organized Wealth and Power*. Boston: Little Brown and Company, 2015.

Frost, Robert. "Trap Nests." *The Collected Prose of Robert Frost*, ed. Mark Richardson, 35–37. Cambridge, Mass.: Belknap Press, 2007.

Funk, M. "Hatcheries." *American Poultry History: 1823–1973*, ed. John L Skinner. United States: American Poultry Historical Society, 1974.

Galen. *Galen on Food and Diet*, ed. Mark Grant. London: Routledge, 2000.

Garrison, W.P. "The Isms of Forty Years Ago." *Harper's New Monthly Magazine* 60, no. 356, (January 1880): 182–193.

Gaswirt, Harold P. *Fraud, Corruption, and Holiness: The Controversy over the Supervision of Jewish Dietary Practice in New York City 1881–1940*. Fort Washington, N.Y.: Kennikat Press, 1974.

Georgia Poultry Times, 17 February 1954.

Giedion, Siegfried. *Mechanization Takes Command: A Contribution to Anonymous History*. London: Oxford University Press, 1948.

Goody, Jack. *Cooking, Cuisine, and Class*. Cambridge: Cambridge University Press, 1982.

Gordon, John Steele. "The Chicken Story." *American Heritage*, September 1996.

Gordy, J. Frank. "Broilers." *American Poultry History: 1823–1973*, ed. John L Skinner. United States: American Poultry Historical Society, 1974.

Graham, Sylvester. *Philosophy of Sacred History.* London: Horsell & Caudwell, 1859.

Gray, Lewis Cecil. *History of Agriculture in the Southern United States to 1860.* Glouchester, Mass.: Peter Smith, 1958.

Gray, Robin. Agricultural Attaché to Moscow. Email, 2016.

Griffin, Emma. "Sports and Celebrations in English Market Towns, 1660–1750." *Historical Research* 75, no. 188 (May 2002): 188–208.

Grimes, William. *Appetite City: a Culinary History of New York.* New York: North Point Press, 2009.

H. Chen, et al., "Establishment of Multiple Sublineages of H5N1 Influenza Virus in Asia: Implications for Pandemic Control," *Proceedings of the National Academy of Sciences of the United States of America* 103, no. 8, 2845–2850.

Hagen, Ann. *A Second Handbook of Anglo-Saxon Food and Drink: Production and Distribution.* Norfolk, Va.: Anglo-Saxon Books, 2002.

Hargrove, James L. "History of the Calorie in Nutrition." *Journal of Nutrition* 136, no. 12 (December 2006): 2957–2961.

Harris, Marvin. *Good to Eat*. Long Grove, Ill.: Waveland Press, 1985.

Hart, E.B., H. Steenbock, S. Lepkovsky, and J.G. Halpin. "The Nutritional Requirements of Baby Chicks III: The Relation of Light to the Growth of Chickens." *Journal of Biological Chemistry*, no. 58 (1923): 33–42.

Hart, E.B., J.G. Halpin, and H. Steenbock. "Use of Synthetic Diets in the Growth of Baby Chicks: A Study of Leg Weakness in Chickens." *Journal of Biological Chemistry*, no. 43 (June 1920): 421–442.

Hays, Willet M. "Address to the First Meeting of the American Breeder's Association." *Proceedings of the American Breeders' Association, vol. 1*. Washington, D.C., 1905.

Hays, Willet M. "American Work in Breeding Plants and Animals." *Proceedings of the American Breeders' Association, vol. 2*. Washington, D.C., 1906.

Heig, Adair. *History of Petaluma: A California River Town*. Petaluma, Calif.: Scotwall Associates, 1982.

Henry, Richard, and Graeme Rothwell. "The World Poultry Industry." World Bank (1995).

Hoge, Tim. "Meat Pot Pie Has a Colorful History." *Los Angeles Times*, 5 July 1985.

Horowitz, Roger. *Putting Meat on the American Table: Taste, Technology, Transformation*.

Baltimore, Md.: Johns Hopkins University Press, 2006.

Hudson, Nicola. "Food in Roman Satire." *Satire and Society in Ancient Rome*, ed. Susan H. Braund. Exeter, England: University of Exeter Press, 1989.

Hunt, Carolina L., and Helen W. Atwater. *How to Select Foods*. Washington, D.C.: Government Printing Office, 1917.

Hunt, William R. *Body Love: The Amazing Career of Bernarr Macfadden*. Bowling Green, Ohio: Bowling Green State University Popular Press, 1989.

Husak, Ryan Lon. "A Survey of Commercially Available Broilers Originating from Organic, Free-Range and Conventional Production Systems for Cooked Meat Yields, Meat Composition and Relative Value." *Retrospective These and Dissertations* 50 (2007), Paper 14523.

Hutchinson, Woods. "Some Diet Delusions." *McLure's Magazine*, April 1906.

Jakle, John A., and Keith A. Sculle. *Fast Food: Roadside Restaurants in the Automobile Age*. Baltimore, Md.: Johns Hopkins University Press, 1999.

Jefferson, Thomas. *Farm Book, 1774–1824*. www.masshist.org. 8 January 2016.

—————. *Notes on the State of Virginia*. Richmond, Va.: J.W. Randolf, 1853.

Jeon, HJ., J.H. Choe, Y. Jung, Z.A. Kruk, D.G. Lim, and C. Jo. "Comparison of the Chemical Composition, Textural Characteristics, and Sensory Properties of North and South Korean Native Chickens and Commercial Broilers." *Korean Journal of Food Science* 30 (2010): 171–178.

Johnson, Samuel. *A Dictionary of the English Language.* London: Printed for T.T. and J. Eggs, 1833.

Joselit, Jenna Weissman. *Our Gang: Jewish Crime and the New York Jewish Community, 1900–1940.* Bloomington: Indiana University Press, 1983.

Kane, Marion. "Nugget Man." PRX, www.prx.org.

Keating, Joshua. "Playing Chicken." *Slate,* 7 August 2015.

Kellogg, J.H. *Pork—or the Dangers of Pork-Eating Exposed.* Battle Creek, Mich.: Good Health Publishing Company, 1897.

Ketchum, Alton. "The Search for Uncle Sam." *History Today,* April 1990.

KFC. "About." www.kfc.com, 28 August 2015.

————. "Colonel Sanders." www.colonel sanders.com, 5 June 2015.

Kollatz, Harry. *True Richmond Stories: Historic Tales from Virginia's Capital.* Charleston, S.C.: The History Press, 2007.

Lam, Francis. "What Do 'Free Range,' 'Organic'

and Other Chicken Labels Really Mean?" *Salon.com.* 20 January 2011.

Lawler, Andrew. *Why Did the Chicken Cross the World: The Epic Saga of the Bird that Powers Civilization.* New York: Atria Books, 2014.

Lee, Jennifer. *The Fortune Cookie Chronicles.*

Leonard, Christopher. *The Meat Racket: the Secret Takeover of America's Food Business.* New York: Simon & Schuster, 2014.

Levenstein, Harvey. "The Perils of Abundance: Food, Health, and Morality in American History." *Food: A Culinary History*, eds. Jean-Louis Flandrid and Massimo Montanaro, 516–530. New York: Columbia University Press, 1996.

——————. *Paradox of Plenty.* New York: Oxford University Press, 1993.

——————. *Revolution at the Table.* New York: Oxford University Press, 1988.

Lewis, Harry. "America's Debt to the Hen." *National Geographic*, April 1927.

Li, Wang, and Chris Frederick. "China's Poultry Demand Remains Sluggish." United States Department of Agriculture, Foreign Agricultural Service, *GAIN Report.* 26 February 2015.

Liebig, Justus von. *Animal Chemistry, or Organic Chemistry in Its Application to Physiology and Pathology.* Cambridge: John Owen, 1843.

—————. *Researches on the Chemistry of Food*. London: Taylor and Walton, 1847.

Linshi, Jack. "How Did the Chicken Cross the Pacific? Kentucky Fried Chicken's Appeal to China's Culinary Tradition in Creating Its Fast Food Empire." *Yale Review of International Studies* (May 2014).

Litton, Timothy D. *Kosher: Private Regulation in the Age of Industrial Food*. Cambridge, Mass.: Harvard University Press, 2013.

Liu, Warren K. *KFC in China: Secret Recipe for Success*. Singapore: John Wiley & Sons, 2008.

Longman, N.Y.E. "U.S. and South Africa in AGOA Chicken Trade Row." *African Business Review* (18 February 2015).

Louisiana State Agriculture Center. "Seasonal Price and Production Influences in the Broiler Chicken Industry." www.lsuagcenter.com, 24 February 2016.

Love, John F. *McDonald's: Behind the Arches*. New York: Bantam Books, 1986.

Lowry, Thea. *Empty Shells: The Story of Petaluma, America's Chicken City*. Novato, Calif.: Manifold Press, 2000.

MacDonald, Betty. *The Egg and I*. New York: J.B. Lippincott Company, 1945.

MacDonald, James M. "The Economic Organization of U.S. Broiler Production." United States Department of Agriculture, *Economic Information Bulletin* No. 38, June 2008.

Maragon, S and L. Busani, "The Use of Vaccination in Poultry Production," *Scientific and Technical Review of the Office International des Epizooties* 26, no. 1 (2006): 265–274.

Marshall, Bonnie M., and Stuart B. Levy. "Food Animals and Antimicrobials: Impacts on Human Health." *Clinical Microbiology Review* 24, no. 7 (October 2011): 718–733.

Martin, Denise. "Birds." *Encyclopedia of African Religion, Vol. 1.*, eds. Molefi Kete Asante, Ama Mazama. SAGE Publications, 2009.

Marx, Leo. *The Machine in the Garden: Technology and the Pastoral Ideal in America.* Oxford: Oxford University Press, 1964.

Maximus Valerius. *Memorable Deeds and Sayings: One Thousand Tales from Ancient Rome*, trans. Henry John Walker. Indianapolis, Ind.: Hackett Publishing Company, 2004.

May, Robert. "The Accomplisht Cook or, The Art & Mystery of Cookery." 1671.

McAdams, Christine. "Frank Perdue Is Chicken." *Esquire*, April 1973.

McDonald's Corporation. "McDonald's USA Nutrition Facts for Popular Menu Items." www.nutrition.mcdonalds.com, 29 August 2015.

——————. "The Ray Kroc Story." www.mcdonalds.com, 4 February 2012.

McKenna, Maryn. "The Father of the Chicken Nugget." *Slate*, 28 December 2012.

McMahon, Sarah F. "A Comfortable Subsistence: The Changing Composition of Diet in Rural New England, 1620–1840." *The William and Mary Quarterly* 42, no. 1 (January 1985): 26–65.

McWilliams, James E. *A Revolution in Eating.* New York: Columbia University Press, 2005.

Meinig, D.W. *The Shaping of America: A Geographical Perspective on 500 Years of History.* New Haven, Conn.: Yale University Press, 2004.

Merton, Thomas. *New English Canaan, in The Literature of Colonial America: An Anthology,* eds. Susan Castillo and Ivy Schweitzer. Oxford: Malden-Blackwell Publishers Ltd., 2002.

Michael, Marvin L., Lorin Kay, and Lee Cary. *Slavery in North Carolina, 1748–1775.* Chapel Hill: University of North Carolina Press, 2000.

Miller, Adrian. *Soul Food: The Surprising Story of an American Cuisine, One Plate At a Time.* Chapel Hill: University of North Carolina Press, 2013.

Miller, Joseph A. "Contracting in Agriculture: Potential Problems." *Drake Journal of Agricultural Law* 8 (2003).

Mills, John. *A Treatise on Cattle.* Dublin: Printed for W. Whitestone, J. Potts, J. Hoey, W. Colles, W. Wilson, R. Moncrieffe, T. Walker, C. Jenkin, and C. Talbot, 1776.

Mizelle, Brett. *Pig*. London: Reaktion Books, 2011.

Modell, John. *Family Budget Study* [computer file]: *Massachusetts 1874*. Ann Arbor, Mich.: Inter-University Consortium for Political and Social Research, 1978. http://nrs.harvard.edu/urn-3:hul.eresource:harvardmitd, 25 November 2011.

Montagu, Lady Mary. *The Lover: A Ballad*. www.poetryfoundation.org.

Mullendore, William Clinton. *History of the United States Food Administration, 1917–1919*. Stanford, Calif.: Stanford University Press, 1941.

National Band and Tag Company. "Anti-Pix" Promotional Material, 1940.

National Chicken Council. "Is Your Chicken Safe? NCC Responds to *Consumer Reports*." 19 December 2013. www.nationalchicken council.org. 4 January 2016.

——. "National Broiler Production." 9 December 2011. www. nationalchicken council.org, 21 February 2012.

——. "Per Capita Consumption of Poultry and Livestock, 1965 to Estimated 2016, in Pounds." www.nationalchickencouncil.org, 8 January 2016.

——. "U.S. Broiler Performance." www.nationalchickencouncil.org, 10 February 2016.

——————. "U.S. Chicken Industry History." www.nationalchickencouncil.org, 12 July 2015.

——————. "Vertical Integration." www.national chickencouncil.org, 29 August 2015.

National Park Service. "Exchange Hotel." www.nps.gov, 10 November 2015.

Nestle, Marion. *Food Politics*. Oakland, California: University of California Press, Ltd., 2002.

New Jersey State Board of Agriculture. *Report of the 16th Annual Session*. Trenton, N.J., 1889.

Newburger, Harry W. "The Gangster in Business." *The American Hebrew*, 8 January 1915.

Nicholson, Arnold. "More White Meat for You." *Saturday Evening Post*, 9 August 1947.

Nierenberg, Danielle. "Factory Farming in the Developing World." *World Watch Magazine* (May/June 2003): 10–19.

Noble, David. *America by Design: Science, Technology, and the Rise of Corporate Capitalism*. New York: Alfred A. Knopf, Inc., 1977.

Norris, L.C. "The Significant Advances of the Past Fifty Years in Poultry Nutrition." *Poultry Science* 37, no. 2 (March 1958): 256–274.

Office of the United States Trade Representative. "U.S.–Russia Reach Agreement on Poultry, Pork and Beef Market Access." 29 September 2003.

Ogle, Maureen. *In Meat We Trust: An Unexpected*

History of Carnivore America. New York: Houghton Mifflin Harcourt, 2013.

Olcese, Orlando, J.R. Couch, and Carl M. Lyman. "Vitamin B12 Concentrates in the Nutrition of the Mature Domestic Fowl." *Journal of Nutrition* 41, no. 1 (May 10, 1950): 73–87.

Opie, Frederick Douglass. *Hog and Hominy: Soul Food from Africa to America.* New York: Columbia University Press, 2008.

Orange County Visitor's Bureau. *Gordonsville: Fried Chicken Capital of the World.* www.visitorangevirginia.com, 12 August 2015.

Ozersky, Josh. *Colonel Sanders and the American Dream.* Austin: University of Texas Press, 2012.

Page, Irvine H., Edgar V. Allen, Francis L. Chamberlain, Ancel Keys, Jeremiah Stamler, and Frederick J. Stare. "Dietary Fat and Its Relation to Heart Attacks and Strokes." *Circulation: Journal of the American Heart Association* 23 (1961): 133–136.

Palmer, Hoke S. *1928 Annual Report,* Extension Poultryman of the University of Delaware.

Payne, L.F. and H.M. Scott. *International Poultry Field Guide for Flock Selection.* Kansas City, Mo.: International Baby Chick Association, 1934.

Pearl, Raymond Pearl. *The Nation's Food—A Statistical Study of a Physiological and Social*

Problem. Philadelphia and London: W.B. Saunders Company, 1920.

Pearson, Lu Emily Hess. *Elizabethans at Home.* Stanford, Calif.: Stanford University Press, 1957.

Penner, Karen Pasaresi. "Salmonella and Eggs." Kansas University, Department of Animal Sciences and Industry, Food Sciences Institute, April 2003.

People for the Ethical Treatment of Animals. "Chickens Used for Food." www.peta.org, 24 February 2016.

Perdue Farms. "Perdue Farms At a Glance." www.perduefarms.com, 24 February 2016.

Perdue, Mitzi. "Mitzi Perdue on Frank: It Took a Tough Man to Choose the Right Ad Agency." *Ad Age, 3* August 2011.

Petaluma Museum Association. "The Man Who Invented Petaluma." *Quarterly Newsletter* 23, no. 2 (Spring 2013).

Peters, Lulu Hunt. *Diet and Health, with Key to the Calories.* Chicago: Riley and Lee Co., 1918.

Pew Charitable Trusts. "The Business of Broilers." www.pewtrusts.org, 21 February 2016.

Phone Interview with Professor Robert Lawrence, the Albert L. Williams Professor of International Trade and Investment at the Harvard Kennedy School of Government, 10 September 2014.

Piro, Anna et al. "Casimir Funk: His Discovery of the Vitamins and Their Deficiency Disorders." *Annals of Nutrition and Metabolism* 57 no. 2 (2010): 85–88.

Platt, Frank L. "How Will the War Affect the U.S. Poultry Industry?" *American Poultry Journal*, no. 1 (October 1939): 577–579.

Plotkin, Stanley, ed. *History of Vaccine Development*. New York: Springer, 2011.

Pollan, Michael. *The Omnivore's Dilemma: A Natural History of Four Meals*. New York: Penguin Press, 2006.

Posner, Bruce G. "Seeing Red: Animalens Inc. Makes and Markets Red-Tinted Contact Lenses for Egg-Laying Chickens." *Inc.*, 1 May 1989.

Potter, David M. *People of Plenty: Economic Abundance and the American Character*. Chicago: University of Chicago Press, 1954.

Poultry Meat Processing, ed. Alan R. Sams. Boca Raton, Fla.: CRC Press, 2001.

Pryor, Elizabeth Brown. "Colonial Poultry Husbandry Around the Chesapeake Bay." *National Colonial Farm Research Report, No. 15*. Accoceek, Md.: Accokeek Foundation, 1983.

Quigley, J.T. "A Kentucky Fried Christmas in Japan." *The Diplomat*, 11 December 2013.

Rabsch, Wolfgang, Billy M. Hargis, Renee M. Tsolis, Robert A. Kingsley, Karl-Heinz Hinz,

Helmut Tschäpe, and Andreas J. Bäumler. "Competitive Exclusion of *Salmonella* Enteritidis by *Salmonella* Gallinarum in Poultry," *Prospective* 6, no. 5 (October 2000): 443–448.

Rifkin, Jeremy. *Beyond Beef: The Rise and Fall of Cattle Culture*, 240. New York: Penguin, 1993.

Rimas, R. Andrew, and Evan D.G. Fraser. *Beef: The Untold Story of How Milk, Meat, and Muscle Changed the World*. New York: HarperCollins, 2008.

Riviere, Dujarric. "Pasteur of France." *The Rotarian*, June 1937.

Rogers, Ben. *Beef and Liberty: Roast Beef, John Bull, and the English Nation*. London: Vintage, 2004.

Rogers, Richard T. "Broilers—Differentiating a Commodity." Foor Marketing Policy Center Research Report, No. 18, December 1992.

Rosner, Fred. *The Medical Legacy of Moses Maimonides*. KTAV Publishing House, Inc., 1998.

Rubel, William. "Eggs in the Moon Shine with Cream. A Selection of Egg Recipes 1500–1800)." *Eggs in Cookery: Proceedings of the Oxford Symposium of Food and Cookery*, ed. Richard Hosking. 2007.

Schlosser, Eric. *Fast Food Nation*. New York: Houghton Mifflin, 2001.

Scott, George Ryley. *The History of Cockfighting.* United Kingdom: Spur Publications Company, 1975.

Scott, J.M. and A.M. Molloy. "The Discovery of Vitamin B12." *Annals of Nutrition & Metabolism* 61, no. 3 (2012): 239–245.

Selin, Helaine, ed. *Encyclopedia of the History of Science, Technology, and Medicine in Non- Western Cultures*, 2nd ed., vol. 1, A-K, Springer Reference.

Shakespeare, William. *Cymbeline: a Tragedy* (1623); reprint, London: G.G. and J. Robinson, et al., 1794.

Shapin, Steve. "Descartes the Doctor: Rationalism and Its Therapies." *The British Journal for the History of Science* 33, no. 2 (2000): 131–154.

Shapiro, Laura. *Perfection Salad: Women and Cooking at the Turn of the Twentieth Century.* New York: Farrar, Straus, and Giroux, 1986.

Sheasley, Bob. *Home to Roost: A Backyard Farmer Chases Chickens Through the Ages.* New York: MacMillan, 2008.

Shepler, Ida M. "Prevention and Cure of Disease." *Successful Poultry Journal* 12, no. 1 (July 1908).

Singer, Peter. *Animal Liberation.* New York: HarperCollins, 2002.

Smith, Andrew F. "Did Hunger Defeat the Confederacy?" *North & South*, May 2011, 41.

Smith, Page, and Charles Daniels. *The Chicken*

Book. Boston: Little, Brown, and Company, 1975.

Smith, R.C. "Factors Affecting Consumer Purchases of Frying Chickens." *University of Delaware Agricultural Experiment Station Bulletin*, no. 298 (July 1953).

Smith, Richard Norton. *On His Own Terms: A Life of Nelson Rockefeller*. New York: Random House, 2014.

Spier, Robert, F.G. Spier. "Food Habits of Nineteenth-Century California Chinese." *California Historical Society Quarterly* 37, no. 1 (March 1958): 79–84.

Sprague, Gordon Wadsworth, Alexander Sturges, and James Hugh Radabaugh. *Economic Survey of the Live Poultry Industry in New York City, Volumes 276–283*. Washington, D.C., August 1937.

Squier, Susan Merril. *Poultry Science, Chicken Culture*. New Brunswick, N.J.: Rutgers University Press, 2011.

Staff of the Select Committee on Nutrition and Human Needs, United States Senate. "Dietary Goals for the United States." Washington, D.C.: U.S. Government Printing Office, 1977.

Stanton, Joe. "Tastes Like Chicken." *Annals of Improbable Research* 4, no. 4.

State of Michigan. "Highly Pathogenic Avian Influenza." www.michigan.gov, 18 February 2016.

Strehl, Dan. "Egg Basket of the World." *Eggs in Cookery: Proceedings of the Oxford Symposium of Food and Cookery*, ed. Richard Hosking, 2007.

Striffler, Steven. *Chicken: The Dangerous Transformation of America's Favorite Food*. New Haven, Conn.: Yale University Press, 2005.

Stull, Donald D., and Michael J. Broadway. *Slaughterhouse Blues: the Meat and Poultry Industry in North America*. Belmont, Calif.: Thomson/Wadsworth, 2004.

Sunde, Milton L. "Nutrition." *American Poultry History: 1823–1973*, ed. John L Skinner. United States: American Poultry Historical Society, 1974.

Temkin, Owsei. *Galenism: Rise and Decline of a Medical Philosophy*. Ithaca, N.Y.: Cornell University Press, 1973.

Termohlen, W.D., J.W. Kinghorne, James H. Radabaugh, and Edgar Lovett Warren. *An Economic Survey of the Commercial Broiler Industry*. Washington, D.C.: U.S. Government Printing Office, 1936.

The California Culturist, vol. 1, 1859.

The Humane Society of the United States. "An HSUS Report: The Welfare of Animals in the Meat, Egg, and Dairy Industries." HSUS Reports: Farm Industry Impacts on Animals, Paper 2 (2009). *The Practical Magazine: an*

Illustrated Cyclopedia of Industrial News, Inventions and Improvements 2 (1873).

Thomson, Vicki A., et al. "Using Ancient DNA to Study the Origins and Dispersal of Ancestral Polynesian Chickens Across the Pacific." *Proceedings of the National Academy of Sciences of the United States of America* 111, no. 13: 4826–4831.

Tobin, Bernard F., and Henry B. Arthur. *Dynamics of Adjustment in the Broiler Industry*. Boston: Harvard Business School, 1964.

Tompkins, Kyla Wazana. "Sylvester Graham's Imperial Dietetics." *Gastronomica: The Journal of Critical Food Studies* 9, no. 1 (Winter 2009): 50–60.

Tonsor, Glynn, James Mintert, and Ted Schroeder. *U.S. Beef Demand Drivers and Enhancement Opportunities*. Kansas State University, June 2009.

Toussaint-Samat, Maguelonne, and Anthea Bell. *History of Food, 2nd ed.* Hoboken, N.J.: Wiley-Blackwell, 2009.

Trollope, Anthony. *An Autobiography of Anthony Trollope*. New York: Dodd, Mead, & Company, 1912.

Trollope, Anthony. *North America, Volume 1*. New York: Harper & Brothers, 1862.

Trusler, John. *The Honours of the Table or, Rules for Behavior During Meals; with the Whole Art of Carving*. London: Literary Press, 1788.

Tryon, Thomas. *Health's Grand Preservative.* London: printed for the author, and are to be sold by Langley Curtis near Fleet-Bridge, 1682.

Tsoulouhas, Theofanis, and Tomislav Vikuna. "Regulating Broiler Contracts: Tournaments Versus Fixed Performance Standards," Selected Paper, AAEA Annual Meeting, July 30–August 2, 2000.

Tyson Foods. "Facts About Tyson Foods." www.tyson.com. 21 February 2016.

U.S. Congress, House of Representatives, Committee on Agriculture. *Hearings, Poultry and Egg Prices, Part I.* 86 Cong. 1st sess., 1959.

U.S. Poultry & Egg Board. "Economic Data." www.uspoultry.org, 12 July 2015.

United States Department of Agriculture, Bureau of Agricultural Economics. *Chickens and Eggs, Including Commercial Broilers.* Washington, D.C., April 1964.

——————. *Chicken on Farms, January 1, 1925–1938.* Washington, D.C., 1938.

——————. *Farm Production, Disposition and Income: Chicken and Eggs: 1944–1945.* Washington, D.C., March 1946.

——————. *Farm Production, Disposition, Cash Receipts, and Gross Income: Chickens on Farms, 1952–1953.* Washington, D.C., March 1953.

United States Department of Agriculture, Economic Research Services. "Agriculture Plays Important Role in Economic Recovery." *Agricultural Outlook*, October 1975.

United States Department of Agriculture, Food Safety and Inspection Service. "Pathogen Reduction; Hazard Analysis and Critical Control Point (HACCP) Systems; Final Rule." *National Register* 61, no. 144 (25 July 1996).

——————. "Chicken from Farm to Table." www.fsis.usda.gov, 26 March 2016.

——————. *Poultry Products Inspection Act.* www.fsis.usda.gov, 12 January 2012.

United States Department of Agriculture, Foreign Agriculture Service. "Livestock and Poultry: World Markets and Trade." October 2015.

United States Department of Agriculture, National Agricultural Statistics Service. "U.S. Broiler Industry Structure." 27 November 2002.

——————. "Poultry Slaughter, 2014 Summary," www.usda.mannlib.cornell.edu. 3 December 2015.

——————. "Livestock Slaughter, 2014 Summary," www.usda.manlib.cornell.edu, 3 December 2015.

——————. Young Meat Chickens Slaughtered in 2010." www.poultryegg.org. 29 November 2011.

United States Department of Agriculture. *Chicken of Tomorrow.* Directed by The National

Chicken-of-Tomorrow Committee. 1948; Massachusetts: Bay State Film Productions, Inc., 2010. *YouTube*. http://www.youtube.com/watch?v=GmdFoTRvNEQ. 12 December 2011.

—————. "Help Feed Yourself." Special Collections, National Agricultural Library. www.nal.usda.gov, 12 January 2012.

—————. "Washing Food: Does It Promote Food Safety?" www.fsis.usda.gov, 7 April 2016.

—————. *The National Poultry Improvement Plan*. Washington, D.C., 1938.

—————. "Uncle Sam Expects You to Keep Hens and Raise Chickens." *Poultry Tribune* 23, no. 1 (September 1917).

United States Department of State, Bureau of Diplomatic Security. "Significant Incidents of Political Violence Against Americans, 1991." Washington, D.C.: Department of State Publications, June 1992.

United States Food Administration. *Ten Lessons on Food Conservation, Lessons 1 to 10*. Washington, D.C.: Government Printing Office, 1917.

University of Kentucky, College of Agriculture, Food and Environment. *Poultry Production Manual*, 26 March 2014.

Vaughan, William. *Approved Directions for Health*. London: T.S. Roger Jackson, 1612.

Veit, Helen Zoe. *Modern Food, Moral Food.* Chapel Hill: University of North Carolina Press, 2013.

Velten, Hannah. *Cow.* Reaktion Books: London, 2007.

Vialles, Noelie. *Animal to Edible.* Cambridge, New York: Cambridge University Press, 1994.

Wei, Wang, Zhu Yong Zhi, Song Yu, and Zand Hang Muhan. "Comparative Study on Flavor Quality of Chicken Soup Made of Different Chicken Breeds," *Acta Agriculturae Jiangxi* 24, no. 6: 149–152.

Weihoff, Dale. "How the Chicken of Tomorrow Became the Chicken of the World." *Institute for Agricultural and Trade Policy.* 26 March 2013.

Weingarten, Susan. "Eggs in the Talmud." *Eggs in Cookery: Proceedings of the Oxford Symposium of Food and Cookery*, ed. Richard Hosking. Oxford, 2007.

What's My Line. *Chicken Eyeglasses.* Directed by The National Chicken-of-Tomorrow Committee, 16 January 1955. *YouTube*, https://www.youtube.com/watch?v=lCTnrsa UY2g, 12 June 2013.

White, E.B. Introduction to Roy E. Jones. *A Basic Chicken Guide for the Small Flock Owner.* New York: W. Morrow and Co., 1944.

Williams-Forson, Psyche A. *Building Houses Out of Chicken Legs: Black Women, Food, &*

Power. Chapel Hill: University of North Carolina Press, 2006.

Williams, William H. *Delmarva's Chicken Industry: 75 Years of Progress*. Georgetown, Del.: Delmarva Poultry Industry Inc., 1998.

Worster, Donald. *The Wealth of Nature: Environmental History and Ecological Imagination*. New York: Oxford University Press, 1993.

Young, Alexander. *Chronicles of the First Planters of the Colony of Massachusetts Bay from 1623 to 1636*. Boston: Charles C. Little and James Brown, 1856.

YUM! Brands. "Restaurant Counts." www.yum.com. 22 March 2016.

Zinn, Howard. *A People's History of the United States: 1492 to Present*. New York: Harper Collins, 2009.

Acknowledgments

I may be the only one listed on the front cover but the making of this book was in no way a solo endeavor. Firstly I would like to thank my editor at Pegasus, Jessica Case, for taking a chance on this strange little work, and my agent at Foundry Literary and Media, Matt Wise, for doing likewise well before all of these bird-brained ideas were fully formed. A special thank you as well to Eric Rayman, the man behind the little email that changed it all, and to Peter Steinberg, who took over the reins for me at Foundry knowing only that I was the girl writing about chickens. But even before all these wonderful humans came Professor Joyce Chaplin, my thesis advisor and historian extraordinaire at Harvard University, who helped these ideas hatch back when *Tastes Like Chicken* was simply a requirement for me to graduate from college. In the years since, she has answered my infinite questions about the scary world of publishing and endured my many, many, many frantic emails throughout the whole process. For her knowledge and patience, I am eternally grateful.

A big thank you must go out as well to the research librarians of the world, who are gods and goddesses among us mere mortals. Most particularly I am thankful for the help of the wonderful women of the Schlesinger Library at the Radcliffe Research Institute, the patient staff of the National Agricultural Library, and the incredibly knowledgeable folks at the Cornell University Rare Manuscript Collections, the American Museum Library at the Smithsonian Institution, and the Library of Congress. And when it comes to the ideas behind this work, I must thank as well historian of science Steven Shapin, whose class on the history of dietetics changed the whole course of my intellectual career.

After all those endless hours of research finally made it to paper, I would be nowhere without my readers, the most important of which was my mother, the biggest and most hardcore chicken fan of them all. An agricultural economist to the end, she was always willing to stay up late reading my drafts, to point out the relevant USDA statute when I was getting off course, and to remind me endlessly that chickens are "slaughtered" and not "killed." And to my many other readers as well, who took the time to read what were probably unreadable drafts of this thing, including my father, Andrew Rude, and my friends Grace Chang, Noah Rayman, Jessica Chao, Ahren Remel, Katie O'Hanlon, Phillip Zhang, Rachel Granetz, and Kathleen Wanio.

And finally a big thank you to everyone who

has supported me in the years that this project has taken, particularly my brother Julian, who has never hesitated to remind me that even though I have a book contract, I am still an idiot, and to Fronds, for enduring almost half a decade of fun facts about chickens.

Center Point Large Print
600 Brooks Road / PO Box 1
Thorndike, ME 04986-0001 USA

(207) 568-3717

US & Canada:
1 800 929-9108
www.centerpointlargeprint.com